The Battle Between Faith and Justice

Memoir

Marci Janell

Copyright ©2024 **Marci Janell**

All rights reserved. No portion of this book may be reproduced, stored in a retrieval system, or transmitted in any form or by any mean-electronic, mechanical, photocopy, recording, or other-except for brief quotations in printed reviews, with the writer's and publisher's prior permission.

Some of the contents of this book originally appeared in *My Memoirs of...* *"Bomb the Church," the war with the GIANT, and Lady Bishop.*

Unless otherwise indicated, Scripture quotations used in this book are from the Holy Bible.

Library of Congress Cataloging-in-Process

Marci Janell

ISBN (soft cover)

Printed in the United States of America

TABLE OF CONTENTS

Introduction 2

Destruction 6

"No Church Like It" 14

Fraudulent Mattie 19

Our Lives 21

Growing Up 24

Lots of Love 31

A Spiritual Rehabilitation Center 35

A Clean Sweep 39

Alvin's Short War 48

"My Daughter" 50

The Purported Vote 62

Chaos 67

Prayer Meeting 71

The Plot Thickens 80

Collection Bag 90

Esther 99

Jim 105

Dismissed! 113

Hospital 119

No Time To Mourn 130

Walkout, Riot, GUNS, and Dogs 145

Sabotage 159

The New Lawsuit	170
The Giant	173
Investigation	180
Aruba	187
In High Praise	195
Bloody Warfare	199
Pro Se-- On Our Own	213
An Election Is Inevitable	229
Opening Statement	236
The Trial Begins	241
The Law Firm Focuses	251
Saving the Best for Last	255
Is Justice A Game?	262
JIM ARRIVES	267
Never Mind What the Law Says	280
The Court's Election	284
Costly Convictions	287
A New War	290
The Red Sea	295

Dedication

To the memory of my father and mother.

To each of my siblings.

I am much indebted to those who were trailblazers for me.

Finally, my heartfelt thanks to those who assisted in editing and inspiring me to share my story, including my editor, Richard.

Marci

INTRODUCTION

This is my story of the endless battles between the renowned Chicago Bethlehem Healing Temple, a former affluent Pentecostal Church, and the Giant law firm that represented the plaintiffs in their goal to prevent me from becoming a Pastor – firstly because I am a woman, and secondly, so that they could exploit the organization for their benefit and purpose.

My memoir draws upon my experiences and resonates with the experiences of countless other women as we have struggled to promote and support the critically important roles of women of all ages in our religious organizations.

I believe that the themes and hard-earned lessons of this story of a war between faith, the law, and justice apply to various faith-based institutions across denominations and traditions.

Those deeply disturbing lessons emerged from the struggles around the pastor ship of Bethlehem Healing Temple, the then-famous church where I was raised and where my father followed tradition by appointing me to succeed him as Pastor. Yet they also apply to traditionally stable institutions and religious organizations, large and small, which rarely contend with so much as a whisper of controversy.

My theme focuses upon the powerfully fierce resentment of armies of traditional men in faith-based institutions and upon their unchallenged determination – often disguised in deceptively reverential language -- to dominate and control their spaces with inflexible rules in words and actions.

Many men who are active members of religious institutions, especially those appointed by official roles, believe they follow principles in their daily and religious lives. And indeed, many men do lead such principled lives. Nevertheless, as my experience demonstrates, vast numbers, perhaps the majority in many churches, respond as males who justify their radical actions, beliefs, emotions, and dominance in the name of justice.

I have experienced firsthand that faith and justice can too often become opposing forces in American and other societies, mostly in religious life. In extreme cases such as mine, the pressures, betrayals, and threats can become nearly – or actually – fatal. Furthermore, my experience battling endless lawsuits confirms that the cause of justice itself to counteract these forces can be twisted to serve manipulative, unprincipled conspiracies.

Few, if any, religious institutions in twenty-first-century America are immune to the pernicious effects of traditional male dominance. Even the Catholic Church has officially recognized and begun to address the global dilemma of how to reconceive the role of women in the church. The Highest Office of the Catholic Church challenged individuals worldwide to participate in a synod designed to reconceive the future of the Church itself.

Although the synod's focus would be upon reflection rather than negotiation, major topics would address questions about the fundamental roles of women that no longer remain sacred, despite having been hollowed for centuries, including whether the church allows women to assume significant leadership roles and become deacons. And can women become priests?

Such global questions lie far beyond the scope of the following chapters and fall outside of my personal experience. I do not want to share my views about how another institution should define or organize its principles, values, or priorities. Nevertheless, such questions remind us that the roles and functions of women – and the respect accorded to all women in religious institutions – can no longer be taken for granted, nor can our desires for change be ignored.

No matter how controversial the critical issues may become, they must be addressed.

Inevitably, they will also be acted upon, one way or another, and unpredictable and earthshaking consequences may eventually follow.

The Pentecostal community in which I grew up was compelled to confront the explosive decision to appoint me as Pastor, including bomb threats and worse. We waged a holy war sustained by a massive lawsuit sustained by a conspiracy among leaders of our congregation – an all-male group of plaintiffs disguised behind a woman who desired for her husband to be the Pastor.

A prominent Chicago law firm led the lawsuit, pro bono, determined to prevail purely (and explicitly!) for the sake of winning a war of attrition.

Its consequences will continue to affect the entire community and beyond for many years.

My purpose in describing what happened to the beloved Pentecostal congregation in which I had spent my entire life and the assault by means of a prolonged lawsuit is to bear witness to needless tragic calamity.

I have chosen to forgive the male plaintiffs and the lady who led the revolt against me and the spiritual legacy of my father, Dr. AC Richards.

In bearing witness to what occurred and explaining how an entire religious community became victims to forces of greed and the drive for personal and collective power, I have written this cautionary tale in a time when "polarization" has become a household word. The battles for the soul of our institutions confirmed how we live in a perilous era when social, political, and cultural tensions have become so severe that there has even been talk of civil war.

The conflicts within and around the institution arose with minor disagreements about roles and responsibilities within a large and prominent religious institution at the center of an economically and socially distressed and rapidly changing urban Black community – the West Side Area of Chicago. The seeds of those conflicts that had been planted and cultivated over half a century before had grown to become a poisonous jungle that overwhelmed the community, irretrievably separating old and young individuals, neighbors, and families.

This is the story of losing the area's priceless religious and social resources. While the community is increasingly changing, the institution's community continues to struggle economically and socially for many reasons, including a lack of professional and twenty-first-century leadership.

My story of the holy war that began with my appointment as Pastor emphasizes another major cause of community distress – the loss of a community held together by the compelling traditions of religious commitment among residents of all ages.

1
DESTRUCTION

"Those of you sitting in this church shall come against it to destroy it".
– **Mattie B. Poole.**

I begin this story with the startling, correct prophecy by the world-famous founder of our church, Mattie B. Poole, to emphasize the inescapable fact that the church was founded, led, and became world-famous by a woman. Those who claim that a woman should never assume a significant role, such as a Pastor, much less lead a congregation, must deny historical facts to preserve and promote their prejudicial delusions.

Unfortunately, the results can be tragic when those delusions transform into action.

"Who Would Do Such a Thing? And why?"

The disabled Black lady, Jean, who sat on her porch daily, hands flopped at her side and her head permanently tilted, maintained a record of what was happening in the neighborhood. She often kept me informed.

She spoke to me about observing the transformation of the once notorious West Side, where prostitution and drugs had ruled the streets for decades, and where Bethlehem Healing Temple had become a beacon to guide a fresh beginning. In the early eighties, my father, Reverend Arcenia Richards, labored to beautify the dilapidated church building, formerly a classic Masonic temple, installing all-new glass doors and stained-glass windows and completely reconstructing five sanctuaries.

As his retirement approached, my father appointed me to succeed him as church pastor, just as he had been appointed. Although I was fully qualified to assume the pastor ship, the congregation reacted with much confusion and many distressing rumors, especially among the senior citizens, who were unsure what to believe, and especially among the men who felt empowered to lead the congregation.

A Shocking Phone Call

It was nearly 6:00 a.m. when the telephone rang. "There has been an incident at the church. Someone has broken the windows and doors. You should go immediately and verify the incident. I was told that it was Dennis. It was reported to me that glass was flying everywhere and now surrounds the entire church."

My father was a relaxed man who did not panic at rumors. He told me that if the vandalism had occurred, the perpetrator would have turned out to be a respected church member like Dennis, but he warned me not to jump to conclusions based on a rumor spread by a phone call.

I volunteered to check it out.

I arrived there within minutes and began walking toward the church in disbelief. Standing there, capturing a picture of the former beauty of the glass doors, I stepped inside the broken entrance door. I stopped short. Six other doors leading into the corridors were also broken. I picked my way through gigantic pieces of jagged glass. The entire first floor of the church was covered with broken glass.

Who could have possibly committed this madness?

I was distraught – bewildered as well as saddened -- but I had to remain focused because hundreds of people would soon arrive to attend Bible study. What would the members think?

I scurried throughout the church to identify the places that needed immediate repair and telephoned the custodians, who arrived within fifteen minutes to clean up the mess.

Glancing across the street, I noticed my friend Jean sitting on her porch. She said, "Marci, I witnessed the entire event. I know who busted out the doors and windows."

"Did you telephone the police?" I asked.

"No."

"Why not?"

"Because it was one of the members of the church."

My throat tightened. That telephone call to my father was correct. It was indeed a member of the church. But who could it be? "Who would do such a thing and why?"

"It was Dennis. He did it," Jean said.

"Dennis?" I could not believe my ears. "Not Dennis!"

"Yes, Dennis. Dennis took an object and threw it at the door, and it broke. He went inside, and I heard the sound of glass breaking."

I was dumbfounded. Dennis was eighty-six years old and had been a church member for over 50 years. I have known him all my life! Dennis was one of the kindest, gentlest people one could ever hope to meet and was a prominent deacon, totally committed to the church.

"Jean, are you certain it was Dennis?"

She nodded emphatically. "I know it was him. I saw his face when he looked over at me."

I immediately telephoned my father.

He remained perfectly calm. "Did you place calls to have the windows repaired?"

I assured him that I had.

My father telephoned Dennis' wife, a woman in her nineties who could not believe her husband could have done such a thing. She claimed that Dennis had been asleep in the next room when the attack happened.

My father asked her if she would please check where he was sleeping in the adjacent room. He waited for her to return.

"He ain't here. I don't know where he is," she said. She kept repeating herself.

My father comforted her and told her that he would call her later.

Before my father could call Dennis' wife back, she called him. "Dennis is home, and I asked him where he had been. He says he has not been anywhere. But I kept asking until he told me the truth. I am so sorry this has happened. But he did not take his medication."

My father asked me to speak directly to him, "How are you, Brother Dennis?"

"I'm mad because they told me that I'm going to be put out of the church when Marci becomes pastor," he responded.

My father tried to assure him that those were false rumors.

Things seemed to settle down.

The telephone lines were ringing wildly, for it did not take long for word to spread that, in addition to the broken doors and windows, there had been a bomb threat. Within an hour, a glass company had repaired all the doors. Nevertheless, it was impossible to replace all the original stained-glass windows. The custodians and the glass company made the repairs so quickly that when the members arrived for Bible study that evening, I doubted that anyone could tell the doors and windows had been broken.

The destruction opened a series of wounds that began the tense drama unfolding despite my father's belief that things would settle down.

You're going to put us in jail!

One summer day a month later, I walked through the park and chatted with senior citizens. Seated on park benches were seniors who had left the church. As I approached them, Bea, a former church lady in her early eighties, grabbed me.

Refusing to let me go, Bea cried uncontrollably. "Why did you put me out of the church? I love you and the church. They told us we can't come back."

I was floored. "Who told you that? That's not true at all. I did not put you out of the church."

With tears in her eyes, she continued, "But they said you are going to put us in jail!"

Shaking my head, I responded, "That is not true."

"They told me you said we can't come back – that you'll take us to jail."

I hugged Bea as tears swelled in my eyes. I repeated, "That is not true. That is not true at all. I did not put you out of the church. You can come to the church whenever you desire. You are always welcome."

Having regained her confidence, Bea shared other startling news.

I told her, "There are a lot of rumors going around. Try not to pay attention. Always remember our relationship and your love for me since you have known me." I sympathized with her, having had to hear such lies.

Bea and I reminisced about the good old days, and I asked Bea to visit us. As I hurried away, my heart felt shattered. How many other seniors had been told that I had put them out of the church or that I would send them to jail? As I feared, other seniors came to me with similar tales.

Lillie

Lillie, who was ninety-two years old, would often telephone the church asking someone to pick her up so she could get to the church. Before she was forced to leave, Lillie attended daily Bible studies. Following her absence from the church, Lillie explained her longing to continue her membership. During one of the seniors' Bible studies, Lillie informed all present that her primary reason for not returning to the church was because she was held captive by those who had formed a conspiracy against me and the Board of Directors of our church. Lillie cried over and over as she shared how the conspiracy had ensnared her.

Kate

Shortly after my conversation with Lillie, another senior telephoned. I immediately recognized Kate's voice. She started her conversation by saying she missed me and asked if I would visit her at her senior complex. Without hesitation, I replied "Yes" and visited her the following day.

As a former employee for the city's department who assisted senior citizens, I frequently assisted seniors with their travels, shopping, and medical needs. I often took Kate grocery shopping and helped her with her personal affairs.

I had some fresh fruit and some dinner. She told me that she would speak with me despite having been forbidden. I remained silent as Kate shared how seniors were forced to leave the church. As I continued to oil Kate's feet, she explained how she had been deceived into leaving the church, "We were tricked into leaving the church. They planned a walkout a long time ago. I know because they called us. They think we are so stupid. We aren't stupid at all."

After listening to Kate share those details with me, I asked Kate one question, "If you know that I would not do the things that I am being accused of, why did you follow them?"

Kate responded, "I am not stupid, Doctor Marci. We have been tricked, and we know we have been tricked, but we are senior citizens. They walked away from the church and tricked us into going with them. They use us for their gain. They planned it. Please don't tell them that I talked to you. They will get so mad. They don't want us to like you."

I remained with Kate for two hours. Walking out of the complex, I realized that the situation was too emotional for me to continue consistently visiting her. However, Kate continued to telephone me when she needed assistance with her doctor's visits and other errands. She also called me when she moved to another location and needed new furniture for her home. I assisted Kate each time she called me. Yet our relationship would never be the same.

The Suicide of a Senior Member

It became increasingly difficult for some of the seniors as they watched the unfolding of the growing division within the church. One day, I received a telephone call from Mother Littlejohn, one of the twins and pillars of our church for over fifty years, "Sis. Minney is dead. She was at this church for over forty years. She left with them and committed suicide." Stunned, I felt overwhelmed.

Mother Littlejohn continued to tell me that Minney had laid her clothes out and planned the details of her funeral before her suicide. Following her plans, she put on several coats, despite the eighty-degree heat, and went to the lake front to end her life. When I asked what the purpose of the coats was, Mother Littlejohn explained that the coats would weigh Minney down when she jumped into the lake.

My immediate reaction was to ask a flood of questions:

Where were those who deceived her into leaving the church?

Who and where were those spreading such deception to confuse and hurt such devoted members?

Why were not any of those people around to help care for Minney or to answer the questions that caused her so much pain?

Had Minney, like Dennis, acted impulsively on false information? Had she also thought she would be thrown in jail if she tried to return to her beloved church?"

Pastor Jackie later informed me that her daughter was a dispatcher at the Jiffy Cab Company and received a telephone call from Minney asking for a ride to the lakefront. Sharon dispatched the call to the driver. The driver later reported that Minney gave him thousands of dollars and asked that it be given away, as she would not need money where she was going. The driver indicated, before dropping Minney off, that she never indicated that she had decided to take her life by drowning.

I buried my head in my hands, wondering what, if anything, I could have done. Although I had previously counseled others, there were too many unanswered questions this time. Unlike those who came to me for counseling, I had no one to turn to.

2
"NO CHURCH LIKE IT"

Most of those fearful senior citizens had been members at the church for decades – their entire adult lives -- and had witnessed some of the greatest miracles and healings ever told. Although I was too young to have been a part of the glory days, I heard so many stories from my parents and the seniors about Mattie Poole's trials and triumphs that I felt inspired.

Each of those seniors held their testimony of witnessing the power of God operating in the "glory days" of the church. The miracles they experienced were as authentic as originally and repeated repeatedly through testimonies. Therefore, I felt that not one of those seniors who left with those who had staged the walkout was to blame for being compelled to sign affidavits stating that I had put them out of the church. They had been deceived.

Most members arrived at the church early and stayed until nearly midnight daily. We were a community and possessed all the resources we needed: self-made custodians, homemade mechanics, self-made culinary experts, or caretakers. Whatever the needs, all could be found inside the church's community. Almost every kind of self-made service existed.

Many senior citizens knew little else outside of the church. The church had formed the center of their lives.

The Glory Days

Bethlehem Tabernacle, later named Bethlehem Healing Temple Church, was a Black Pentecostal church founded by its late pastors, Mattie and

Bishop Charles Poole, and the time with the Pooles represented the original "glory days" of the church.

Mattie B. Poole had a gift of faith and healing. People traveled from around the world to have Mattie lay her hands on them to receive the power of her healing and to witness Mattie touch individuals in the "name of her God" to be healed.

Many verifiable miracles took place during Mattie's years of teaching and preaching. As a result of the glory days in the late 1940s or early 1950s, one Bishop, Samuel Hancock, declared, "There shall be no church like it."

Mattie Bell Robinson Poole was born in Memphis, Tennessee, and at the age of seventeen, Mattie traveled to Chicago and met and married Charles E. Poole. Although Mattie and Charles had no biological children, they opened their home to many gifted as well as autistic children.

Praying for hours, Mattie was deeply concerned about the welfare of others. She labored tirelessly, night and day, aiding those who, she believed had strayed from The Movement: the depressed, the despondent, the sick, and the afflicted. It was her usual manner to be in prayer and reading the Holy Bible "at the crack of dawn," Because of her great labor, love, fidelity, and dedicated life for others, she diligently worked to fulfill the great commission of Christ and trained as many as she encountered to become followers of Christ.

An Uncompromising Tradition

Mattie's teachings were of faith, heaven, and a burning hell worldwide. Mattie did not hesitate to excommunicate those who were not abiding by the church's government. One act of excommunication included publicly displaying one's name to demonstrate that the person was no longer a part of the church.

Mattie was a tough, uncompromising woman who believed that keeping strict holiness provided more authority with God. She pushed everyone around her to live more holy lives dedicated to the "God of Mattie." Having been previously excommunicated from two organizations because of their strong convictions in healing, the Pooles founded their organization, All Nations Apostolic Welfare Workers.

The Pooles Established Their Theocracy

The Pooles' convictions were so strong that Charles and Mattie established laws within their organization as a theocratic government. Therefore, if their congregants broke those laws, they could no longer be a part of their organization. Mattie consistently expelled individuals that she believed embarrassed or harmed God.

As a result of the healings and miracles, Charles and Mattie established churches and corporations across the nation, expressly from a theological view, nothing outside of the Holy Bible would take priority within the church.

While traveling worldwide, teaching and preaching, Mattie and Charles laid hands on the sick, afflicted, and diseased. Their faith was so strong that they planted multiple churches, such as Bethlehem Healing Temple of The National Organization. Charles and Mattie believed in appointing all those who served in their organizations. Each appointed individual served on their board and in their ministry. There were no elections of any kind. Charles and Mattie appointed those individuals, as recorded in the Book of Acts, Chapter Six by the Apostles.

Because Mattie and Charles held to the strong beliefs of a theocratic government, the Pooles established a hierarchy of appointments based on Biblical principles. With both organizations functioning as monarchies, God was the sole source that the Pooles consulted with for advice on an appointment of any position.

If anyone opposed the Pooles' leadership, that individual was immediately excommunicated from the church, and that person's name was placed on a church wall for public viewing. Mattie then announced to the entire congregation that anyone found associating with an excommunicated individual would also be excommunicated. Mattie was as austere as she was holy. Her commitment to holiness and the gift of healing solidified her successful ministry. No one challenged her authority.

Years later, when my father appointed me to succeed him as a pastor, senior members of our church continued to believe in and adhere to the theocratic principles declared by Mattie Poole.

No wonder they reacted to threats of expulsion in extreme ways!

My father, Arcenia, chauffeured Charles, and Mattie. Arcenia later became the Pastor and Presiding Bishop of the church and The National Organization.

The Power of the Holy Spirit

As Mattie traveled extensively to healing campaigns across the country, thousands were baptized into water and filled with the Baptism of the Holy Spirit. As recorded in the book "You Can Be Healed," countless individuals testified to being miraculously healed of various diseases and afflictions through baptism in the name of Jesus.

We believed in the power of the Holy Spirit. Following Jesus' ascension into heaven, we believe He left His Holy Spirit to complete His work on earth.

Furthermore, we believed it was normal to be extremely animated as we worshiped. It was common for individuals to scream, holler, and shout during worship as a display of being touched by the power of God. Often, many rolled around uncontrollably. We also spoke in "tongues" -- other incomprehensible languages -- as a sign of the presence of the Holy Spirit. We prophesied and believed that those prophecies from God would come to pass.

The Word of Healing Spreads

In the early 1930s, Mattie and Charles opened a mission on d the West Side of Chicago named Bethlehem Tabernacle. After many years of witnessing to individuals about the mighty working power of God and watching as individuals were miraculously saved, delivered, and healed, the mission relocated to a garage on North Leavitt and Washington, which became the central place of worship.

The church remained there until the mid-1940s when it migrated to a storefront on a corner near their home. At that location, through much dedication, prayer, suffering, and persecution, Mattie felt the power of God and the gift of healing amidst their services in another supernatural way.

The storefront church was filled until the mid-1950s when Mattie and her congregation were forced to build a new church building adjoining the Mission. This new structure could seat hundreds, with room for expansion and growth. Mattie performed many miracles. The lame walked, the blind saw, and the deaf could hear. The word of healing spread throughout the city, the country, and the larger world as people visited to experience the mighty moving of the Holy Spirit when Mattie, along with Charles, encouraged individuals from all ethnic backgrounds to believe in a miracle.

Mattie soon began a radio broadcast named Living Witnesses, which aired on several radio stations.

In the mid-1950s, the church was renamed Bethlehem Healing Temple Church. Following the renaming, Mattie founded and presided over yet another organization. Charles agreed to assist Mattie and became her vice president.

Mattie felt that it was time to begin a new organization of her own. After concluding a revival in Detroit, she returned to the city to launch the organization as its President.

3
FRAUDULENT MATTIE

B elieving in the laying-on of hands and the laying-on of prayer cloths, Mattie began using pieces of cloth through prayer and anointing of oil to mail to individuals who requested the cloths. As word of the clothes spread, Mattie soon had many requests for prayer clothes. Her mailing list grew to more than 25,000.

Then, the Federal government investigated Mattie for mail fraud. Mattie soon became known as Fraudulent Mattie throughout the litigation. Mattie's name appeared along with Charles's in the court documents as "Mattie is a Fraud."

After a severe battle with the United States Postal Service in 1955, Mattie and Charles were summoned to Washington, D.C., to answer questions about her beliefs and the use of prayer cloths in the United States. The Supreme Court finally cleared Mattie of fraud. The United States Postal Service even commended her in 1959 when she and Charles received the Blue Ribbon seal of recognition and respect.

Mattie's four-year litigation resulted in a celebration called "The Day of Thanks." The celebration commemorated the victories of the children of Israel after being delivered from slavery under Pharoah. Mattie set this day aside annually to give testimony to God for the crossing of the church's own "Red Seas" and deliverance from modern enemies.

Following the victory, Mattie enlarged her borders and planted additional churches in other countries, traveling extensively overseas to create Schools of Ministry.

Bishop Hancock correctly said, "There will be no church like it." There was no church like Bethlehem Healing Temple within our city, state, nation, or abroad.

Mattie was God's gift to humanity. She appointed each of her leaders as directed by the Holy Spirit.

Theocratic Government

Mattie believed in theocracy. She believed God spoke to man, as Moses did with the Children of Israel. Therefore, throughout Mattie's and her successor's tenure, the members of the Board of Directors and all officials or leaders were appointed. Mattie telephoned any church members she believed would be assets to her organization and appointed them to join her Board of Directors. Everyone who was ever a part of Mattie's leadership or corporation knew there was never an election. If anyone spoke of holding an election to determine leaders, Mattie would immediately excommunicate them.

A Charter in Name Only

Although our organization had a charter, the corporation and organization operated fully independent of its charter. Bethlehem Healing Temple's history was clear. Our religious beliefs, practices, and organization's polity were selected solely by appointment.

All related organizations were organized the same way. The leaders taught according to the scriptures. The members were led as the children of Israel had been led. God spoke to a man, Moses, responsible for speaking to God's people.

4

OUR LIVES

Having been reared in a Pentecostal church with an uncompromising theological view and environment, we were forbidden to engage in activities considered to be worldly. The almighty God was our focus, and anything outside Him was considered an ungodly distraction.

Families were encouraged to read the Holy Bible, pray, and study daily to determine the mission of God for their lives. They adhered to authoritarian principles, including a strict dress code and sacred periods of fasting. Everyone who entered the church left with a story of being touched by God and witnessing the mighty power of God. Everyone knew that God was with Mattie. It did not matter that she maintained a religious philosophy that was rigorous, difficult, and judgmental. Everyone desired to be touched by the God of Mattie.

Mattie's services sometimes lasted six hours, but no one would leave. During a service, there would possibly be a one-hour intermission, which would resume until one o'clock in the morning. There was no time limit in the presence of the God of Mattie.

Mattie strongly believed in the God who parted the Red Sea for the children of Israel. She taught that God would show mercy to people committed to living holy lifestyles. Preaching that Jehovah would judge evil, and that right would ultimately prevail, she encouraged everyone to practice that philosophy with all their hearts and minds, acting daily upon the principles of those beliefs.

Changing the church's name to include the word "Healing" was a testimony to the miraculous events witnessed within it and reminded everyone of God's miraculous power through prayer.

Bethlehem became the talk of the religious community. Churches and organizations worldwide recommend the church for spiritual and natural healing. Anyone who needed a miracle could visit the church and anticipate that the God of Mattie would provide healing and direction.

The power of God continued to be with the Pooles despite the growing dissension within the organization around them. The Pooles were influential and had abundant resources. Those seeking political office regularly visited the organization seeking advantages for upcoming elections. Individual leaders, pastors, businesses, and corporations approached the organization because of its incomparable reputation and extremely large families.

"Keep Them Barefoot and Pregnant:" The Lifelong Role of Females

"And you, be ye fruitful, and multiply, bring forth abundantly in the earth, and multiply therein." – Genesis 9:7

The saying "keep them barefoot and pregnant" was the norm in our church. Having been reared in a family of twelve siblings and over fifteen foster children, I thought having many children was common. We did not believe in birth control under any circumstances. Mothers were taught to follow the direct command of the Bible to be fruitful.

Merely considering birth control methods was considered an offense to God. Most of the older mothers were careful to talk to the younger mothers to inform them of the "no birth control method" policy. Therefore, numerical advantage became extremely vital to church politics. To resolve an internal disagreement, everyone had to call upon the larger families, and those with the most family members joining the fight would win.

Exceptionally large families granted people several advantages in church planting. When the time came to plant a church, there was no need to seek any outsiders to join. It was often easy to determine who would be the next Pastor to plant a church.

Families increased from children to grandchildren, grandchildren to nieces and nephews. Jack, a former church member, had a family of more than twenty children. As a result of Jack's family being alone, his congregation consisted of a membership of nearly two hundred people.

Our small community had many connected relatives; everyone seemed to be related. One man in our church had nineteen children, and after the passing of his first wife, he married a woman with seventeen children! And there were grandchildren, nieces, nephews, and other family members. Having such large families and extended cadres of relatives proved to be an asset when we needed to assemble large numbers of supporters.

The members of the church believed that not only did you *not* have to use preventive methods for birth control, but, if necessary, God – who was all-powerful – would prevent unwanted pregnancies. I remember testimonies of ladies asking God to "close their wombs" to stop having children.

If you did not have a large family, you were considered abnormal. I vividly recall my father sitting in a meeting with three other associates, laughing because the four had over seventy children.

The Childbirth Advantage

Later, when the plaintiffs launched their lawsuit, they immediately contacted all their siblings, children, and as many downstream relatives as they could contact, and based on hearsay, they made them all parties to the litigation.

5

GROWING UP

The early days of my childhood, being reared in a household full of children, were wonderful. My parents often spoke of the civil rights movement when we learned to appreciate our freedom. During the presidency of John Fitzgerald Kennedy, my mother was expecting her fifth child. President Kennedy impacted my parents' lives so much that, following his death, my mother named one of her sons after him. We were taught that we must never forget the times when Dr. Martin Luther King fought for civil rights. As a liberated people, we learned that our forefathers established our rights by their actions, anchored by their faith and prayers.

The Early Days

We were reared in a strict, holy environment and were taught to obey many rules. We did not visit movie theaters. As a young girl, I recall receiving permission from my parents to visit my grammar school teacher, Ms. Mabel, along with a few other students. Ms. Mabel took us out to dinner and shopping. When Ms. Mabel said we were going to the movie theater, we were having the time.

I was overjoyed. I dared not tell Ms. Mabel we could not go to the movies. I was so excited that I refused to telephone my parents for permission. I could hardly wait. We did not own a television. I would finally have an opportunity to go to the movies. I will never forget walking into the theater. As I sat in the seat waiting for the movie to appear on the enormous screen, I recall thinking of the wonderful opportunity I was experiencing and wishing my siblings could have this opportunity.

What was the harm in us visiting the movie theaters to view a movie? I wondered. Not once did I remove my eyes from the screen. As the actress Pam Grier appeared on the screen, I thought, "She is one of the most beautiful women in the world." I could hardly wait to share this secret with my sister. Being reared in an environment where the movie theater was prohibited, the movie theater trip became one of my life's most memorable moments.

I did not visit a movie theater again until I was an adult.

We were also taught that television was a sin against God. When I was a child, someone gave our family a television set. My father locked it in a basement area, which we called "the cubbyhole" -- my father's office. No one dared enter "the cubbyhole" without Dad's permission. However, during one of our classes at school, my siblings and I were instructed to view a certain television program. I sat silently as my teacher instructed us to write an essay about the program. I was embarrassed to raise my hand and inform the teacher that I could not watch television.

That evening, my parents were not home. As my siblings and I sat in the basement talking about the television program, we remembered the donated television, and my oldest brother, Winston, managed to unlock "the cubbyhole," and we viewed the required television program. Afterward, Winston returned the television to its hiding place. We thought he had placed it in its original position.

When my parents arrived home, Winston immediately went to my father to confess, and my father went to "the cubbyhole" and concluded that Winston was telling the truth. He did not return the television to its original position. We were set for punishment. My father later explained that it was not our act of watching the television program but the act of entering that area that he most objected to. It was most comforting to know that while he held close to the church's ordinances, my father did not believe it was a sin for us to watch television.

As ladies, we were not allowed to wear makeup or jewelry, nor were we allowed to wear pants, for all three acts were sinful. I recall when my sister Montoria (we called her "Money") was in high school and was preparing to wear pants to school without my parents' permission. I was on the lookout as Money prepared to walk outside, looking beautiful in her pants and outfit as if she were going to a party.

As Money walked down the stairs gracefully, I said, "You look so cute. I cannot wait until I get to high school. I am going to wear pants." As I was speaking, I could hear footsteps approaching. I whispered as loudly as I could, "Someone is coming."

Money ran back upstairs. The sound of the footsteps was my mother. Turning to me, she asked, "Where is your sister? She does not want to be late for school." I sighed. My mother continued, "Tell her I want to see her before leaving for school."

That was the end of our ten-minute pants party. Money and I were grossly disappointed. Money reached into the closet and pulled out a dress that needed ironing. I asked, "Are you going to iron your dress?" Money shook her head, no. She did not have time to run the iron over the dress. I walked my sister downstairs to hear what my mother had to say. My mother was on the telephone when my sister walked into the room. As my mother got up to walk my sister to the door, she looked at her and said, "You are going to be late. Get going." She then took a second look and asked, "Why did you not iron your clothes?" My sister did not respond and left the house wearing those wrinkled clothes as my mother continued talking on the telephone.

We were also forbidden to wear any open-toed shoes. At a very young age, I broke my toe and had to wear sandals while my toe healed. One of the ladies from the church took me shopping and purchased a pair of white sandals. When I put those sandals on my feet, I joyfully wore them as if I had received a Christmas present in the summertime. It did not matter what outfit I wore; I would wear white sandals with every outfit. Even when my toe was completely healed, I wore those sandals until my toes leaned over the front. When it was time for me to stop wearing them, I hid them in my closet, hoping to wear them again someday. We grew up believing that strict holiness (as depicted in the Old Testament) was essential. Anyone who did not conform to the standards of holiness, as preached within the churches, became an outcast. We did not believe we were missing out on anything.

We were taught and required to pray. Prayer was a way of life. I recall we gathered for prayer each morning before going to school. Each night before bed, we gathered for prayer as a family. Prayer was such an integral part of our lives that it did not matter what other priorities we had to ignore to pray. If we ran late for school, we would have to stop and pray for God's protection. Prayer was to us as essential as food.

"Be Grateful for the Smallest Deed…"

Being reared in a large family, we were taught, "Be grateful for the smallest deed; there are so many people who are worse off than you." Often, we did not have enough resources to sustain us. Our parents believed in the power of prayer ever since childhood. There were other times we observed from behind doors as our parents petitioned God, asking Him to help their little children. Somehow, through every crisis, the very nucleus of my parents' prayers and faith sustain us through crises, and we were given enough food and resources.

Our parents reminded us daily that God provided for us and that we should not take His kindness for granted. Our parents further reminded us of the power of God in Mattie B. Poole and her services and that we must honor her church for the rest of our lives. My mother often spoke of the miraculous healing of my oldest sister, Patricia, who, as a baby, crawled on the floor, took an electrical cord from the socket, and put it in her mouth. As Patricia turned blue and lost her breath, my mother telephoned Mattie, screaming for the life of her child. Mother shared with us the power of God that was with Mattie, explaining that Mattie told her to lay her hands on my sister's body, and as my mother followed Mattie's instructions, Mattie prayed and commanded death to leave my sister's body and said that the God in heaven would return life into my sister. As Mattie continued to pray, Patricia started coughing up all the poison that was in her body; she spat out blue blood and coughed up all sorts of substances. What mattered most was that life instantly returned to Patricia. As a reminder of the near-death experience, Patricia carried a scar on the right side of her mouth.

Mother reminded us of the dangers we faced living on the West Side of the city, growing up during a very depressing time for African Americans. During the night, my mother hardly slept, and we could hear her petitioning God to please protect her children from the evil of this life.

A burglar once interrupted my mother's sleepless nights in prayer when he tried to enter our house through the back porch window. Mother noticed the burglar's shadow. As she continued to pray, she confronted the burglar, who jumped out of the window. I recall many nights being awakened by prayer. I remember in the middle of the night, as my mother prayed for me, she was leaving the room, and one of my siblings woke up and said, "Mama, don't forget to pray for me." We would immediately fall asleep following my mother's prayers.

Early Morning Prayer Meetings

My mother often spoke of the miracles during Mattie's life. "Those were the days of miracles. When your sister, Pat, died, Mattie prayed for her, and God gave us a miracle and brought her back to life. You've got to believe in God. He is real. His words are real." Equally, my father would often speak of the miracles that took place – which had never been seen in the history of the West Side – that Mattie performed at the storefront church in early Morning Prayer meetings.

My father testified, "I brought a blind man to church. I walked out the door, and someone called me back screaming, 'Brother Richards, the blind man you just brought to church is running around the church. God has blessed him with his eyesight."

My parents told us about miracle after miracle, sharing their testimonies. "We had no food for y'all on Christmas. We had no money. God touched somebody's heart. Someone put bags of toys and food on our doorstep on Christmas morning. Believe in God."

My father would awaken every day at 4:00 a.m. and prepare to go to church for prayer. Often, he would allow us to go to prayer with him.

I trained myself to hear my father's footsteps when he prepared for prayer. He promised that if we would get up without him having to wake us, he would allow us to attend prayer services at five o'clock. Many rushed inside at five o'clock to attend this prayer meeting, enduring sleet, storms, and below-zero weather, and my father never missed prayer services. As I traveled to prayer services with him, I would rush to keep pace with him. Looking up at him, I often said, "Daddy, I can't keep up with you. Your legs are too long." Sensing my eagerness to keep pace, he would pick me up and carry me.

As my father's shift changed during his working schedule, there was once a time in the heart of winter when my father arrived early to prayer and found that no one else had yet arrived. He could not get into the building and could not find any of the custodial workers. Indeed, Dad would turn around and go home. But, no – instead, Dad prayed at the window by the prayer room door. As cars drove by, people would stop to listen to him pray. Prostitutes stopped asking my father for prayer. For over one hour, Dad stood there on the side of the street and prayed.

My dad often allowed us to participate in all-night prayer meetings held every Tuesday and Friday night, beginning at midnight and lasting until six o'clock and ending with a series of testimonies and praises to God for the blessings He shared with us.

As a young girl, I went to those prayer meetings to be blessed by God. I had heard of so many of the miracles performed by God that I was faithful to the ordinances and governments of the church. The church held non-stop, consistent prayer meetings. During the first hours, some watched as those praying would make their petitions -- every petition one could think of -- known before God. During the last hours, they would watch as God allowed all sorts of miracles to occur. The power of the Holy Spirit took over as supernatural miracles took place, keeping the church's lifeblood flowing.

Young Adult Years

As a young adult, I wanted to become an elementary school teacher. I admired my teachers and determined that I would one day become one as well, but as I grew older, my goals changed, and I began studying Business Management. Upon graduating from high school, I took my first trip to the Bahamas, one of the most exciting times of my life, as I fulfilled my dreams of meeting different nationalities. I was encouraged to continue my travels among other cultures after completing my first undergraduate year. I discovered that the world was much larger than I had imagined and became determined to expose myself to other cultures.

During my studies, I accepted a position as a manager to pay for my undergraduate degree. As I continued my education, I became interested in starting my own business and opened a boutique for women. I struggled to continue working to earn my undergraduate degree while hiring additional staff to help operate my business. Unfortunately, as I struggled to continue my education, one of my staff, Lucy, embezzled company funds. By the time someone discovered Lucy's theft, it was too late. Our company lost thousands of dollars.

When I confronted Lucy, she confessed. I found it in my heart to forgive her and to count each experience as a blessing. Following that experience, I entered Bible College and worked on my advanced degree. This was one of the most rewarding experiences of my life. Bible College was where I belonged. My graduate school class experiences prepared me for my position as Pastor. I was determined to excel, even though I was the only young Black female in almost every class among traditional men. The challenges I faced at that time prepared me for the upcoming war.

My life took a turn in a different direction. After pursuing my post-graduate degrees, I traveled extensively, teaching doctrines of faith in Christ and conducting seminars and workshops. I soon accepted my destiny. As I taught across the country and abroad, I maintained an extensive teaching schedule as we spiritually transformed the church and community by empowering others to increase their social consciousness.

After graduation, I received my ordination papers.

6

LOTS OF LOVE

My Father's Love

I cannot overstate the power of a father's true love in a young lady's life. As a teenager, I spoke daily about my father to my friends and teachers. There was no doubt that my father loved me and my siblings. The love that existed between my father and me was pure and passionate. We were best friends. My father -- an extremely kind, patient, gentle, and wise man -- knew how to share his time, love, and energy as if we were only children.

I took my first airplane ride with Bishop Charles Poole at a very young age. Bethlehem was hosting a Healing Crusade in Georgia. I begged my dad to let me travel to the crusade with him. When my father informed Bishop Poole that he would allow me to accompany him to the crusade, he insisted that I travel by plane. I recall standing in the airport, looking at the airplane on the runway, and wondering who was responsible for building such a large airplane. The airplane seemed so enormous that it took up the entire runway. I ran from the window to where Bishop Poole was sitting and asked if I could telephone my dad because I wanted my father's presence before boarding. Bishop Poole smiled as he placed me upon his lap and said, "Your father will meet us in Georgia."

I held Bishop Poole's hand for our trip to Georgia. When we arrived in Georgia, my father, who had driven there, awaited us. I cried as my father picked me up in his arms. When my dad asked me if there was a problem, I begged him never to leave me to travel alone.

From then on, I began traveling with my father to crusades across the country. I listened to my father's messages of faith and hope. I often thought that following Daddy's messages, he makes you feel like you can fly.

What awe-inspiring messages he taught!

Before each service, my father introduced me as his daughter, and he invited me to share the platform with him after each message.

My father continued to shower us with his love as we grew older. When my father was not traveling in a crusade, he would drive me to school. During my high school years, my father drove me to school and picked me up from school. My father drove me to work when I was hired for my first paid job. My father would come to my job each week and have lunch with me and some of my co-workers. Twice a week, we would have dinner together. Our bond was strong. Surely, every young lady should have an opportunity to be as loved by her father as I was by mine.

My Mother's Love

My mother was the nucleus of our family. There were times in my life that I am quite certain if it had not been for my mother's love, I would not have been strong enough to manage the challenges I faced. My mother seemed to have had the answers to all my problems. She knew when I was ill and did not wish to inconvenience her. She knew when I had to make significant decisions, and she was there to encourage me.

My mother understood the true discipline of nourishing. She was not only my mother, but she was also my friend. She made me laugh and allowed me to cry. During the most severely testing time of my life, my mother visited me and stayed all night with me until the dawn of a new day, assuring me that there was not one challenge in life that God would not see me through.

A true woman of faith, my mother personified love and hope. She allowed the gift of love to outshine the forces of darkness and taught us how to love. My mother taught us that without love, you die. There may not be a natural, biological death; however, there is something inside of you that eats away at the very fiber of your existence until a person deteriorates.

Mother believed that love would conquer one's greatest enemy. My mother lived a life of love. Every decision she made was a direct result of her love.

My mother showered me with love and taught us the principles of love and wisdom, sacrificing her children to benefit from an excellent education. She worked midnight shifts so that we could have a better lifestyle. She personified wisdom among her enemies, who came to feed off her selfless love.

My mother understood how to meet the needs of each of her children.

My mother, a profoundly spiritual lady, enjoyed direct communication with God and taught us to pray, read, and rely on the Holy Bible. She taught us to believe in the power of Almighty God, that God loved us, and that God was directly involved in the lives of His children. We understood that nothing that happened in our lives was purely coincidental -- that God allowed certain events and circumstances to occur. My mother was confident that even unpleasant circumstances would eventually lead to a good experience. My mother was also a woman of valor, blessed with such a buoyant spirit that I remember her crying tears of joy and hardly ever sorrow. One of the few times I witnessed her shedding tears of sorrow was at the passing of my father.

My mother was compassionate and instilled compassion in each of her children.

My mother's love outshone any cloudy day.

A Daughter's Love

As much as I felt my parents' love for me, so was my love for them. It was a blessing to be reared in a home where there was no question about the love of either of my parents. The love between my parents and me extended beyond the borders of our home. We were closely knit, and everyone around us knew of my love for my parents.

As I started to travel and teach across the country and abroad, I spoke of the love my parents and I had for each other. Upon my travels to Africa, I shared with the audience the need for love to permeate the hearts of those we meet throughout our lifetime. I took the message of my parents' love and began spreading it to a hopeless generation.

Love was our primary reason for existence. That was the message I shared with others, as a direct influence of my love for my parents.

7

A SPIRITUAL REHABILITATION CENTER

The ecclesiastical life of Arcenia Cornelius Richards, Sr. was one of great valor, humility, and service. Educated in the primary and secondary schools of New Orleans, Bishop Richards, under the tutelage of Mattie and Charles Poole, confessed his belief in Christ at the Bethlehem Healing Temple Church and immediately became Mattie's and Charles's assistant. Recognizing Richards' humble spirit and his love for God and mankind, as well as his ability to lead, Bishop Poole required Bishop Richards to advance his studies to become a minister.

Bishop Richards further educated himself in theology and Christian education.

After being properly trained and educated in the ministry school, Richards ministered for several years and became Pastor at the Revival Tabernacle Church. After he continued his training, education, and further testing, he assumed the office of Elder and District Elder over many churches within The National Organization.

His pastoral dedication and zeal destined him to further distinctive promotions. After his appointment to the office of Bishopric, he became the Assistant Presiding Bishop of The National Organization.

Making enormous changes in rebuilding every uninhabitable sanctuary, Bishop Richards established and mastered the art of transforming Bethlehem into a more progressive organization. With virtually no assistance from the previous administration and no resources to provide for renovations, Bishop Richards sought the assistance of friends and those who believed in the organization's mission. By hiring outside consultants and contractors, Richards renovated Bethlehem Healing Temple Church, Inc. Laboring relentlessly, ministering to those who were in prison, on drugs, downtrodden, and ill, Bishop Richards coined the phrase that he backed up with his actions, "It's a simple solution, Only Believe." Teaching and believing that all things were possible through Christ, Bishop A. C. Richards watched as God transformed the lives of those joining Bethlehem Healing Temple Church.

While being mentored to become the succeeding Pastor and Presiding Bishop of the church and corporation, Bishop Richards accompanied Mattie as she traveled to healing campaigns nationwide. Upon Mattie's death, Charles continued to mentor Richards for the organization's leadership.

Charles continued his wife's legacy. As President of The National Organization, he named and appointed his assistant, Bishop Richards, who was by then well-trained, equipped, and educated in the school of ministry.

Charles traveled from state to state, continuing Mattie's teachings, and principles of faith, but he was more engaged as Pastor of Bethlehem than with establishing churches.

Because Mattie had taken care of most of the business details of the organization, Charles was unfamiliar with operating the church's business. Lacking the sense of direction that Mattie had helped to provide, Charles lost several churches through litigation. He decided it was time to allow Bethlehem Healing Temple Church to become independent again. In 1980, Charles incorporated Bethlehem Healing Temple Church, Inc.

Charles appointed Bishop Richards as Presiding Bishop of The National Organization and Senior Pastor of Bethlehem Healing Temple. When Charles Poole died in 1984, Bishop Richards assumed his assignment with diligence and care and became Pastor, shepherd, and friend to the flock of Mattie and Charles Poole, following in the footsteps of his former leaders.

During the early years of his ministry, Bishop A. C. Richards's primary responsibility was to assist Mattie in her healing campaigns worldwide.

Richards' position allowed for personal training from both Bishop Charles and Mattie Poole.

He rejoiced as he witnessed how Mattie would heal people. As a young minister and trainee, Bishop Richards introduced a legally blind man to the Healing Temple. The experience of watching a miracle unfold as the blind man regained his sight changed Bishop Richards's life forever. Bishop Richards resigned from his secular position after nearly twenty years.

Upon his elevation to the bishopric, A. C. Richards faced the challenging transition of trying to follow in the footsteps of greatness. Having the signatures of the Board of Directors and the records from the late Bishop Poole's appointment, in an act of humility, Bishop Richards allowed himself to be confirmed as the senior Pastor. As Bishop, Arcenia was, by ecclesiastical practice, the over-shepherd of the church and did not need this process. That confirmation was simply another sign of his unassuming nature.

Historic Achievements

Bishop Richards became the leader of one of the most renowned Pentecostal churches in the world for the next two decades. In the late 1970s or early 1980s, The National Organization was dissolved. As Pastor of the Bethlehem Healing Temple Church, Bishop Richards noted the dissolution of The National Organization and prepared to incorporate a new version of The National Organization.

The National Organization under Bishop Poole's tenure had been dissolved. Despite litigation and other administrative challenges, Bishop Richards incorporated The National Organization, Inc. as a separate entity. Despite battles over integrity and viability, The National Organization became a thriving corporation. In response to the transformation of the City's Near West Side community, Bishop Richards decided to organize under the charter of its already existing practice, thereby establishing its By-Laws and Constitution according to the longstanding practice of the Bethlehem Healing Temple Church, Inc., and The National Organization.

Advocacy for Women in Ministry

Thoroughly trained under a female pastor, Bishop Richards fought to provide many opportunities for women preachers and became an advocate for women in ministry. However, Bishop Richards did not favor any woman without the calling of God, or the rigorous training associated with ministerial skills. Bishops held the responsibility of selecting and appointing the Pastor of Bethlehem. Equally, the person shared his selection with the Board of Directors, the Board of Deacons, the Trustees, and the lay leaders.

Like his predecessors, he also appointed his successor. He then appointed me as Pastor, an almost automatic decision securely rooted in tradition, but that would also have unforeseen catastrophic consequences. The board agreed and confirmed my appointment.

8

A CLEAN SWEEP

God Shall Sweep This Church Clean

In awe of Mattie's teachings on faith, I asked my father how Mattie had been able to withstand the conflicts and litigation that she faced within and outside of the church.

"Listen to the recordings of Mother Mattie," my father responded. "It is easy to tell of the dissension that had grown within the church. Mattie spoke openly and candidly about the division that continued."

I listened to various tape messages from Mattie's Bible teachings. On one tape-recorded thirty years earlier, I heard, "They say, Sister Poole, you were right up in front, and they had a meeting and read your name absent."

"I ain't absent…Whoever heard of putting the man who started the organization? Y'all sitting right here are against this church."

Mattie spoke of those who were holding conspiratorial meetings to form a corporate takeover of her organization and prophesied, "God shall sweep this church clean. Those of you sitting in this congregation will one day come against this church to destroy it."

Mattie repeatedly shared with the congregation her fear that the church – once favored with countless miracles – would be torn apart. While continuing her mission of faith and healing, Mattie was careful to openly share her conviction that the organization she had founded and led would be destroyed by those determined to overthrow her leadership.

Mattie was gifted – no one could deny that – but those who envied Mattie did not have her gifts or share the fiercely passionate strength of her faith. Jealous enemies would eventually arise to destroy the name of Mattie and the organization that she founded.

Mattie herself had to fight prejudices and personal insolence. She had been sued for her faith and convictions. She understood the spiritual and judicial dynamics among religious organizations, yet she maintained her prophecy for many years.

One day, as I prepared to defend myself for accepting the call to Pastor, my brother Alvin left a compelling voice recording of Mattie's fatal message, "… God shall sweep this church clean." What chilling words!

Her resounding prophecy would prove true. Mattie knew that something appalling would happen within the organizations she had incorporated. Not long after making that prediction, Mattie Bell Robinson Poole passed away.

Jamaica – The Prophecy

It was the beginning of the year, and several of my sisters, mother, and aunt decided to take a trip to Jamaica. I was reluctant to join them because I did not want to leave my dad and felt a sense of urgency to visit my cousin, Eric. Eric and I grew up together as if we were siblings and shared nearly all our childhood. We remained extremely close as we grew older, and several times during the year, Eric moved in with me, and we shared our hopes and dreams. All week long, I had tried unsuccessfully to reach Eric.

My sisters convinced me I could use the break, so I reluctantly agreed to go to Jamaica.

The Saturday before leaving for Jamaica, I finally reached Eric. As we chatted, Eric asked if I would visit him in his new apartment in the suburbs. I told him, "Yes, it would be my pleasure. However, I have some errands to run first." As I wrote the traveling instructions to Eric's new apartment, I told him I sensed that it was extremely important to see each other that day. He agreed. I left the paper on the kitchen table with the traveling instructions to Eric's apartment.

It seemed there was not enough time in the day for me to run all my errands. I needed to visit my father, pay bills, and tie up loose ends. Before long, the day had gotten away from me. It was late when I returned home, and there was only time to pack the items I would take to Jamaica (my sisters had scheduled an early flight), so I could not visit my cousin before my trip.

During the flight to Jamaica, I thought about Eric. He and I had visited Jamaica together previously, and we'd had such a wonderful time that I wished that Eric could have taken this trip with us and promised myself he would be the second person I would contact upon my return. I would visit my father first and then travel to Eric's new apartment.

Jamaica was great. My sisters were correct; I needed that trip. The food and the people were wonderful. We had our driver named Marc. My sister, Gwen, had warned me about Marc. She told me he would fall in love with me as soon as he took one look at me. I said, "Do not worry – I did not come to Jamaica to fall in love."

Gwen was correct. As soon as Marc met me, he could not take his eyes off me. Each day, Marci was there to escort us; he told me he would be my guardian angel. I had traveled to Jamaica several times and was not afraid of dangerous areas. We grew up in a dangerous area of the city, and I was accustomed to keeping my eyes open and being aware of my surroundings.

Nevertheless, my family convinced me to allow Marci to escort me each time I left the cottage. This wonderful place had so much to do, and Marc was the perfect gentleman and tour guide. We visited the little shops and the stores. Every place we traveled reminded me of when Eric and I visited Jamaica. Why was Eric so heavily on my mind?

We were in the middle of enjoying ourselves at the beach. I suddenly told my sisters and mother, "I must leave. I must get home to see Eric." I could not explain why, but I knew my intense feeling was urgent.

"We have three days left for our vacation. We are not scheduled to leave until Sunday, and it is only Thursday," my sister Money responded. "Yes, I understand, but I must return to the States. Somehow, I sense that it is urgent," I stated. I did not know why, but I could not be persuaded to ignore my sudden feeling.

My Mother's First Prophecy

As I prepared to leave, my mother walked into the bedroom I was sharing with my sister, Money. My mother began to pray for me. I could tell from the prayer that something was challenging and that my life was about to change. My mother was a prophetess. She could see into the future. She would often share future events with us. I knew that I should not take whatever she said to me lightly.

My mother's first words were, "There is a great and effective door open for you, but there are many adversaries." She continued, "Your life is about to change, but God will be with you every step of the way. Do not forget to seek His guidance in everything that you do." She became very emotional and continued, "It will be very difficult. It will be very hard. You must not give up." She repeated, "There is a great and effective door open for you, but there are many adversaries." My mother wept over me as she embraced me with all of her might. She ended her prayer with, "May the God of heaven be your guide and grant you strength for the task ahead. And Lord, may her faith be stronger because of her test."

"What is it?" I inquired. She did not immediately respond.

Sitting there deep in thought, she finally said, "God is with you."

The time had come. I was leaving my family and returning to the States alone. My mother's words were so strong. I had no idea what was about to happen; nonetheless, I reminded myself that God was with me and that there was a great opportunity, but there were also many enemies. Who are these enemies? I wondered. I have no enemies that would cause me great harm.

Leaving Jamaica

Marc escorted me to the airport and waited to ensure I would get on the plane, as I did not have a reservation to travel that day. Once he was assured that I would make the flight, he gave me a genuine pearl seashell and asked if I would always remember him. I assured him I would and headed down the corridor to take the flight back to the States.

Once I sat on the plane, thoughts of Eric flooded my mind, along with the words my mother had spoken to me a few hours earlier. Leafing through the pages of the Bible, I read the verse of scripture written by the Apostle Paul from the passage my mother quoted to me. The words from the Bible seemed to leap off the page at me. I read First Corinthians 16:9, "For a great and effective door is opened unto me, and there are many adversaries." I read the verse over and over again. What is this great door, and who are these adversaries? I wondered. Why would anyone want to hurt me? I could not think of any enemies. There were so many questions and very few answers. After I closed my Bible and prayed, my anxious thoughts returned to Eric. Was there some important reason that he wanted me to visit him?

Upon my arrival in the States, I tried to call Eric, but there was no answer. Never mind, I thought. I will surprise him and go to his new apartment.

Upon arriving home, I visited with my dad for the rest of the day and showered him with the gifts I had purchased for him in Jamaica. Again, I had no opportunity to visit with or hear from Eric at 1:00 a.m. I was still trying to reach Eric but continued to reach his voicemail. I prayed for Eric and fell asleep, but I was unusually restless. I tried to read for a while but was distracted.

Early in the morning, I decided to go to the beauty salon closer to Eric's apartment. As I left for my salon appointment, I accidentally left the directions to Eric's apartment on my table. Eric's parents lived near the beauty salon, and I could find his new address from his mother.

Horrible News

The stylish Pat was putting the finishing touches on my hair when the salon telephone rang. Pat handed me the telephone and said, "It's for you."

I asked, "Who is it?" She responded by saying, "It's your office."

As I answered the phone, Kelle told me, "You need to get in touch with your sister, LaVena!" What could be so important this early in the morning?

Never mind, I thought. I will surprise him and go over to his new apartment.

When I reached LaVena, she told me that one of Eric's brothers was looking for me. My thoughts immediately rushed to Eric's brother, Curtis, who had been ill. Has something happened to Curtis? Was he okay? Is that why I needed to contact Eric? My heart started racing.

LaVena continued, "Eric was involved in a terrible accident."

I started shaking and asked, "Is he okay? Where is he? I will go there." She paused and said, "Eric was killed. He did not make it."

I responded, "No, this cannot be possible!" My breath left me, and I fell to the floor.

Pat came over and began consoling me. I could not think! I could not breathe! There had to be some terrible mistake.

The hairstylist took the telephone from my hand. I do not remember speaking to my sister again.

I said to Pat, "I have to go." She offered to say a prayer for me.

I was unable to make sense of these events. This had to be a mistake. Perhaps Eric had been in an accident, but I knew he still had to be alive. There was no way this could be true.

I left the salon and rushed to Eric's parents' home. Someone would surely tell me where Eric was recovering. Eric's sister, Deborah, answered the door. As I stepped inside the house, it was dark and silent, and suddenly I knew. No one had to say a word.

I entered the kitchen and fell into a chair. Deborah knew of my relationship with Eric. The two of us embraced, and without saying a word, I cried uncontrollably.

How could this have happened? I could not stay there.

I asked to speak with Eric's mom. There were very few words between the two of us. Eric's mother's heart was completely broken.

I told Eric's family that I would return, and I left to visit Eric's wife, Delta, a few blocks away. I was in a state of shock and overwhelmed with grief.

The look on Delta's face told me she was expecting me. She said," I have been trying to reach you. I am so sorry." I was overcome with grief. Delta consoled me as she explained the few details she had received. I told her that I would assist in the funeral preparations and left.

Eric had been my big brother. Who was going to take care of me? Who would protect me from the vultures? Why did I not change plans or make more time to see him? Was one of the reasons I felt compelled to return home earlier from Jamaica due to Eric being in trouble? I had many unanswered questions. Whatever happened, I knew I would never know all the details surrounding Eric's passing. Eric's last words were, "I can't wait to see you. I love you so much."

With so many unknown adversaries, I would have needed Eric to guide me through the tough days and whatever awaited me.

Eric's death began the most stressful year of my life. When I returned home, I walked into the kitchen and saw the directions to Eric's new apartment. I sat there with a deep longing to hear Eric's voice one last time, but I was left with only the memories of Eric's last words to me.

My Mother's Second Prophecy

Following Eric's death, my life changed. My father urged us to spend more time together as a family. We decided to meet every Saturday at 7:00 p.m. for prayer and dinner. It was a time of great reflection, spiritual guidance, strength, structure, and love for our close-knit family.

Eric's death drew me even closer to my father. We focused more on my father's health and encouraged him to take better care of himself. My father took time to establish departmental restructuring and implement a more organized and progressive ministry involving the Board of Directors, the Deacons, and other leaders.

Upon hearing of my father's decision to restructure the Christian Education Department, we prayed for him and God's direction for the ministry. We did not worry about Dad's decisions since he had been pastoring for nearly 40 years with great success.

We did not hint at the betrayals, conspiracies, and trials – courtroom confrontations and emotional ordeals- that awaited us.

In the middle of one of our prayer sessions, my mother began to prophesy, sharing with us what God spoke for us as a family, "There will be many tough days ahead, but God is with us." I thought we had had enough tough days; we could use some good days.

My mother turned to me, saying, "There is a great anointing, but it will cost a great sacrifice." She continued, "Mattie Poole had a great calling but experienced many trials. Her gift of healing cost her nearly everything she believed in. With every great anointing comes a great price."

Who was seeking a great anointing? Why was my mother speaking those words to me? There were other family members present. Why me?

I did not fully understand the first prophecy about a great, effectual door with many adversaries. Now, here was another prophecy I could not grasp. I was standing as my mother spoke. My feet seemed to give away. I was not prepared for a greater anointing.

We kept a bottle of oil in each of our homes because we believed in the power of the pouring of oil as symbolic of the anointing of God. Mother came and laid hands on me with the oil. My mother continued to prophesy over and over to me that there would be a great price to pay for the anointing of God upon my life. I not only had no concept of what Mother was referring to, but I also refused to consider what could happen because I was still grieving over Eric's death and wanted to spend time with my family. I wanted to enjoy time with them, not to seek a profound message about my future.

I did not take my mother's prophecy lightly. I prayed and asked God for strength to confront the future that awaited me and continued my travels and itinerant speaking engagements.

9

ALVIN'S SHORT WAR

"…Alvin Went To Jail"

I felt uneasy as I sat on the plane returning home from Phoenix, Arizona, where I had been one of the guest speakers at a Pentecostal National Conference. I knew there would be many changes in my life, yet I wondered why I felt such urgent tension.

My brother, Alvin, pastor of Revival Tabernacle Church, was engaged in a serious lawsuit with plaintiffs who wanted to control his church. He was also the friend and relative of members of Bethlehem Healing Temple. No wonder I was worried!

At the airport, I phoned home, and my sister, Ebony, answered, "Girl, there was a fight at Revival today, and Alvin went to jail."

What in the world are you talking about? Went to jail? For what?"

"Because of the lawsuit! Perci and his group want to be the Pastor of the church. Alvin was served with additional court documents. Of course, you know those people are the family members of those who don't want you to be pastor at Bethlehem. Those people went crazy. Who would want to be Pastor over those people?"

"Is Alvin still in jail?"

He's fine. Girl Alvin took off his shoes and was ready to fight for what he believed. The police surrounded the place. Those people are c-r-a-z-y! That's the reason I took a job far away from here. Alvin told the police he was ready to go to jail. The last I saw; he was being pushed into the back of the police car."

"Where is Dad? Where is Mama?"

"They are okay. But Daddy is in Bethlehem. You better get there fast. You and I know the people at that church have been fighting since the days of Sister Poole."

Alvin's Short-Lived War

Alvin was released from jail and resumed his responsibilities as Pastor while he continued to fight the lawsuit. When the plaintiffs claimed charges of defamation of character and lies, the court refused to listen, and the judge allowed our legal counsel to present all our evidence. The plaintiffs brought another lawsuit, which the second judge also dismissed.

My brother's war was short-lived, but the plaintiffs' relatives from Revival Tabernacle were determined to wage a vicious attack to prevent me from being pastor of Bethlehem Healing Temple.

It was the first salvo in a long war.

10
"MY DAUGHTER"

Genesis of the Conspiracy: "My Daughter Will Be the Pastor"

My father's announcement -- "My daughter will be the Pastor of this church" – focused on a vast conspiracy which had been brewing for more than fifty years. It had come to a head during the spring, when my father, like his predecessors, announced his successor.

There was also a Board of Directors and leaders' meeting held with the Director of Christian Education to restructure the Christian Education Department and request Mike, the current leader, to resign his post because he had missed many deadlines, and because there were financial and other concerns about his ministry.

The neighborhood had rapidly changed, so we agreed with the President's decision to reorganize several departments with innovative and trustworthy individuals.

A potentially explosive confrontation seemed to dissipate when Mike agreed to resign. The board granted Mike three weeks to introduce the new director to the staff and familiarize her with the responsibilities of the department. But that illusory sense of peace and harmony would soon be disrupted.

That Sunday, Clay, a board member, asked to meet me in the finance room. I agreed, but when I opened the door, I stepped back. There were ten people sitting inside of the room, including staff of the Christian Education department.

"What is this all about?"

Everyone started yelling at me. "You better put Mike back in!" Tray, their spokesman, finally spoke up and said, "Either put Mike back in place or we will see you tomorrow."

"You understand I was not responsible for removing Mike as the Director. Is that a threat? If it is, I guess I will see you tomorrow." I left amid cat calls.

A Mob Threatens

Monday afternoon an angry mob confronted me. There were family members of one of the Deacons, Tray, who had fifteen children, and the Rogers family, who had thirty-six children.

It was a long walk through the agitated crowd, who formed a tight circle inside the reception area. The shouts grew louder, yet I was not in the least intimidated. It was as if the Holy Spirit had paved my way.

One by one those who were shouting threats moved to the side, allowing me room to pass directly through the chanting crowd toward the Pastor's office.

When I arrived at the door. I knew that I was about to enter the lion's den. The click of the knob reaffirmed my acceptance of the call to become Pastor.

Once I was safely inside the office, I shut the door and fell to my knees thanking God for my safety and for not having to defend myself physically. Inside the Pastor's office sat the ones suspected of embezzling funds from the corporation and were now part of the conspiracy.

Along the back wall sat Tray, Mike, Clay, and Don. Don was rather quiet and informed me that he knew what they did was wrong. However, being friends with them made him a party to the conspiracy.

Clay and the others were watching the security cameras. Until then I did not realize that they had been cheerleaders for the conspiracy.

Clay immediately confronted me. "We want a meeting with the Pastor or else..."

I interrupted him, "Or else what?" My voice rose, "Or else what? Your conspiracy started before my father became the Pastor of this church. You were always against a female being appointed as Pastor. I listened to the tapes from Mattie Poole where she stated you and your former wife were conspiring to try and take over the corporation. Mattie was the founder. You were jealous of my father's relationship with her. You should never forget that he was the appointed successor. But my father is not present to defend himself, and you are taking it out on me. Is this the reason you brought me in here -- to make threats?"

Tray, the assistant chairman of Christian Education, spoke up next to make more demands, but I had had enough.

I began to make my own demands.

"Let me start by informing all of you that since there is a Pastor of this church, he makes the decisions. Each of you has bullied and terrorized members for years, behaving like a street gang. Unlike others, I am not afraid of either one of you. Do you all get that? This does not frighten me. Now I am giving each of you three seconds to get out of this office or I will call the police on each of you and your bullying family members."

As I opened the door for them to leave, I picked up the telephone to call security. Clay asked me when a suitable time might be to schedule a meeting with the Pastor.

"When he gets here, you talk to him and do not forget to tell him where you have been hiding the money you took. Now, get out!"

Later that evening I received a telephone call from Ann, one of the Christian Education staff. "Mike has just telephoned several of us and asked us to have a meeting with him immediately."

"When will this meeting take place?" I asked.

"Tomorrow evening."

"Who has been invited?"

"Most of the staff."

"Did he mention the purpose of the meeting?"

"Yes, he said that he was being replaced and we have got to do something right away because you are going to be the Pastor and you are trying to get rid of him."

I instructed her to attend the meeting and take notes.

Perjury

One day Clay, whose wife Mattie had excommunicated decades ago, walked into my office, and said, "Just you wait. I know there wasn't an election. Bishop Poole appointed your father. I don't care 'bout no election. We all signed a letter for your father when he became Pastor. But when I get to court, I will swear on the Holy Bible that there was an election."

Clay was admitting that he planned to perjure himself in a possible upcoming trial.

I responded, "Are you planning to take me to court? You are still angry that Mattie excommunicated your deceased wife for an attempted conspiracy."

He pointed at me. "Just you wait, we are going to hire a Giant law firm to crush you."

Conspiracy

Following Mike's agreement to step down quietly as director, he apparently used his requested time to prepare a revolt. I phoned Ann to find out what happened in the meeting.

"You had better be ready for a fight! He is out to get you for sure this time."

"What do you mean, this time?"

"They hold you personally responsible for Mike being removed as Director."

"Who are *they*?" I insisted.

"Clay, Mike, Tray, his wife and fifteen kids, Lucy, and the Jones family, you know it's a bunch of those Jones," she answered.

"Was Clay there?"

"Of course! You know he was there. Did you even need to ask that? Tray is out to get you as well. He is just a silent snake."

"What makes you say such a thing?" I asked.

"You remember I told you years ago that each Friday night I sat in the baptism room where they held meetings to have you removed when you were the Youth Director?" Ann asked.

I told her that was a long time ago -- more than eight years.

Ann was emphatic, and I could hear the concern in her voice. "Well, it has escalated. They wanted to force you out of this church nearly ten years ago. And as long as you were in college, they were forming an alliance. They've been having private meetings with us for years. Another thing, Lester has been holding private meetings at his house. The letter we talked about several months ago came from me."

"What letter?" I asked.

"The anonymous letter to your father," she admitted.

"Are you speaking of the letter written to my father regarding Lester's private meetings to elevate himself as Pastor?" I couldn't believe this.

"Yes!"

I was astonished. "I had no idea that you wrote that letter."

"I couldn't tell you that it was from me. But you can ask James. We sat in your father's office when Clay, Dexter, and Tray demanded that your dad get rid of you. I have got to say, you are in for a big war because you have got so many people who are fighting for the throne. And please beware, the biggest threat is Mattie Poole's foster child, Deb. She has her hand on the seniors. She is slick. She is poisonous because she manipulates from behind the scenes," Ann warned.

"You should not talk about people that way. It's not nice."

"I'm telling you, that lady told me personally, she'll do whatever it takes to get what she wants. Read the book regarding Mattie's life."

"I have read that book many times," I replied.

"Be naive if you want to. I won't be the one to say I told you so, you'll see. It's deep, girl, they want your blood, bad. You just remember there's more than one person involved in the plot. It will thicken."

"I hope your theory is not true."

"Call it what you want, time will prove what I'm saying. Call me tomorrow," Ann finished.

I did not want to believe what Ann was telling me -- that there was such a conspiracy against me.

I recalled my dream about the locked doors.

Chain Locked Doors

It was the middle of the night when I awakened from a frightening dream. Earlier I had had a puzzling dream about a changing of guards, in which students were changing military uniforms. I did not understand that earlier dream, but this new dream had awakened me.

In the scene, my family and I were seated with many others at the back of the main sanctuary. Something terrible had happened to my father; someone else was at the microphone. I recognized Mike and Clay. Where was my father? I wondered. Why was the sanctuary so dark?

I prepared to walk to the front of the church to determine what was happening and why my father was absent. When Mike and Clay tried to stop me, I could feel that no matter how hard I searched for my father, he would not appear.

I suddenly realized that my father had passed away and that we would never see him again. What would we do? Who could we count on? My father had given his life for his ministry and his family.

As I left the sanctuary, I turned to go into another part of the church, but all the doors were locked. I felt as if someone were following me. When I turned around, I saw Mike and Clay carrying all of the keys to the church. They smiled at each other as they continued to lock other doors.

My family and I were refused access to the church.

As Mike and Clay turned their backs to lock more doors, someone opened the door to the outside office. My family and I tried to enter my father's office, but the office door was locked. My siblings stared at me, clueless. I had no answers.

The Holy Spirit directed me to place my hand on the doorknob to my father's office. This time the door opened. I entered the office and told my siblings, "They could not lock us out of this office."

When the members of the church saw me inside of my father's office, they seemed relieved that I was able to enter locked doors, to overcome those who were attempting to lock me out. The Holy Spirit spoke to me, "Each door you touch will be unlocked. You need only to place your hand on the knob."

I awakened from the dream. It was one of the most frightening dreams I had ever had. It felt so real that I sat up in the bed with tears rolling down my face. The thought of losing my father was too intense for me. I wrote down the dream of the locked doors in my journal and underlined the words, "You need only to place your hand on the knob."

What a profound dream! At the time, I did not know the significance of the dream, nor did I realize how many times I would have to refer to it. How many times would I have to remember to touch the door in faith and simply believe that the locked doors would open to me? Only God had the answer to that question. He alone held the keys to unlock any doors in my life.

Ann's Warning

After I had time to reflect on Ann's theory, it was time to return her call.

"Marci, they're having a meeting,' Friday," Ann told me, "The Deacons and Mike. They are planning on calling all their family and friends."

"What in the world are you talking about?"

"They are demanding that the Bishop be there. You better get ready. They will try to make Bishop put Mike back in as Director of Christian Education."

They cannot make anyone put Mike back into place because the Pastor has made his decision," I reminded her.

"Well, like I told you, they think you decided to replace Mike as Director," she repeated.

"What time and where is the meeting?" I asked.

"They are going to call the Bishop. Don't say anything until you hear about it."

I thanked Ann. People were already choosing sides: those, like Ann, who believed in my position as Pastor versus those who were determined to replace me.

First Public Meeting of the Conspiracy

The following Thursday, Mattie Poole's foster daughter, Deb, and the conspirators met to plot against the Pastor and distributed flyers announcing a church meeting on Friday. But on Friday, a meeting with the Deacons' Board became a meeting with the conspirators, their family members, and their friends.

The meeting opened with the Pastor asking, "Why are we here?"

Tray, the Assistant Superintendent of Sunday school, and his wife Linda began belligerently shouting at the Pastor. The Pastor immediately interrupted Tray and Linda as each posed the question, "Why can't we have Mike return as Director?"

The answer was direct and logical: "The Sunday School is not growing, and we need to begin making progress within. The neighborhood is rapidly changing, and we are not compatible with the upcoming changes of our neighborhood. The new Director is innovative and creative."

The meeting turned sour as the disgruntled group became more confrontational.

The following Sunday, the conspirators met with the Board of Directors and my father in his official role as Pastor, to again insist that the new Sunday School Director be removed or else they would organize and carry out a plot against him.

Without hesitating, the Pastor informed the conspirators that the new Director would remain in position. The threat of open warfare intensified as members of the Board of Directors contended with the disgruntled group. They declared that the Pastor could make appointments and decisions as he deemed necessary.

The conspirators then refused to work with the new director, but the members of the Board agreed to work with the new Director. The meeting was adjourned, and the disgruntled group met in another part of the church.

On Tuesday, the Pastor met again with the conspirators and an attorney. In that meeting, the conspirators demanded Mike's reinstatement. The Pastor questioned Clay about financial accounting, but. Clay refused to answer.

On the following Friday, the Pastor held another meeting with the conspirators and an attorney. The Pastor stated that the board needed to address the issue of whether Clay had taken money without permission, and after chaotic discussion the meeting adjourned.

The following Sunday, the conspirators met again with the Pastor and insisted that they were ready to act if he did not return Mike to his position, regardless of unaccounted funds. When the Pastor rejected the demands of the conspirators, they distributed another flier announcing a meeting the following Monday.

The Pastor attended the meeting; however, when Clay became angry, the audience became agitated, and the Pastor left the meeting.

The conspirators stated that there would be another meeting the following Tuesday, but the Pastor dismissed the meeting.

As I left the sanctuary, my mother's prophecy in Jamaica came to mind, "There is a great and effective door and there are many adversaries."

Where were these enemies coming from? Were these the adversaries my mother spoke of? How could this be happening so rapidly? I then recalled my dream of Mike and Clay locking all the doors to keep me from entering.

What had started as a manageable disagreement had sparked a war.

The War – The Public Announcement

As agreed, approximately a month later, there was a public announcement of the new director, Lisa. Immediately Clay, along with Tray, the Assistant Director of the Christian Education Department, and their supporters made threats and accusations toward me and distributed a flier announcing a gathering on Monday to demand the reinstatement of the former director.

On Monday, Marie and other members of our Board of Directors attended the gathering, which became another platform to hurl accusations and insults at our Board of Directors, but the meeting ended abruptly when our Board of Directors refused to continue being insulted.

The Deacons' Demands

The Board of Deacons met with the Pastor and our interim attorney, Gregory, on Tuesday. That evening the conspirators met with the Pastor and demanded to join the Board of Directors. My father agreed to another meeting with the conspirators. During that meeting, the Deacons asked whether he was certain that I would be Pastor. Clay, the spokesperson, asked, "Are you still going to name Marci to be the Pastor?"

My father replied, "That's old. She's already the Pastor."

On Thursday, the conspirators received letters demanding that they discontinue their meetings. The following Sunday Clay announced that there would be a prayer meeting on Monday. On Sunday, the conspirators met with the Pastor and continued to demand that he reinstate the former Director. The Pastor refused, stating that Sunday was a day of worship and agreed to meet with them on Tuesday instead.

Again, on Sunday the disgruntled group demanded that they become members of the Board of Directors, adding that if they were not immediately appointed directors, they were prepared to telephone their friends and relatives who would incite more division among the congregation.

On Tuesday, the Pastor agreed to have yet another meeting with the conspirators, but in that meeting requested an audit from each department leader. The conspirators said they were not interested in discussing finances and continued to demand that Mike be reinstated and be given a platform to speak.

They also demanded the Pastor's resignation.

The following Sunday, the conspirators again insisted on becoming members of the Board of Directors and would proceed either with a public march or with physical force to remove the Pastor.

Could it be that the prophecy of Mattie Poole would come to pass? Would the church be swept clean?

11
THE PURPORTED VOTE

nn informed me about the meeting organized by the Deacons and their self-promoted secretary. "They have galvanized members of their family and friends and distributed flyers announcing a meeting Wednesday as they try to get rid of you. The flier said it's supposed to happen during the week before the holiday or the week after Memorial Day."

"What is scheduled to take place?" I asked.

Ann said, "Those people are crazy. They say there is going to be a meeting so they can vote."

"Vote? An election? For what?" I asked.

"They are going to try and put themselves in position as the leaders of the church," she stated.

"Do you know who's going to participate in their purported, so-called, voting?"

"Girl, they have called up the dead to be at the church next week to come in to put themselves up."

Shocked, I replied, "Summon the dead? Are you referring to a – a séance? People chanting to the dead?"

Ann laughed so loud and long I could not understand why she was laughing. Finally, she said, "Girl, all I'm saying is they are going to call in people who haven't been at the church in years to set themselves up as the Pastor over you."

"Well, I know that you will be there, and I am sure that you will call and give me the details."

"You know I wouldn't miss this for the world. They don't even like each other. This should be really good," Ann replied.

Wednesday arrived and the conspirators met. The other participants were Lloyd, the Assistant Bishop of The National Organization, and Lester, who wanted to set himself up as Pastor. I was home when Ann telephoned me from the church and said, "They are all up there making people sign their names to some kind of list. Girl, there are so many people who are so mad that they are doing this. It is so chaotic."

"Have you seen Marie or anyone from my family?" I asked.

"Your mother is here, so is your brother and some other members of your family. I saw Marie around here somewhere."

"Ask Marie to telephone me when you see her."

Marie called, frustrated, to say, "You would not believe this. A McDaze woman and her relatives are sitting at a table in the lobby asking people for their signatures, telling everyone that Bishop has decided to resign. When I asked if I could see the documents, McDaze told me no. They are sitting up there, and their secretary is sitting at the offering table in the middle of the church."

I tried to encourage Marie by saying, "Just as her name is, McDaze, and so let it speak for itself. The unknown names missing from the purported list of signatures are now surfacing. The organizers have come to the front of the table. Don't worry. There is no way that you will be able to keep up with that conspiracy."

Marie responded, "I have been at this church over thirty years, and I have never seen such foolishness."

I asked Marie where my mother was, and she told me that she was in the outside hall talking to some people she had not seen in over forty years.

Marie continued to observe a self-styled gathering coordinated by those aspiring to be in leadership at the church. It was essential to note some of the parties in attendance in this meeting; these parties were key witnesses for the upcoming litigation and trial against us and our corporation. Along with the plaintiffs, the key witnesses in the Brownlow and Rogers vs. Richards's lawsuit were Deb, Lester, Clay, Lloyd, Rogers, McDaze, Jimmy, Lucy, and Mike.

The days ahead proved to be exceptionally testing following the tumultuous circumstances confronting my father and me, the Board of Directors, and the ministry.

The conspirators were not a well-organized group. At first sight, it seemed that their primary goal was to have Lisa replaced as Sunday School Director. Mike was unemployed and was primarily responsible for directing the funds from our Christian Education and for our banquet hall. It was well known that Mike wanted to be Pastor.

The people organizing the conspirator's meetings managed to keep their names and faces out of the litigation as long as possible. Since Deb's mother's former position was corporate secretary of our organization, upon her mother's death, Deb received all the corporate records along with the complete history of the corporation. As a result of her numerous conversations with me and others, we knew that she was carrying out her own personal agenda.

Clay had told me, "I had nothing to do with initiating the lawsuit, although I'm a part of it.

Clay did not know his attorney's telephone number, nor did he even know his name. I picked up the telephone, dialed Jim, and requested Clay's counsel's information so that Clay could call him.

I had known Clay all my life; he was neither an organizer nor a public speaker. Clay also had a speech impediment and avoided speaking before large groups.

Several members informed the Board of Directors that the plaintiffs' secretary was working behind the scenes to set her husband Jimmy up as Pastor. Like Mike, Jimmy lacked the charisma to be the next leader. Lloyd, who was appointed the assistant presider of The National Organization and appointed Pastor of another church, laid claims to be the assistant Pastor of our church. Lloyd was also a close friend of Mike's.

On the other hand, it appeared that there was not enough support to reinforce Lloyd's desire to be appointed as the next leader of the church. One other person -- Lester -- was trying to emerge as leader and was having meetings to position himself as the next Pastor.

Although all these individuals had their own personal agendas, they joined forces to bring the lawsuit against me and the corporation.

Within Bethlehem's organization there existed several entities within the corporation. Given the autonomy and liberal structure of the organization, most of the managers within the corporation took full advantage of the liberality and ran things the way they wanted to. Although my father was aware of the eccentric management style of several of the managers, it did not pose a public threat to the overall structure of the organization -- a mistaken impression that would prove nearly fatal.

The Pastor did not address the significant behaviors of managers, who positioned themselves as dictatorial leaders who developed and divided clusters of followers. Most of these clusters included their family members and friends, some of whom had not even been members of the church.

While there existed much divisiveness among these groups, the time came when they would form an alliance based upon lies.

When the initial demands of Clay, his friends, and the conspirators were not met, the conspirators distributed flyers announcing a Wednesday meeting, where they attempted to overthrow my father for appointing me as his successor.

On the eve of the self-styled gathering of these clustered groups, there was a gathering of the family members including family who were not a part of the organization or those who had not been a part of the organization for more than thirty to forty years. These outsiders came to participate in and observe the actions of the disgruntled group.

The conspirators asked their families and friends to sign their names to a petition in their relentless efforts to try and seize control of the corporation. Upon receiving many of the outsiders' and family members' signatures to support their actions, the conspirators began the overt attempt to seize control of the assets and resources of the corporation.

The following Sunday, Clay finally revealed to the Board who was responsible for bringing the lawsuit. "Our secretary prepared the papers for us. She's working on getting us a big law firm to help us and we are going to see y'all in court. Everything is going to be on lock down."

12

CHAOS

Lockdown

The day after the vote, I received telephone calls from the receptionists of the church who were mostly senior citizens. "They have locked down the church. Chains are everywhere. We can't get out and nobody can get in."

"Who are they?" I asked.

"Clay and his group," Essie said.

Dillie telephoned my father. "Please come and help us. We are locked up inside the church. Cindy, who is a convicted felon, is holding us hostage."

I phoned one of the custodians and discovered there was indeed a group of senior citizens locked up inside the church. Essie told me, "They are not allowing anyone access to the church."

I immediately called the fire marshal. Along with several other people, I arrived at the church at the same time the fire marshals arrived and saw chains on all the doors. The marshals demanded that the doors be unlocked and informed Cindy and others that they could not lock individuals inside of a building, Cindy and her followers left the grounds.

My father arrived at the church, along with my brother Arthur, who reminded me of the Incredible Hulk. Arthur started removing the locks and chains on the outside doors and went through the entire church snatching all of the chains and huge padlocks off all of the doors. He also had someone remove the other dead-bolted locks placed on the office doors.

As the locks were being removed, I heard a scream. I headed upstairs to my office and approached Kelle's screams. Tyler, a mentally ill man who obviously had not taken his medication, was breaking, and entering my office.

Tyler was yelling at Kelle, "Clay and Deb told me to break into Marci's office and take all the files and change the locks."

I immediately understood what had happened. Clay and Deb had tricked this loyal and obedient but mentally ill man, Tyler, to do their dirty work, stealing my files and locking my office for the conspirators.

I stopped in my tracks as Tyler then threatened me and Kelle with a gigantic power chain saw. "I'm going to kill you. C'mon!

I yelled, "Kelle, he has mental issues. Don't go any closer."

Kelle was a petite lady, but her stature in no way reflected her valor.

Ignoring me, Kelle continued to walk toward Tyler and screamed at him, "You had better get away from Doc's office right now."

The ladies from the cafeteria were preparing food, heard the screams, and came running upstairs. Mother Littlejohn screamed, "Tyler is crazy. He's been on medication for years. Get away from him."

With the gigantic power saw in his hands, Tyler rushed towards Kelle. I watched as Kelle did not move or blink an eye. She screamed, "I dare you to lift that thing at me."

What a bodacious lady! I continued to yell, "Kelle, he's crazy."

While Kelle and Tyler were screaming back and forth, one of the other employees telephoned the police. Tyler was arrested and taken to jail

The conspirators' revolt had spread in unexpected ways as they manipulated innocent, vulnerable bystanders like Tyler to do their bidding, regardless of consequences. If Tyler had injured or even killed one of us, he – not Clay or Deb, who had told him what to do -- would have suffered those consequences.

Following Tyler's arrest, we successfully managed to remove all the bolted chains from the other doors and continued with the order of the day until that evening's Bible study. Following the morning chaos, we entered a lion's den which was supposed to be our Bible study meeting.

I noticed Clay and their secretary talking and went to interrupt the conversation to ask who gave the command to change the locks, when I noticed the plaintiff's secretary giving Clay instructions, "Go in there and hand this letter to Bishop and tell him it's for him to leave."

Clay nodded. As I was about to address the plaintiff's secretary, I turned my head toward the commotion in the sanctuary and watched Cindy, assisted by the other conspirators, abusively threaten my father. Before I could get to the stage, my mother demanded that Cindy show respect.

I walked up to Cindy. "How dare you stand on that sacred pulpit like you are a saint? You have got a lot of nerves! When your father died, you arrived at this church in a paddy wagon. The police brought you to this church from the penitentiary in handcuffs, in an orange jumpsuit, with chains strapped all around you. That is how you arrived at your father's funeral! It was my daddy who demanded that the police remove the handcuffs and chains from you, allowing you to attend your father's funeral like a decent human being. It was my father who came to the hospital to visit you when you were shot seven times and left for dead, drowning in your own blood. And this is the thanks you show him? You should be arrested and returned to the pen from where my father prayed for your release."

Cindy did not respond. The police were summoned, and we ended Bible study.

During the following weeks we endured chaos.

13

PRAYER MEETING

━━━━━)|•|(━━━━━

The Days Following the Vote

It was not unusual for my father to miss a Sunday morning service, and every fourth Sunday he would teach at the Revival church. The Sunday following the conspirators' purported election, my father did not appear in church. That Sunday felt like a high-powered action movie. There was never a dull moment as those suing us were constantly thinking of methods to carry out their plot.

Deb, Lester, Clay, Mike, and their friends held a celebration that morning. Their friends from long ago were in attendance. They made the entire Sunday morning worship a spectacle. Parading up and down the aisle declaring their victory over their enemies, they pointed at me. They placed banners in their children's hands and encouraged them to clap as they clapped. They encouraged the children to stomp their feet as they stomped their feet. They encouraged them to jump as they jumped.

I was incredulous and decided to exit the sanctuary in search of my mother

Those in the audience were in total consternation. Visitors had no clue about what was happening. The conspirators' supporters approached the stage, one after the other, making a spectacle of the Sunday morning services. This scene continued for nearly two hours until finally someone decided that enough was enough. One of the leaders of the church stood and demanded the supporters of the conspirators leave the audience. It was quiet following the group's exit.

The following Monday was like an ordinary day. The conspirators did not come near the building. The office staff continued to carry out their assignments, and no one spoke of the day before.

On Tuesday, my father taught Bible study as if the actions of the conspirators were meaningless. During the week, there were many rumors circulating that my father was no longer Pastor.

The following Sunday morning was like an ordinary Sunday. My father appeared at the church and walked into his office speaking to everyone as he prepared to go inside the sanctuary. As Dad prepared to leave the church, those standing in the audience gave him hugs as he walked through the halls. Upon arriving in the sanctuary, my father took his usual seat. Finally, it was time for my father to address the audience. Turning the microphone over to him, the praise leader said, "Please stand with me and receive our pastor, Bishop Arcenia Richards."

The audience applauded and the first words from dad's mouth were, "I am still the Pastor."

The audience continued to applaud, and Dad continued the service as if there had been no interruptions. Every person in leadership, including the conspirators and their supporters submitted themselves to his authority. No one questioned my father's authority, words, presence, or leadership. As Daddy stood at the microphone, he gave Clay some directions as to the offering and Clay followed suit as he always did when given directions by the Pastor.

The words "I am still the Pastor" rang throughout the hallways as the supporters of the conspirators sat in the back of the service in total disbelief, watching as their plan was foiled.

Prayer Meeting or Planning Meeting?

Among her other duties, Marie was also one of the announcers at the church. One Sunday, as Marie stood to make the announcements, Clay passed Marie a note which read, "There will be a prayer meeting tomorrow night at 7:00p.m. We are asking everyone to be at the prayer meeting.

Come one, come all." After making the announcements, Marie looked over at me, handed me the note, and said, "Let's attend this."

I nodded, thinking that this would be a great time for all of us to come together and pray.

On Monday, I sat upstairs in my office working. Vickie, one of the daughters of the Bishops of The National Organization, came to my office and asked if I knew what was going on downstairs. I said, "I believe it is a prayer meeting."

She responded, "I think you should go down there."

I went downstairs and stood outside of the sanctuary. I noticed Clay standing at the microphone and overheard someone say, "We are losing momentum. We cannot continue to hold the people. We have got to do something."

I looked inside to see who was speaking. Sitting off to the side in what we called the handicapped section of the church was McDaze, a plaintiff who was very ill, in a wheelchair, and on oxygen.

I then noticed Cindy, who stood and said, "Marci is going to catch on to what we are doing, if y'all don't hurry up."

I looked in the back of the room and saw Marie sitting with her hands folded, listening. Marie looked at me and nodded, as if to say, "I told you that we needed to be here."

I interjected, "What happened to the prayer meeting? Or was this really a planning meeting?" Stepping all the way inside, I watched the surprised faces of those in attendance. Many gasped as if they'd been caught doing something naughty. No one answered my question.

I continued to stand there as Cindy spoke. This time she did not say my name. Instead, she said, "She is not stupid. They are going to find out what we are doing"

McDaze said, "We were calling her name, so why stop just because she walked in the room?"

I spoke up, "Do not mind me. I thought this was a prayer meeting, and I wanted to be a part of the prayer. Apparently, I am the only item on the agenda and it's not prayer; therefore, I am interested in this meeting since I am the topic of discussion."

With those words, I took a seat along the side of the wall. My presence made the group uncomfortable. They could hardly believe I had entered, much less taken a seat and interrupted their meeting. Finally, someone stood and said, "We better get a lawyer."

Clay said, "We are working on something so real big. Let's talk about this later. Give y'all names so that we can call y'all." Then they dispersed.

There was never supposed to be a prayer meeting. The group used the meeting to continue their conspiracy.

Known and the Unknown Names

Following the meeting, Marie and I located a copy of the alleged signed petitions from the conspirators and their supporters.

We studied the list of names carefully. We were familiar with some of the names, although there were many we did not recognize as members of the church.

I had conversations with several of them and discovered various reasons they had signed these petitions. One of the seniors informed me that she was told that the Pastor was ready to retire and needed her signature to do so.

Another said that he was told it was the Pastor who required his signature and, since the leaders were given so much independence, he did not think to question their motives. He further explained that during a conversation he was informed of the actions of the conspirators and went to the Pastor to inquire about the need for signatures. When he learned that there was no such need, he immediately went to remove his name, only to be told that he could not remove or scratch out his signature.

The Perspective from the Lakefront

I often drove to the lakefront to watch the waves, as if it were a small sea. I would sit on the lakefront allowing my thoughts to reflect on the winds as they carried away the pain and disappointment of whatever misfortunes I experienced. The scene from the lake provided me with serenity.

There were different cultures and lifestyles represented on the lakefront; the wealthy and the poor enjoyed equal pleasures there. You could purchase ice cream and climb from one rock to another. Or you could sit and meditate. Sometimes I dozed off into a deep sleep as I listened to the sound of the waves and felt the cool breeze wash over me, flushing out the mundane activities and responsibilities and demands of my everyday affairs and tensions.

I knew that there was something strong working against us. The scene of the lakefront allowed me to focus on positive events.

I had made copies of the opponents' petitions. One day, as I prayed at the lakefront, I took the list of those who had signed their names to the petitions and tossed the entire list into the water. I prayed that God would bless the innocent and naïve and deceived people who had signed their names on that list. I also prayed for my family, asking God to forgive us for any sins that we had committed and to protect us from the evil powers of darkness.

I reflected on the story of Moses and the children of Israel crossing the Red Sea and then cautiously tore each page of the petitions into tiny pieces and scattered them from one end of the lake to the other, praying as the tiny pieces of paper disappeared. Some pieces would rise to the top for a few moments. I stayed there determined to watch until each piece of paper disappeared into the lake while thinking of God presiding over a vast sea. As I stood looking at the clear waters, I believed that God heard my prayer.

Bible Verses Under the Seats

I phoned Marie and asked her to help me type Bible verses. Without asking questions, she typed the verses in bold and large print on hundreds of pages. We enlisted the services of a dear friend of mine, Danny, to place the Bible verses under every pew and every chair in the sanctuary.

Marie and I walked for hours with Danny from the first section of the sanctuary to the final section. We covered every seat with pages of Bible verses.

There was a platform where all the ministers, elders, and teachers sat. We stapled pages under each seat, under the podium where each speaker taught, under the instruments, and other areas that were not even visible. There were pages placed under the collection table, and we filled the collection baskets. There were pages under the communion table. We dared not miss a spot.

There was also a baptistery and the choir's stand with seats for the choir members. "This area must be covered as well," I told Danny. The steps in the choir area were much closer together. Danny was such a tall, long-legged gentleman that it was nearly impossible for him to staple the sheets of paper under the seats between the choir steps.

I insisted, "We are nearly done. Please don't give up now." Finally, the job was nearly finished. There was just one seat off to the side.

As I reached for the paper I said, "I would like to place the Bible verse under this seat." He handed me the paper and helped me kneel. I fell to my knees and read aloud the verse on the paper. Substituting the word "my" for the word "his" within the verse, I read from Deuteronomy 33:11, "Bless, Lord, my substance, and accept the work of my hands...." I stapled the sheet and stood. Standing up and sweating, I took a seat in that chair and repeated the verse again.

All of us held hands, as I led us in a prayer. We turned off the lights and left the church.

The Prayer Chapel

The Prayer Chapel was one of the most sacred places in the church -- the place where we prayed to receive answers from God. No one dared talk in the Prayer Chapel except to pray. We were taught that the Prayer Chapel was the place that Mattie had labored and talked to God for the miracles. Therefore, if there was one place, I believed God would hear me, it was the Prayer Chapel.

You could always hear people praying in the Prayer Chapel. Even at times when you believed you would have some alone time, you would discover that others were ahead of you, only they were praying silently, petitioning God.

Prostitutes came off the street and fell to their knees begging God to forgive them. Daily, I recalled the voices of those within the prayer room petitioning God for answers. Time after time, I interrupted my personal prayers to ask God to answer those who were crying out for His guidance.

There, in that sacred place, where people would pray to the God of Mattie, I prayed. My faith was in God Almighty. He, I believed, was in total control of the affairs of my life.

Exhausted, I believed that was the end of my assignment. I allowed myself to relax in the Prayer Chapel.

Then I decided to visit my father.

"You Will Never Understand Betrayal"

Upon arriving at my father's house, my eyes were swollen from the tears that I had shed as a result of the betrayals. I found my dad kneeling in prayer. He looked up at me and must have noticed the swelling in my eyes. He spoke softly, asked if I would kneel beside him, and as I knelt, he placed his arms around me.

His first words were, "I want to share something with you that may help you throughout life's journey. Betrayal is extremely complicated. You will never understand betrayal. Therefore, you must be in constant reminder that Jesus was betrayed by his closest friends."

I waited a few moments and said, "We are not Jesus."

"But we have Jesus living on the inside of us. Matthew 10:24, the Bible clearly teaches us that the servant is not greater than the Master. So, if we are to be true disciples of Christ, we shall experience similar circumstances, including being betrayed by friends."

Indeed, what my father was sharing was too convoluted for me. Theologically, I understand the betrayal of Jesus. I also understand, according to the Bible, that although Jesus was crucified, He was sent into this world as God's Son to die for the sins of humanity. In my heart of hearts, though, I was not ready to experience what Jesus experienced. I could not understand the reason for the betrayal. Why, all the conspirators had been appointed and promoted by my father.

It was Mattie's brother, Henry, who told my father, "Bishop, these men (referring to the Deacon Board) are nothing but good janitors, why are you promoting them? They are not capable of the leadership you're giving to them. Giving someone power beyond their ability will ultimately end up in abuse."

To completely understand why certain puzzling events occur, one must understand the history of the actors. Inevitably, behind each event of division and war there are underlying factors of greed, jealousy, ambition, lust, pride, and personal gain. To ignore or deny these issues is self-deceit. If those issues are not confronted, then betrayal becomes the measure by which those who are responsible promote themselves.

Behind Betrayal

There are enemies in the camp of every organization, though they may not be readily apparent. Even in families, there are often those who seek to be the heir to the throne who have neither the right nor the qualifications.

Mattie Poole's foster daughter was the daughter of the former corporate secretary, yet she eventually became secretary of the plaintiffs.

Jean, a member of the church and one of their supporters told me, "Bishop and Sister Poole adamantly opposed her ascendancy to leadership." One could almost understand the plaintiff's secretary's desire, as her mother, Mrs. James, was personal secretary to the founding Pastors. Mrs. James served not only as the secretary of the founding Pastors, but she also served as the secretary of Bethlehem's corporation until her death. Therefore, Deb, Mattie Poole's foster child, saw it as a natural course that she would ascend triumphantly to the leadership of the church and the corporation.

After her mother's death, she became obsessed with the quest for this almost holy grail of leadership. In several conversations she stated her passionate desire to be secretary of the corporation. "I know all about this church. I was born in it, and this is my church. I will be the one who determines what happens at this church."

Upon the removal of Mike as the Christian Education director, Deb and Mike joined their friends and relatives as co-conspirators. The self-appointed pastor of their separated church, plaintiff Lester, appeared eager to become Pastor of Bethlehem. I was informed weekly of the numerous meetings held among those suing us. We received scores of letters informing us that Lester was meeting with several factions from the church to ensure his eventual position as Pastor.

When all those conspirators could not effectively gain control of the church and corporation, they aligned themselves with others to start another church and corporation. The plaintiffs, along with their friends, were otherwise completely divided, but they formed an alliance and sued us. My mother was correct. There were many adversaries. Unfortunately, I did not recognize all of them.

14
THE PLOT THICKENS

The Conspiracy

It was at the birthday party of Vickie, one of the Bishops from The National Organization, that Marie, the General Secretary of The National Organization and I were informed that Clay and Lloyd were privately meeting with others at the same time. Vickie asked, "Did you know the deacons from your church and Bishop Lloyd are having a private meeting with the other bishops? They called my father. They said your father wasn't invited."

It seemed that this had been a personal meeting to elevate Lloyd to the position of Presiding Bishop and President of The National Organization.

Annual Report

It was approaching time to file our annual report with the Secretary of State; however, there was much turmoil within the corporation that we needed to avoid distractions. One day, as two members of the Board of Directors approached the church as my father was leaving, they hesitated to stop and ask him if they could meet with him. We understood that when he was ready to leave the office, you risked everything by asking him to stay, because he did not believe in any delays. This particular day: however, he immediately agreed to meet with them, and they asked me to join the meeting.

As my father headed back to his office for the meeting, he said it was time to file the annual report. At the end of the meeting, one man said, "File the annual report now."

The annual report was completed, the meeting concluded, and we left the church. None of us had any clue that filing the annual report prior to the deadline would prevent the conspirators from carrying out a plan to seize control of the organization.

"She Has Always Thrown a Rock and Hid Her Hand"

I had no idea what the 85-year-old lady's statement meant: "She has always thrown a rock and hid her hand."

"Who?" I asked.

"Mattie Poole's foster daughter," she responded. "I have known her since she was a child."

I replied, "Well, I have always been taught what is done in the dark will come to the light."

The elderly lady smiled. "You have no idea. This war started before you were born. You just happened to be caught in the middle of it."

I returned her smile and walked off.

The Letter from the Secretary of State

A few weeks later as we were managing the affairs of the organization, we received an unexpected letter in the mail from the Secretary of State, which stated that the Secretary was returning the falsified records filed by the conspirators. As I continued reviewing the papers, I noticed a letter from Mattie's foster daughter, Deb, on our letterhead. This was no longer just some misdirected family squabble. The war had apparently turned into a major case of perjury.

At the bottom of the letter were the signatures of each of the plaintiffs. Mattie's foster child, as secretary, had filed the papers on behalf of the corporation.

We immediately contacted our attorney, Jim, and sent him copies of the information. Jim sent letters to those seeking to seize control of the corporation and informed them of the gravity of their actions and the legal actions that could be taken against them. The conspirators were now stepping over all kinds of boundaries to attempt to carry out their plan.

The plaintiffs and their secretary had sworn and taken an oath before a notary public and filed with the Secretary of State's Office a falsified Annual Report purporting to be the official annual report from the corporation. The false Annual Report also contained names and signatures of individuals who equally misrepresented themselves as board members, thereby furthering their gross acts of perjury.

The Secretary of State returned the original documents filed by the secretary and the plaintiffs to the offices of the corporation. Along with that incident, there were other incidents in which the plaintiffs' counsels assisted the plaintiffs' secretary with a signed notarized letter addressed to the Secretary of State, fraudulently misrepresenting people who were never members of the official board.

Did the actions of the plaintiffs and their secretary indicate that any individual could file a false report to try and gain control of an organization? All of the above fraudulent misrepresentation of facts and people had violated the General Not-For-Profit Corporation, which exposes culprits' liability.

The plaintiffs and their secretary willfully disregarded the letter from our counsel advising the plaintiffs to cease and desist from filing false reports, including warning them of their acts of perjury and right to pursue all available legal actions, both criminal and civil. The letter from the Secretary of State would not be the end of the plaintiff's attempts to coerce the Secretary of State into making them the official Board of our Corporation.

Hospital and Post Office Visits

One of the former board members, Dillie, who was a part of the finance team, became ill and was absent from the church for an extended period. Rubi informed me that both she and Mattie's foster child had made several trips to the hospital to visit Dillie to have her sign documents against the Pastor.

While Dillie was gravely ill, Deb admitted having visited the hospital to obtain her signature. "I visited Dillie today in the hospital. I tried to get her to sign documents against the Bishop. She told me that she could never go against the Bishop and that she supported me and you." Dillie had made her decision and told Rubi and Deb how appalled she was at their insistence that she revoke her unfailing support of the Pastor. Deb also informed me that Dillie unequivocally told her that she would never sign any documents against the Pastor and fully supported all of his decisions. Dillie was overwhelmed by the chain of events, never left the hospital, and died a few weeks later.

I often wondered why Deb informed me that she had visited Dillie. That was a bizarre incident. However, it would not seem bizarre compared to the next chain of events.

Following Deb's conversation to me about Dillie, she phoned me to ask for my oldest brother, Winston's number.

"I don't have his number in front of me. I can relay a message for you. What would you like me to tell him?"

"I would like to talk to him as the oldest child. See, I am the oldest in my family. I thought I would like to try and convince him to talk to the Bishop about leaving the church," she explained.

I replied, "I have always thought there was something wrong with you, but I could not put my finger on it. I have heard for years that you are as crazy as you look. First, he is not the oldest child in my family. Secondly, because you have the audacity to call and ask me for my brother's number to ask him to convince my father to leave the church; I am going to give it to you. This should be quite interesting. I just want you to know that I will not be responsible for what happens during that telephone call."

I relayed the message to Winston. "Mattie's foster child wants to speak to you so that you will convince Dad to resign as Pastor."

"Does she think that I am a fool? That is one crazy dummy. She doesn't want to talk to me. I will be there Sunday."

"Please don't come. It's not worth it."

I made Winston promise me that he would not come to the church that week.

A visit to the post office was also revealing. While retrieving the mail for the church, a representative at the post office stopped me. "Someone has informed the post office that the Pastor, Bishop Richards, is deceased and that the postal address should be changed."

"Who was the person, and did they give you an address by which to forward the mail?" I asked.

"Yes, Lucy." The address to forward Dad's mail belonged to the plaintiff. Astonished, I told my father and told him what I had learned.

"Did you tell them that that is not true?"

"Absolutely, but you really should address these incidents. They are getting out of hand."

"You have to choose your battles," was his reply.

With one lie following another lie, the conspiracy thickened to support the covert and disruptive efforts of those who had formed an alliance opposing my pastorship.

The Insurance Policy

Dillie's funeral was on a Saturday, and as I sat in the sanctuary mourning our loss, I noticed that Rubi was absent. I wondered why.

The two of them had worked in the office together for more than thirty years and were primarily responsible for the financial affairs of the church. I felt an urgency to go to the office to see what time my father was scheduled to give Dillie's eulogy.

The postal carrier stopped and handed me the mail as I approached my father's office. I noticed Rogers, who had traveled to the city for Dillie's funeral services, sitting in my father's office whispering in his ear. When I opened the door unannounced, Rogers stood and abruptly left. When I asked my father what Rogers had been telling him, he stated, "Just the fact that there are those in the conspiracy who desire to be Pastor, including himself."

In the following weeks, as a Giant law firm promoted a lawsuit on behalf of Rogers, I would often recall that scene as I watched Rogers whispering in my father's ear.

I decided to step outside of the office. I told myself that if there were those who wished to share their views with him, it did not concern me. How many others were there who would vie for position as Pastor?

I decided to take a seat in the receptionist's office and watch Dillie's funeral services from the television cameras. I noticed that I was still carrying the mail as I sat at the desk. I was not accustomed to managing the mail, so I decided to drop the mail off in Rubi's office. As I glanced down at the mail, I noticed the first letter had the name of my father's insurance carrier as the return address. I looked at the addressee and noticed that it was addressed to Rubi.

Why would my father's insurance company mail a letter to Rubi? Rubi was not one of his family members, much less a beneficiary. I decided to open the envelope. I nearly dropped the letter as I read the words from the insurance company addressed to Rubi.

The letter stated that the company had received the information to change the name, address, and documents concerning the policy of Arcenia C. Richards, to Rubi, adding that all future correspondence concerning the insurance policy of Arcenia C. Richards would be forwarded to her address.

I sat down in total disbelief. I did not know how to respond. I decided that it would be best if I did not inform my father about the letter.

As I was sitting there in shock, my father walked out of the office and said, "You look as if you have seen a ghost. Are you okay?"

I could not bring myself to share the details of what I had just read. I pulled myself together and asked him if he was ready to do the eulogy. He said he was ready to attend the service, and as we proceeded into the sanctuary, I felt grateful that Rubi had elected to skip Dillie's funeral. I wondered for the rest of the weekend how I should discuss the details of the insurance policy with her.

After Dillie's funeral service, I decided to share the details of the letter with my mother. She, too, was shocked. I placed the letter in a safe and thought about how to correct what I had discovered.

Who is Responsible?

On Monday morning, it was urgent that I reach my father's insurance company. As I waited for an agent to answer the telephone, I wondered how this could have happened. Can anyone change someone's insurance policy with a mere telephone call and a letter? It had happened to us.

I told the representative that I was holding a letter sent from the company to one of the secretaries of the church indicating that my father's insurance policy had been altered. "Can you tell me who is responsible for changing the insurance policy?"

The representative was extremely apologetic and assured me that this matter would receive the company's immediate attention. I prepared to fax the details proving my relationship with my father while the representative continued to apologize, assuring me that those errors were extremely unlikely. I expressed my concerns that my father had had a policy with this company for almost twenty-five years and allowing someone to alter a policy with a phone call was not a good business practice.

The representative assured me that this policy was not customary and ended the telephone call by immediately faxing the corrected information over to me.

It was several weeks later before I decided to address Rubi about her actions with the insurance company. During our conversation, Rubi expressed her deepest apology to me, but I needed to know what could have possibly convinced her to do such a revolting, fraudulent thing. Rubi informed me of the goals of the conspirators and the pressure she felt to commit such an act. I decided not to speak with her about that matter again.

The Secretary of State Returns Our Letter

There was much confusion among the conspirators. Yet there were also many innocent people who were witnessing the events. There was no way to continue administering the affairs of the organization while also monitoring the actions of the disgruntled group.

It was Sunday afternoon during worship service, as Jimmy and Gabriel competed for control of the services in front of the entire congregation. The plaintiff's secretary, Deb, who was also Jimmy's wife, shook her hand in Jimmy's face and told him to take control of the service.

I decided to follow her as she left the sanctuary. It was time to speak to her concerning the letter from the Secretary of State. The plaintiff's secretary arrived in the office before I did.

My father, who was extremely weak, was on the telephone. I walked in to see the receptionist hand Deb the telephone to speak to my father. As she spoke to him, I went into his office and picked up the telephone to ask him not to speak with anyone.

We could not understand the sacrifice and labor of my father in the ministry only to experience the escalating betrayal and conspiracy. Dad was too weak and did not respond. He said to me, "Baby doll, Dad does not feel well."

I knew there was something seriously wrong.

I ran into the outside office and approached Deb with these words, "You can no longer throw a rock and hide your hand. The letter and the papers you sent to the Secretary of State were mailed to me."

There were many people listening to our conversation. The plaintiff's secretary asked if I would step inside my father's office for a private conversation.

"Sure, as long as we have a witness."

I asked my brother, A. C., to come along as a witness. Deb asked where the papers from the Secretary of State were and attempted to explain her actions.

The story was rapidly unfolding.

They had roped in too many innocent senior citizens. I had had too many personal conversations with the seniors who had informed me of the lies and misinformation they were being told.

Besides, these seniors loved my father and their ministry. Those who understood the truth would never have consented to the behavior of the conspirators. The unknown names were now being revealed.

As the plaintiff's secretary continued to state her illogical reasons for the attempted takeover of the corporation, she turned to A. C. and asked if he understood her reasoning.

Before A. C. could answer, there was a loud knock on the door. It was her husband, Jimmy, screaming on the outside of the door, "Come out here!" Deb returned her focus to me and asked, "Can I have those papers? See, they wanted me to be their secretary." I simply stared at her in amazement.

Opening the door I said, "Please leave. Just get out."

Closing the door behind her, I turned to my brother and said, "This war is much larger than we are."

I soon learned that his comment was an understatement.

15
COLLECTION BAG

"They Took the Collection Bag"

The threats against me became increasingly aggressive. The plaintiffs had persuaded their families and friends. Their supporters now became overt in their conspiracy to take control of the corporation. They were once careful about allowing the Board of Directors to know that they were taking the corporations' finances, but they had become bold.

I was standing inside of the finance office along with Clay and Rubi. Looking at the bag in Clay's hand, Rubi informed me, "They took the collection bag. They took the money."

"Who are they?" I asked.

"Clay and them. Clay is going to take the money from the collection."

I reached for the collection bag in Clay's hand and asked him, "Who gave you the authority to personally take this collection bag? And what do you intend to do with it?"

Attempting to hold the bag close, Clay responded, "My attorney told me to take the money from each service, fundraiser, and any other event that generated finances."

I moved in a little closer and placed my hands on the bag, "I don't think so. I don't think so. Does your attorney pay the bills at this church? No! He does not. I have seen the bills from your attorney, and I have seen where you have been taking the church's money to pay him. This time, it won't happen. This collection is going where the collections should always have been put – in the bank."

I snatched the collection bag out of Clay's hand. He stood up to grab the bag and pushed me. He appeared to be ready to push me again. I braced myself and stepped out of my heels, with the collection bag in my hand, and looked at Clay and said, "You do not want to do that." I repeated, "You really do not want to do that."

Rubi stood up from behind her desk and said to Clay, "Hitting her is counted as an assault."

I looked at both of them. "Clay, you should have listened to Rubi. She told you right. And Rubi, I am not sure what you two have been up to with respect to taking the collections, but I am sure of one thing, whatever it is, your plans will fail. Now if you will excuse me, I will make sure these donations are deposited into the bank."

The Missing Collection Bag

One day I was looking through papers when the receptionist interrupted me.

"How may I help you?" I asked.

"Doctor Richie, you need to take this call," she insisted.

The voice on the other end of the phone asked for Rubi. "Rubi no longer works with the company. How may I assist you?"

The voice responded, "There is a gentleman named Clay here at the bank attempting to withdraw more than $54,000 from your corporate account."

Astonished, I asked, "$54,000? What do you mean?"

The person on the other end of the telephone continued, "Madam, we do not believe that this transaction has been authorized and we would like verification and approval of Clay's request. We need to speak with the President or another authorized employee."

I did not hesitate. "You are speaking directly to the President. I will be at your bank within the next half hour." Hanging up the telephone I paged Marie and repeated what the bank representative said to me. Marie responded, "$54,000? Gone? Where did it come from – the collection bag?" Marie escorted me to the bank.

At the bank, the Branch Manager showed me a copy of the check written by Clay -- more than $54,000 made out to Lloyd and The National Corporation. These funds were directly from the church's account. I was not surprised.

Turning to the bank officer I said, "I knew all along they were not honest."

Back at the church, I read the documents from the previous administration where Clay seemed to have always wanted to control the financial affairs of the corporation. I read from one of the Board meetings where Bishop Charles Poole had written, "Money Matters." As trustee and deacon, Clay was given the fiduciary responsibility to collect and deposit funds for the corporation. It was during that meeting that he tried to take control of money matters.

This led me to suspect that Clay intentionally abused his fiduciary responsibilities by diverting church funds without the approval of the church, its Board of Directors, or the Pastor's knowledge.

Unusual Garbage

One day, I noticed Rubi carrying large black garbage bags to the janitor's closet. I continued to watch her enter the closet with one black bag after another. I thought it was strange for her to have so much garbage to empty from her small office. I waited until Rubi left for the day and asked Kelle, "Will you please retrieve the bags from the closet?"

When Kelle did not return soon, I headed to the janitor's closet and noticed Kelle digging in the large orange garbage cans.

I asked, "Kelle, why are you digging in the garbage?"

Kelle replied, "Pastor, those black bags are in the garbage. There are too many bags for me to manage alone, so help me pull them out."

Looking into the bags, I noticed the black bags were filled with the corporation's financial records from previous years. As we continued to go through the garbage cans, we discovered many legal documents describing the actions of those suing us.

After filing those documents, we visited another finance office where Clay often met with several of those who were a party to the lawsuit and discovered additional legal documents.

Canceled Checks

The next day Rubi, the financial secretary of the corporation, asked to meet with me in my office.

"I threw a lot of stuff out of my office," she confessed.

"I am very much aware of that. Why did you throw away the records?"

"I don't know. But I wanted to tell you something because I know you ain't got no help. They'll use the canceled checks I gave them against y'all for leverage."

"Who's going to use what against whom?"

"All of them. They are working together. They came to my office and asked me for the payroll checks and some other reimbursement checks for you and some other people."

"And…go on," I urged.

"I gave them the copies of the canceled checks."

"You provided them with copies of what checks?"

"Copies of payroll checks and reimbursement checks," she explained.

"Why would you give anyone copies of payroll checks and copies of reimbursement checks?" I asked.

"You remember when you bought that stuff for the church and when Alvin bought the sound system for the church?"

"Yes, I have always made purchases for the church and have provided you with the original receipts."

"Yeah, I know. But they made me give them the checks. They say they are going to try and make you look like you are stealing," she explained.

'Whoever they are, they will be proven wrong. I keep good receipts and I will show *them* copies of my receipts – for reimbursements," I said.

"I'm telling you, they are planning something. They got their lawyer looking at the stuff I gave them," she insisted.

"Can you give me a copy of the items you gave to them? That way, if need be, I will be able to defend myself with copies of receipts for purchases that I personally made."

"Yeah, I can give you copies and I'm also willing to sign a letter stating' that they have been taking' the money for a long time without the Bishop knowing' it. They were planning to give it to Lloyd, then Rubi finished.

Rubi wrote in detail what she shared with me and left the office for the day.

When They Threw Marie – and Civility -- Off the Stage

We phoned the police daily. Although we were not intimidated by the numerous threats, we knew that no threat should be ignored.

Marie was responsible for opening the Sunday morning worship services, and as she stood on the stage singing, "Precious Lord, Take My Hand," Mike approached her with a group of five ladies, including Mary, who weighed at least three hundred fifty pounds.

My friend, Paulie, observed what happened next.

Marie continued to sing as Mike said to the ladies, "Okay, who's going to throw her off the stage?"

Marie continued to sing. Mike said directly to Marie, "Leave the stage."

Marie refused. Then all three hundred and fifty pounds of Mary stepped forward and said, "I'll do it."

As Marie continued to sing, Mary charged the altar. With her two huge arms she tried to lift Marie. Then she shoved Marie to the floor.

Paulie assured me that Marie was shaken up, but okay.

I immediately rushed toward the stage. I dared anyone to touch me, much less to throw me off the pulpit. Someone from the crowd shouted "Here she comes. Y'all better be careful because Marci is not Marie.

You won't hit her and get away with it."

I was not afraid.

I was ready to defend myself.

As I made my way to the pulpit, the intimidating threats did not let up. The group could not frighten me, but the deterioration of longstanding cordial relationships -- basic polite behavior at virtually all levels -- was deeply disturbing. These people no longer formed part of a congregation of like minds and spirits dedicated to Christian worship. Far from it. They were behaving like a violent gang.

The Threats Hit Home

There were many threats against me. One confrontation involved a family member, my aunt Maye, a retired Pastor who led one of our committees and was also a teacher who accompanied the ministers on the platform during Sunday worship.

One Sunday morning during worship services, which consisted of members sharing their testimonies, Aunt Maye stood in the line to testify. As she began speaking, instead of testifying, Aunt Maye shouted, "My niece will never be a Pastor here. I do not care if she is my niece…I will not be a member because she is the Pastor!"

Aunt Maye continued making unkind statements about me.

A few days later, Aunt Maye and I came face to face when she was holding a conversation with my father as I entered the office. She stood up from her seat and left. I followed her to one of the sanctuaries of the church, and we discussed her remarks during the worship services. Aunt Maye told me that she did not approve of my becoming Pastor because she thought I was too young, and that if she had anything to do with it, I would never become Pastor. When I asked her if that was a threat, she told me that I could count on her using her influence to prevent me from becoming Pastor.

"What influence?" I asked. I was becoming accustomed to managing opposing, irrational people whom I'd thought I knew well who were behaving like street gangsters. Discovering a camp follower in my own family, a woman who had known me all my life, was not going to faze me now.

Aunt Maye had voluntarily given up her position as a pastor. After we had several conversations about my preparation for pastoring, she declared that I was not ready; I was too young. I asked her when she thought I would be ready. Would that be when I was her age of seventy-five?

Aunt Maye became irate and did not speak to me again.

The tension between me and other family members intensified. From that day forth, many of our family members within the church sector actively sought to isolate themselves from the war.

An Octogenarian Stands her Ground.

The chain of events unfolded rapidly, and we recorded many occurrences to demonstrate the grave injustices of accusations and lawsuits. Numerous incidents confirmed that many individuals who had actively joined the opposition to me no longer engaged in basic civil behavior. No one was exempt.

Some people refused to be courteous even to elderly women.

Mother Walker, who was 86 years of age, was responsible for answering the telephone. One day, she stood on the pulpit and tried to tell Jimmy, the plaintiff's secretary's husband, that there was a phone call for him.

Jimmy's wife interrupted her, boisterously running to the pulpit and shouting, "You'd better take this service over right now because we need to set this church straight!"

Mother Walker was trying to communicate with the two of them when Jimmy, shoving his way to the microphone, nearly pushed her off the stage. But Mother Walker refused to be pushed around. Although she paced back and forth feeling her way around the pulpit, she stood her ground.

Mother Walker's twin, Mother Littlejohn, rose from her seat. Running over to Mother Walker, she begged her to calm down, fearing she would be greatly harmed, "They are making a scene. You do not want to hurt yourself. Relax and calm down." Mother Walker exited the platform and returned to fulfill her responsibilities as receptionist.

20,000 Flyers

Propaganda featuring ad hominem accusations has always been a powerful weapon of warfare, and the battles within our church fit that pattern when I received a telephone call from the former Sunday School Director, Mike's wife. She explained that a town meeting in her community concerned the distribution of thousands of flyers about Mike. The flyers claimed that there was an alleged pedophile named Mike living in the community and listed Mike's full name and address, cautioning parents not to allow their children to walk alone.

"Flyers were posted everywhere, on every doorstep, and Mike thinks you did it because of the fight."

As I walked through the parking lot, Mike accused me of distributing the flyers. I assured him that I had nothing to do with it. "I do not hide my hand. Whatever it is that I must communicate to you, I will tell you face to face."

Mike walked away and never mentioned that incident – one of numerous ambushes intended to sabotage my trustworthiness -- again.

16
ESTHER

"Following Bishop Richards' Death, I Will Be Pastor…"

He received notice of a lawsuit from Bishop Stanlie from another state. Bishop Stanlie was the nephew-in-law of the late Pooles as well as the Presiding Bishop of another Pentecostal organization. Prior to the war within our corporation, he was one of my father's longtime friends.

My father would often call on Bishop Stanlie to teach. Bishop Stanlie often visited my father at his home. Most of my siblings were quite reluctant to allow Bishop Stanlie to visit our home because he attempted to coerce my father to turn the ministry and the corporation over to him. My father emphatically told him that I would be the Pastor. Nevertheless, Bishop Stanlie continued his bold and calculating approach.

One morning during the pending litigation, Bishop Stanlie was the guest speaker for our services. My father thought he had to go out of town; however, he surprised us by joining us for the service

I was startled when Bishop Stanlie chose as his message the scenes in his previous court cases where he took over churches. He stated that he had an important announcement to read and, producing a document from his pocket, he began reading, "Following the death of Bishop Richards, I will be the Pastor of Bethlehem Healing Temple. I will be responsible for taking care of his wife, with a weekly allowance. Further I will have the authority to appoint each member of the Board of Directors and all positions within the church."

The crowd went into a state of frenzy. There was so much noise it sounded like a sporting event. People were shouting and screaming, "You aren't from here. Get out of here! You don't belong here. Go home!"

Bishop Stanlie was not the slightest bit discouraged. He raised his voice, and it was only when my father rose to the microphone and informed the members that Bishop Stanlie's statements were inaccurate that the audience calmed down.

Bishop Stanlie refused to give up his intention to be Pastor of the church. Several pastors from other states had told me that Bishop Stanlie was known to have entered court battles with churches.

A week or so after Bishop Stanlie's startling announcement, my brother, A.C., and my sister, Gwendolyn, discovered documents detailing Bishop Stanlie's desire to seize control of the church. Included were monetary offers to my father and details of how he would care for my mother.

Each week following Bishop Stanlie's announcement, he would send his son, Stan, to attend our Sunday services. Stan's job was to convince my father to sign documents naming Bishop Stanley as the next Pastor, but my father refused to sign them. It appeared that Stan was not moving as rapidly as Bishop Stanlie had expected him to, so he replaced Stan with his son Gabe, who continued the weekly mission to convince my father to sign the documents.

One Sunday afternoon I sat in the cafeteria while my father was downstairs in his office greeting members after morning service. A.C. was with him. When Gabe walked in demanding to have a private meeting with my father and motioned everyone to clear out of the room.

A. C. rushed upstairs into the cafeteria and pulled me aside. "Get downstairs immediately. Gabe has requested to see Dad in private."

Leaving my plate of food, I rushed downstairs to my dad's office. I entered without knocking and saw Gabe sticking a document inside his coat pocket. I rushed up to him and snatched it from his hand. After a brief tug of war, I had the document in my hand.

Opening the document, I saw that it was the document Bishop Stanlie had previously asked my father to sign. I also noticed a stamp bearing my father's signature and a nearby ink pad on the desk.

Apparently, Bishop Stanlie had not found the proper time to be alone with my father to obtain his signature and had sent Gabe to do the job instead.

Then I noticed that it bore a stamped signature and not an original signature. "Did you stamp this document?"

Gabe would not respond.

I then asked, "What do you think you are doing? Are all of you guys attempting to seize control of this corporation for selfish personal gain?" I continued, "This document should go to our attorney to determine what the proper actions should be against you and your father as a result of your feeble attempts to gain control of our corporation by fraudulently stamping my father's signature."

I then turned to my dad. "Have you read this document?"

"What document? No. I was preoccupied waiting here for A.C. to return. I thought he went to get some food from the cafeteria," he replied.

Suddenly, Gabe disappeared.

Confronting Gabe

The next time I saw Gabe, he asked to speak with me. I thought he was going to apologize for the stunt that he attempted to pull with my father. Instead, Gabe walked up to me and demanded, "Give me those papers that I had with your father's signature on them."

I was not certain if Gabe was referring to the last set of papers or a new set of papers. Therefore, I asked, "What papers are you referring to?"

"You know what documents I'm talking about. My father said I had better not come back home without those papers," he responded.

"I'd like to ask you one question. You are a preacher, right – right? So then tell me – if your father told you to do something against the laws of God, would you do it?" I asked.

Gabe looked at me and said, "Yes."

I stared him directly in the eyes and told him, "Firstly, I do not have papers that belong to you or your father. Secondly, I suggest you step away from me, because the Bible says the law is for the lawless, meaning in your case, you have no respect for the laws of God."

Gabe returned to his home state as I pondered what could possibly happen next.

Esther Goes Before the King

It was Sunday morning. I awakened at 4:00a.m. My heart was heavy as I reflected on the activities of the last few weeks. I did not understand how it was possible for such a renowned church to be confronted with the challenges that we had been facing. I suppose that I should not have been surprised given the history and the many miracles that took place at the church.

I decided to read a verse from the Bible to comfort my heart. I decided that whatever verse I turned to would be my scripture for the day and that verse would sustain me. Opening the Bible, the pages flipped open to the book of Esther.

Esther, the queen, was making her petition in front of the king. Esther's uncle, Mordecai, had refused to bow before one of the King's servants, Haman. Filled with rage and arrogance, Haman discovered a way to have the king sign a decree for the Jews to be executed. Mordecai sent word admonishing Esther that unless she petitioned the king, she would be destroyed along with her people. Mordecai further challenged Esther to take note of her position as queen, telling her that her position was for a specific time. And that time was the moment for which she was positioned in the king's palace.

Looking down the page, I noticed the words, "Esther took her case before the court." Why had I turned to that passage? I continued to read. "Esther took her case before the king in his court."

I thought that this could not have been interpreted that we were going to court. We did not believe in suing each other as siblings from the same religious background and sharing identical beliefs.

I continued to read. The passage did not comment on Esther going before the king as much as it mentioned Esther taking her case before the court. I read and read, underlining as I encountered parts of the story that I believed fit my situation.

I knew without a doubt that we were going to court. I read through the entire book of Esther. In the end I concluded, as Esther had, that soon I would have to appear in court. I continued reading until nearly 7:00a.m. As I closed the Bible, I said a prayer and petitioned that God would be with me as He was with Esther.

As I prepared to go to Sunday morning worship, I reflected on queen Esther going to court and taking her case before the king. I had a sinking feeling that something unusual would happen that day. As I arrived at the church, the order of the day was very quiet. There were no interruptions during the day. The conspirators were very quiet. Their behavior changed. They did not say anything to me.

Speaking to one of the trustees, I said, "The war will soon end."

He smiled as he replied, "They cannot keep anything from you. How did you find out so soon?" I had no idea what he was referring to, so I said, "Whatever they have done in the dark will soon be brought to light."

It was not my father's nature to engage in legal matters, nor did he believe in a sibling suing in the court of law. It was my brother, A.C.'s, telephone call that alarmed me. Marie and I were visiting one of the seniors, Mother

Jackson, in the hospital when the call came in from A.C. "Marci, have you spoken to dad about the court documents?"

"I have no idea what you are referring to."

A.C. explained, "As Dad was preparing to go to bed, he emptied the pockets of his jacket and threw some papers on the bed. I decided to look at the papers and discovered the papers were of a legal nature. Once I read the documents, I noticed that on Sunday, they presented Dad with court documents listing a scheduled court date in two days."

I asked to speak with my dad. I had so many questions, but instead I asked him one question, "Dad, at what point did you receive those documents?" He said that he was given the documents as he was walking toward the platform preparing to give his Sunday sermon.

I asked him why he did not mention this to us before we left the church regarding the documents. He said his philosophy was, "I was at church for Sunday morning services. I was not there to argue or fight with anyone. I am the Pastor. I nourished and appointed all those people, and they really don't know any better. In the end, good always overcomes evil." This was similar to Mattie's theological view that God spoke to man and man spoke to God's people.

I believed that the law would ensure swift relief. We also believed unequivocally that justice was on our side.

Therefore, I was not concerned about the false claims against us. We soon learned that the actions of the plaintiffs showed their unjust methods as well as our naivety. Had we understood the injustices of the law and the room for serious errors, we might have been more adequately prepared.

Following the plaintiff serving us with their lawsuit, I reflected on the story of Esther going to court. My thoughts were correct. We were going to court. The lawsuit named each individual member of the Board of Directors. Since our former counsel no longer represented us, it was time to secure counsel for the upcoming legal battles in what could escalate to become a holy war.

17
JIM

Retaining Counsel

The former counsel, who had represented our corporation for more than thirty years, withdrew as our corporate counsel, leaving us in the lurch for an attorney who had knowledge of corporate and religious law. Once we discovered we needed information to form our defense, we realized we did not have access to our legal documents.

The former corporate counsel had refused to hand over our documents, having explained that the plaintiffs had requested all of our corporate legal documents from his firm. Therefore, he refused to give either party copies of the legal history for our corporation. Included in those documents were volumes of evidence demonstrating the plaintiffs' representation while serving as directors for the corporation.

We were not represented by any other counsel; therefore, we had to gather all the legal documents we could locate. That legal documentation would have exposed the lies and perjuries of those suing us, along with their witnesses if we had been granted access to them.

"We Need Jim"

Prior to securing counsel, I told my brother, Alvin, the Pastor of Revival Tabernacle, and our corporate Board of Directors of our church, that "We need Jim."

"Jim" was simply a name that came to me, a placeholder name for a good attorney expert in religious as well as corporate law. "Jim" would represent us in the near and probably the distant future of the impending holy war.

I also told my father and the Board of Directors that Jim would understand the dynamics of what we faced and would be well equipped to assist us in governing the affairs of the corporation.

We did not know who Jim might be, but the name Jim stayed with me. I asked everyone I met if they knew an attorney named Jim. It was silly and entirely random, I knew, but I also thought that there must be a reason that name had stayed with me. And the name was common enough that it might ring a bell for someone acquainted with the right attorney or with someone who knew about a "Jim" that would suit our needs.

My ongoing search for Jim eventually involved many twists, turns, and coincidences, including false hopes, side trails, and dead ends as we considered numerous attorneys. Some were even named Jim.

One of the most promising candidates stated, however, that the pending court date was too soon for his firm to represent us. Nonetheless, he had a friend who might be willing to look at our case, cautioning us that the law firm that he would recommend did not take average cases and that we must be ready to meet as soon as possible.

Within the hour, he told Alvin to meet at his friend's office. I asked Marie to join us.

Will the Right Jim Please Step Forward?

When we arrived at the law firm, the person we had been instructed to meet shook hands with Alvin and said, "My name is Jim."

What were the odds of this happening?

This is the Jim who will represent us, I thought -- the one who understands corporate and religious law and can help us the most.

I nudged Alvin and said, "I told you that we needed Jim!"

Alvin looked at me and smiled.

Presenting Our Case to Jim

I met with Marie, who agreed to share as much history of both corporations, Bethlehem Healing Temple, and The National Organization, as possible. Whatever counsel represents us must receive all documents and evidence relating to both the church and The National Organization. This later proved to be correct.

The time had finally come for us to present the case to Jim, whose firm Jim proved to be one of the most knowledgeable firms for religious and corporate practices.

Jim was thorough and repeatedly asked question after question about our history, beginning with the birth of Mattie and continuing to the summons to court.

Jim consistently involved himself with details of the case and spoke as if we were the firm's sole client, referring to the case as "we" – a message that we would fight the case together.

As General Secretary, Marie had all the records concerning The National Organization. These records included audio and video recordings of meetings, minutes of meetings, and tapes of services. Marie was primarily responsible for organizing and coordinating the meetings and subsequent records relating to them for The National Organization, including all Bishop Board's meetings and Board of Directors meetings.

The history of The National Organization was particularly important to the case because The National Organization was established out of Bethlehem Healing Temple Church, Inc., and "The National Organization" was first incorporated under the umbrella of Bethlehem.

We were never so confident. The right Jim was now in position, and it was time for us to appear in court.

Our First Day in Court

I had full confidence in Jim's representation. My schedule prevented me from personally appearing in court the first day. Jim was startled by my absence.

I had just sat down at my desk when I received a telephone call from Jim. He sounded alarmed, "Marci, get here as quickly as you can. Who are all these people? There are nearly one hundred people bombarding the courtroom."

We had failed to mention to Jim the numerical politics of the large families and friends who had joined the conspirators in suing the corporation.

A call from Marie interrupted. "I am at court, and they have all shown up."

"Who?" I asked.

"The plaintiffs came with the senior citizens from the church as well as lots of their family members. You know Rogers has thirty-seven children and hundreds of grandchildren and he is only one of the plaintiffs. If each of the plaintiffs shows up with their whole family this is going to be a showstopper."

"This will create a diversion from the purpose of the lawsuit -- exactly what the plaintiffs want. I hope Jim stays focused."

I assured Jim that this would be the scene throughout the proceedings. Jim was focused and courageous and quickly adjusted to the scene.

Our first day in court was extremely brief. Once Jim met with the plaintiffs' counsel and disclosed our documentation, the plaintiffs' first counsel immediately withdrew, and the judge scheduled a continuation.

Riot!

A few days later the annual National Conference was held where thousands of churchgoers converged on the church. As a member of the board of directors, I was expected to attend all conferences. There were rumors festering among those who were a part of the organization incorporated by my father. The Tuesday afternoon of the convention was most startling. There was a lot of tension. The plaintiffs managed to incite people who were extremely violent and had notorious criminal records.

As certain members of the Board of Directors, including Marie and myself, sat in my father's office, conspirators were meeting inside another office. I asked my father if he was going to teach Bible study that evening. My father did not respond and appeared to be in deep thought, so I did not disturb him. Instead, I decided to run home and return later.

Arriving home, I heard my pager sending a message -- Marie paging me from the church.

Driving up to the church, I saw hundreds of people standing outside. Tables and chairs were upside down along the sidewalk. It was a riot! There were other vending tables turned over inside and the place was in an uproar. The food tables were turned over. There were pieces of cheese and chicken scattered on the floor of the lobby. Candy bars were thrown throughout the entire area. Volunteers were picking up the food as people walked in and out of the church. The elderly were sitting in their seats, shocked and shaking. Whatever had happened within the five minutes I left, had set off an explosion.

My first thought was for the safety of my father. I found him standing at the microphone. Despite the hundreds of rioters, Dad was safe. My next thought was to search for Marie. I looked up to see her hurriedly walking through the hallway along with Michael, a security team member who was a former military officer weighing at least four hundred pounds. Marie and my father were safe.

"Gene Snatched the Microphone from Bishop"

Before I could get to Marie, Dad's guard shouted, "Gene snatched the microphone from the Bishop!" Now I knew I had to find Gene, who was Marie's daughter's father-in-law. I noticed Gene as he ran out of the front door.

I shouted, "Gene!" As he turned around, I said, "Did you just snatch the microphone out of my father's hand?"

"I was in a meeting with the plaintiffs when they asked me to take the microphone from your father while he was teaching Bible Class. I wasn't thinking,' I got scared."

As Gene spoke, Mary, the three hundred fifty-pound lady who had thrown Marie off the pulpit, was trying to start another riot by screaming, "I'm ready for some more!"

I was not in the mood to be hassled by this lady. I turned to her and said, "Not today, Mary. I mean it, not today. Get away from here. Go sit down."

Gene's actions resulted in chaos. The mayhem had begun.

Marie was panic-stricken. She rushed up to me. "Your father was teaching Bible study and Gene snatched the microphone from the Bishop. Michael immediately stood up and snatched the microphone from Gene, saying, 'Meet me outside in the parking lot and I will teach you how to respect

Bishop.' At that point those in the audience dared Gene to go outside and fight Michael.

'Gene was so scared. That's why he's running out the door. Michael dared all the plaintiffs and Gene to stand up and fight him. Others stood up ready to fight those people. The explosive reactions occurred at that moment. The plaintiffs and their family members started turning over the vending tables. Chairs were being thrown throughout the corridor of the church. They went wild."

This was the beginning of many riots!

I asked Michael what happened. "They would never have tried this if the Bishop were in better health. That bunch of cowards ain't none of them bold enough to try me. They wait until a man gets sick and then try this bull. Let them come near him again and they'd wish they hadn't."

I did not respond. Michael's loyalty was unswerving. I was convinced he was the proper security person to cover my father at that time.

My father regained control of the event and ended up teaching Bible study as if nothing bad had happened!

Clearly, though, we could never take one more minute for granted. We were engaged in a vicious war.

"Wait Until Tomorrow"

The corporate Board of Directors met in the office of the Presiding Bishop, to recap the events from the day before. The disturbances totally disrupted the National Conference. Immediately, the Board of Directors decided to act against the plaintiffs and their supporters. My father said, "Services will be carried out as usual and we will enlist the services of additional security."

I asked him to wait until tomorrow, since that was our court date, ending confusion and providing us with steps for further action.

Marie walked upstairs to the lounge and noticed the plaintiffs, along with Lloyd and two Bishops, conducting a private meeting. As the General Secretary of The National Organization, she took notes, as she listened to them discuss Lloyd's desire to become President and Presiding Bishop of The National Organization.

When Lloyd decided to go to the Presiding Bishop's office to request a meeting, Marie left the lounge to inform the Board of Directors that the plaintiffs and their supporters were preparing to meet with the Presiding Bishop. Lloyd knocked on my father's door, interrupting his lunch, and said, "We want to meet with you because we did not do right the first time."

My father never looked up from his lunch. He simply stated, "Wait till tomorrow."

Once the plaintiffs exited the office, I asked him what he meant about waiting until tomorrow. He explained, "Tomorrow, God shall vindicate us from this malicious report, and we shall have the victory, for the battle is not our battle. The battle is God's battle, and God always wins."

He continued to eat his lunch in silence. "Wait until tomorrow" were among the most prophetic words my father ever spoke.

The Second Day in Court

It was a long night. It had been a little over a month since we had our first day in court. It was time for Jim to argue our case. Given Jim's knowledge and all the existing evidence, the second day in court ended nearly as quickly as the first one.

18
DISMISSED!

Standing

J im, our defense counsel, immediately addressed the plaintiff's outlandish claims to bring such a case. He argued that they lacked any standing – that is, any legal justification to bring a lawsuit.

According to Jim's statement, "We've made an argument that the plaintiffs lack standing, and I'd like to just define that a little more carefully for the court. If the plaintiffs were corporate members, we understand that corporate members have standing to protect their rights as corporate members. So, if they were the corporate members, we're not saying they don't have standing to insist they have a right to vote on something that corporate members have a right to. We're saying, membership issues aside, if the court agrees with the defendants that the plaintiffs are not members of the corporation, they completely lack standing to bring any of these claims, because the relief sought would all be relief owed to the corporation."

He continued, "So even less than a shareholder, members in this corporation have no rights whatsoever in the church or its property. Only the corporation does, which is undisputed. Only the corporation has a right to that protection. Members of the board could not sue in their own name. It would be just like a business corporation. Members of the board who owe a fiduciary duty to the corporation could bring a suit on behalf of the corporation and arguably, a member of the corporation could bring a derivative action in the name of the corporation, but the relief goes to the corporation, not to those individuals."

The judge asked him, "You're telling me there are no members here?"

"That's correct, Your Honor. A Not-for-Profit corporation, no individuals with a proprietary interest in it whatsoever, organized and operating solely for religious purposes, under the control of its Pastor. Further, the Board of Directors manages the civil corporation with a fiduciary duty to the corporation. In those circumstances, the appropriate person to bring an action on behalf of the corporation is indeed the board."

There it was, according to the law, these individuals had no legal remedy to pursue the lawsuit. So, we believed it!

Plaintiffs Barred By Laches

The plaintiff's complaint and amended complaint was barred. The Legal Doctrine of Laches provides a party, like us, with a defense where long-neglected rights were attempted to be enforced.

Jim said, "We've argued that the plaintiffs' claims are barred by the Doctrine of Laches, and we've cited cases to the Court. We spoke about the diligence of plaintiffs in pursuing their rights and when there is a total failure of diligence and some prejudice on the other side, the claim is barred by laches in the corporate control context. As plaintiffs in equity, those plaintiffs are now barred under Laches to come here and say that the court has to force this corporation to hold an election to its Board of Directors, having benefited from the same system themselves."

"...Four Critical Indisputable Facts..."

Jim addressed the judge: "Your Honor, I'd like to begin by observing what we believe are the four critical and undisputed facts, as established by the record.

Primarily, in the 60-year history of this church, the Pastor has always controlled the church, its operations, its affairs, and its governance.

Regardless of what the papers may say about other institutions, other churches, other organizations, Bethlehem Healing Temple Church has always been under the hierarchical control of its Pastor. Nothing in the records, nothing submitted by the plaintiffs, contradicts this undisputed fact.

Secondly, in the 21-year history of this corporation, every single director who has ever served has been appointed by the Pastor. There has never been an election of the directors to the Board of Directors by anyone other than the pastor. The plaintiffs do not submit one shred of competent evidence to contest this fact. Indeed, Plaintiff Brownlow served on the Board of Directors himself for fourteen years, as established by the annual report submitted with the defendant's reply brief. None of those terms of service were by virtue of an election by the congregation or the corporate members. Every year that plaintiff Brownlow served on the board, he served because the Pastor had appointed him."

He continued, "Plaintiff Lester served on the board for six years and Plaintiff Gene served on the board for one year. These three plaintiffs know full well that there has never been an election in the twenty-one-year history of this corporation for the Board of Directors. Another undisputed fact is that the Defendant is indeed the Pastor as we sit here today. There is nothing in the records to dispute that. In fact, plaintiffs protest loudly that this lawsuit is not about controlling or contesting the identity of the Pastor."

Finally, Jim concluded, "In the evidence, plaintiff Lester, in his personal handwriting, acknowledged acceptance of his appointed position as Board of Director for the corporation. Additionally, plaintiffs Clay and Rogers met with the former counsel of our corporation, representing, and acting on behalf of the Board of Directors of the corporation. Yet in court, each of these individuals deliberately lied and said they were unaware that the corporation was incorporated as an organization. That is why the Pastor has appointed the Board of Directors every year since there's been a corporation. That is why the Pastor serves as an appointee of his predecessor who served as an appointee of his predecessor, the founder of this movement, Mattie."

The court carefully listened to the case. After a long and powerful presentation, Jim proposed a motion to dismiss the Brownlow lawsuit.

The Court Dismisses

Upon Jim's presentation of the truth, the facts, and the supporting evidence of our case, the judge weighed the facts and issued a decision. The hearing judge noted the large attendance by divided members of the church. He said that was why he had given counsel on both sides more time to argue this case than usual. He went on to explain how he saw things, since he thought that many people attending the hearing in the courtroom should be aware of where he was coming from and what was behind his decision.

He spoke of our entire country having its beginning in the seeking and preservation of religious freedom. He said he mentioned this because it had an impact upon how the Founding Fathers of this country looked at religious freedom and the possibility of an intrusive government coming back into the picture. He noted the importance to the Founding Fathers of freedom to practice your religion, and said that it was key that a judge, who is an arm of the government, shouldn't be telling people in any particular religion how to practice their religion or how to run their church.

He concluded that the government, by its very nature, can be intrusive. To fight this potential overreaching from the government, he noted how courts have been instructed, from the beginning, in ways to stay out of religious affairs.

He then agreed with our attorney, Jim, that a case like this does not belong in the courtroom. He even said he found it offensive to the founding principles of our country that our opponents would seek help from some government official in intruding upon religious worship, potentially putting the government in between individual worshippers and God Almighty.

The court dismissed the case in our favor.

The Court's Dismissal Scene

Following the court's verdict, Jim smiled, took up his notes, and went to shake hands with Marie. When Marie asked Jim to interpret the court's decision, Jim replied, "We won."

Marie was all smiles as she shouted, "Hallelujah!"

Outside the courtroom, the plaintiffs stared at her as she performed a Holy Spirit dance. Marie danced for five minutes outside of the courtroom, as someone from the plaintiffs said, "Be quiet." Marie said she refused to be quiet as she remembered the words of my father, "Wait until tomorrow."

Marie told me, "It is over! It is over! God was with Jim and God is with us!" I called the church and told the receptionist, "This is not our battle. Please tell my father that I am on my way to the church. It is over!" The receptionist herself started screaming, "Hallelujah!"

I arrived at the church and went into the office to share further details of our victory with my father. My father was sitting in his chair as I said, "Daddy, this is the Lord's battle. It is not your war. The victory was inevitable. You have always stated that good will overcome evil. Today, good overcame evil." My father sat quietly in his seat. I asked him what he thought it all meant.

Without looking at me he said, "You must never panic. You do not know who your friends or your enemies are in this battle. You must always remember one thing and that is God has a plan." I then remembered the words he had repeated, "Wait until tomorrow."

Ecstatic, I walked through the corridors of the church toward the Prayer Chape to offer a prayer of thanks to God.

As I walked toward the Prayer Chapel, Tray's wife, (who was one of the supporters of the plaintiffs), stood in the hallway on the phone.

I said, "You can hang up now, it is over." Tray's wife stared at me as I walked into the Prayer Chapel with my hands uplifted. She followed me into the Prayer Chapel and asked me to repeat those words.

I kneeled and said, "Thank you, Father, for hearing our case today and granting us victory."

Tray walked out of the Prayer Chapel in total disbelief.

Dad was correct! Tomorrow promised to be a better day and it was victorious.

Back At Jim's Office

Jim invited Marie and me to meet him at his office to share the details of the court's order. A very relaxed counsel greeted our arrival. Jim deserved this win. He understood the battle which confronted us, and he had been valorous.

Following this discussion, I said, "Jim, I don't want to sound mystical but that was the power of the Holy Spirit."

As we were preparing to leave, Jim smiled and said, "I felt the power of the Holy Spirit as I argued our case. There was one other time in my life when I felt the power of the Holy Spirit; however, this was by far a greater experience. I knew it was the power of the Holy Spirit."

I replied, "I have been praying for you to experience the presence of the Holy Spirit. I did not want you to think that we were fanatical. This is the answer to my prayer."

19

HOSPITAL

"For the thing which I greatly feared will come upon me, and that which I was afraid of will come unto me." –. **Job 3:25.**

y father had not been to a hospital or doctor since becoming a member of the church under Mattie's tenure. His witnessing many miracles meant that he was thoroughly convinced that God was a supernatural healer. Whenever he was ill, he trusted God to heal his body. He had such faith that he never went to the doctor for regular checkups or visits. Refusing aid or assistance, he endured severe pain. He never revealed how ill he was.

My dad's face was swollen. He was very conscious of his appearance and did not like the look of his face. My brothers finally convinced him to see a physician.

The visit did not go as anticipated because the doctors ran various tests and discovered that my dad had not only suffered a stroke and a mild heart attack, but also had kidney and prostate problems.

My father was not interested in hearing what the physicians had to say about his present health conditions. He wanted only to learn why his face was swollen.

The doctors admitted my dad into the hospital. He was resolute in his faith and said, "The God of heaven shall heal me." A few days later, my father was released from the hospital.

During my dad's two-week absence from the church, there were rumors that he had passed. Such rumors included that we were too shocked to acknowledge that my father had passed and that we were keeping his death a secret.

The time to grasp for positions had started. Who will be the next in line for the position as leader? There were many empires waiting to rise.

I was under immense pressure with my government job as I contended with the war that was happening at the church. But most important was my father and his condition.

I spent as much time as I could at his bedside. I read Bible verses to him. I prayed with him. I told him that everything was going to be alright.

I could tell the severity of his excruciating pain as I watched the sweat pour down his face. It became very quiet. I continued to read Bible verses to him. I turned to Psalm 41, and I recall reading the entire passage. I told my dad, "God shall heal you and this will be the beginning of more miracles." With those words, my father dozed off to sleep.

I prayed all night asking God to comfort his heart and to heal his body. I petitioned God to honor his faith and to remember the many acts of kindness, his sacrificial life, and the prayers he had always offered for others. I asked God to remember all of the messages of faith that my father had taught for the last forty years. I sat there with little strength as tears rolled down my face. My family had begged my dad to go to the hospital, but he wished not to seek medical assistance. At 7:00am., I told my father that I had to go to work. I promised I would return later in the day.

My employer's primary concern seemed to be pushing out the numbers, and it did not matter that my father lay dying.

I had a previously scheduled meeting at a radio station to organize a march within the community in a few days. As I traveled to the meeting, my thoughts were on my father. I decided to phone home to see if he was better, but my brother told me that Dad had been rushed back to the hospital. My family asked me to meet them at the hospital. I left work early.

I called Marie, asking her to accompany me to the hospital. I had no clue where I was traveling in the suburbs in the middle of rush-hour traffic. We drove for two hours trying to locate the hospital. It was terribly hot, we had no air conditioning, I was experiencing conniptions and getting more and more upset. Where was this hospital?

At The Hospital

After that long, hot ride, I noticed my family members present, including my mother, but the doctors would not allow me in to see my father and insisted that I stay in the waiting room. I continued to insist that the doctors allow me in to see my father until my mother told me to be patient.

I realized that the situation had become critically serious when the doctors informed us that Dad was being moved to the Intensive Care Unit. There was one machine hooked to my father's body. My father was conscious, but very weak. He had not had anything to eat and was very thirsty. I stood holding the cup from which Daddy drank and started singing two of his favorite songs. One of those songs was, "Farther along, we'll know all about it. Farther along we'll understand why." Part of one of the stanzas of the song went "When death has come and taken our loved ones, it leaves our homes so lonely and drear, then we wonder why others prosper, living so wicked year after year."

Neither my father nor I sang that stanza. Instead, we continued to sing the chorus. Finally, we sang another one of his favorite songs "Courage oh my soul and let us journey on, though the night be long it won't be very long, the storm is passing over, hallelujah," my father sang with all of his might. The nurse came into the room and asked if we would step outside as they were preparing to sedate my father.

Daddy looked at me and said, "Don't leave me in this hospital. I am a man of faith."

I responded, "Don't worry. I'll be right back. I will never leave you here."

As my mother and the rest of my siblings stepped outside, I walked into the waiting room where Marie was standing.

I decided to go home and shower. I returned to the ICU room and promised that I would return in a few minutes. I made my brother promise not to leave until I returned. I kissed Daddy and repeated, "I shall return in just a few minutes." I left the hospital to drive Marie home.

The Worst News of My Life

I was terribly exhausted. I went home and fell asleep on the couch. I had no idea what time it was when the phone rang. I jumped up and started searching for my glasses. I looked at the clock. It was 1:00a.m. I did not realize I had slept that long. The telephone call was from my brother, Alvin. "The hospital just telephoned. Daddy has stopped breathing."

I searched for my glasses. I did not know the directions to the hospital. How was I going to drive alone? How could I have slept so long?

I was delirious! "Dear God," I prayed, "Please do not allow anything to happen to my father. I do not believe I can make it in this life without him. Please dear God." I earnestly continued to pray.

I still could not find my glasses.

I telephoned Marie to ask her for directions to the hospital. When I broke the news, Marie told her husband, Gordon. I was disoriented. I grabbed my keys and rushed out the door. I just started driving. I had no idea in what direction I was headed. I drove until I could no longer see the road. I headed in the direction of my sister's house. I searched for my mobile telephone to call my sister, Pat, who lived in the suburbs, which I thought was closer to the hospital than I was. As she picked up the telephone, she said to me, "Calm down. I do not think Daddy is going to make it."

I could not catch my breath. She handed the telephone to her husband, Ernest, who was more relaxed. He asked where I was. I had no idea of my location, but I knew I was in the vicinity of their house. I was too emotional to make it directly to their home; therefore, Ernest met me at the freeway.

When Ernest arrived, I fell to the ground in despair. *"I do not know how to get to the hospital. Please, hurry."* My head was spinning, and my emotions were high. I refused to believe that Dad was not going to be okay. I realized that this was the most difficult moment of my life. Ernest picked me up from the ground and drove me to the hospital. Upon our arrival we walked into the room where my father lay. My mother stood at his side.

I looked at my dad and saw that there was no movement. Then my attention turned to the machine which had been hooked to my father's body. The machine was disconnected.

I suddenly realized what this meant and completely lost control. I fell to the floor as the nurse walked in with sedatives and asked my mother to give me the medication, but I refused it. The pain was too intense. This was the sting of death that the Apostle Paul wrote about in I Corinthians chapter fifteen. I pulled myself from the floor and lay across my father's body. I could feel his body turning cold.

"Please, Lord," I prayed, "I will do anything you ask of me if you will allow my father to live." As I held on to my father, Marie and her husband entered the room. This was the first time I had seen Marie's husband, Gordon, in nearly twenty years. It was difficult for him to deal with the scene, and he walked out of the room as my mother and Marie tried to console me.

There was no way to console me. The thing that I feared most in life had come to pass.

During the ride home I was overcome with grief. I repeated so many Bible verses that I must have sounded like a non-stop recording. I placed my hands on the top of my forehead and petitioned God to please help me to maintain my sanity. My mother prayed for me. As I continued to shake my head back and forth, I said, "No! No! No!"

She comforted me, "You must say 'yes' to the will of God even when that will does not agree with your desire. Your father has completed his assignment on earth." Even in my pain, I knew those were thoughtful and true words.

Since I was still grieving Eric's death, I hesitated to phone Eric's wife to ask for the number of the funeral director. I knew that my father would have wished that I call his two angels, Mother Walker, and Mother

Littlejohn. Mother Walker was in tears while Mother Littlejohn informed me that I had important work to do, and I could not afford to waste time grieving over the passing of my father. She told me, "In a war, many soldiers fall and die. You, however, must continue fighting until the war is won."

I then called the new Christian Education Director, Lisa, and finally Eric's wife. and asked for the funeral director's telephone number.

My family and I were sitting in grief when we heard a loud bang on the door. At the door were the plaintiff's secretary, Deb, and her sister, Paullie.

I said, "How bold of her to come to my house! Does she really think that we are fools?" My mother interrupted me and asked if that was the Christian way to behave, even to those who have wronged us. I knew she was right, and I relaxed and sat on the floor as my sister placed her arms around me.

Deb rushed into my living room shouting, "Oh, this is the most awful day!"

I glanced at my sister and asked, "For who, us or them? Is it awful because my father died or awful that I am now the Pastor?"

I knew I had better keep quiet because I was certain that I could not pretend any longer that Rubi shared with me the masterminds behind the lawsuit.

Paullie hugged me. I knew that Paullie cared for me; we enjoyed an excellent relationship. She shared my pain and loss, and she completely understood the deep emotions of grief.

She said very few words as she held my hand as I recognized the motives of others who were behind the plot to oust me as Pastor.

As we sat there, Deb asked if she could assist with the funeral preparations. Knowing my father and my mother would have wanted me to forgive her, I mumbled, "Sure. This is going to be proclaimed as history in the making." I continued, "You have pictures of my father as well as the history of the corporation. I want you to bring the photo for the front cover of the program and put together a list of Dad's favorite songs. Additionally…"

My sister, LaVena, interrupted. "Let's stop pretending. Everyone here knows exactly her ill motives. Do you think it is a good idea to allow her to work on Dad's program?"

"We need everyone's assistance. Daddy was much bigger than the current war. He kept his friends close and his enemies closer," I replied.

I concluded by saying to Deb, "And, by the way, please allow me to get through the burial of my dad before you continue your conspiracy."

Deb exited quickly. I remembered the passage from John 13:21-30. "Jesus was troubled in spirit, testified, and said, Verily, verily, I say unto you that one of you shall betray me.

He, then lying on Jesus' breast, said unto him, Lord, who is it? Jesus answered, He is to whom I shall give a piece of bread when I have dipped it. And when he had dipped the bread, he gave it to Judas Iscariot, the son of Simon. And after the bread Satan entered into him. Then said Jesus unto him; that thou do, do quickly."

I turned to my brother, A.C., and said, "With dad's passing, the battle is about to come to full term. Finally, the truth will be revealed. As the Bible teaches us, Isaac was the Chosen One over Ishmael, as Jacob was the Chosen One over Esau. I will no longer stand for any deception or pretense. But first, we need to properly bury Dad."

A.C. replied, "It's going to be a long uphill battle."

The Pulpit Scene

As I dressed for Sunday worship, I prepared myself to make the public announcement regarding my father's death and to address the congregation about the next goals for our organization.

The plaintiffs and their supporters were prepared to attack. I had received calls informing me that there were shouts of victory from the plaintiffs and their supporters over the death of my father.

I chose not to dwell on it. I had to face the congregation and provide them with the details of the funeral.

At the church, one of the first people I met was Paullie. The look on her face was so comforting that I believed I could manage what was ahead. I tried to assure her that I was fine. As I walked toward the sanctuary, one of the plaintiffs' family members confronted me. I turned around and said, "Today, if you or anyone dare touch me, I will try my darndest to ensure that that hand will never raise itself to hit another person."

I continued to walk until I reached the back door of the sanctuary. I took a deep breath and entered the sanctuary.

Lester was at the microphone. As he spoke, I walked directly to the platform. Lloyd, Mike, Tray, Clay, and approximately twenty other men guarded the platform. The group included Lloyd, the one who held the private meeting to be the Presiding Bishop of The National Organization.

Approaching the pulpit, I said to Lloyd, "How bold of you to stand on my father's pulpit after your deeds towards him! I know you organized the conspiracy with The National Organization, along with Clay and Mike." I then turned to Mike and said, "May God judge each of you for your evil and conspiring actions."

I was completely agitated. My brother, A. C. grabbed my arm. I pulled away from him to address Lester, "I will speak now."

Lester stated, "She has an announcement about the funeral arrangements."

I addressed the audience to share the details of moving forward and the urgency to keep the faith.

I looked down and noticed an outlined program. We had never had an outlined program for a Sunday morning worship service; this was another sign of the takeover. I ignored the program and continued to speak. Finally,

I said, "I see we have a program here, so I will let the order of the program run its course."

As I stepped away from the microphone, Lester walked up to the microphone and said, "She isn't going to let me do nothing, but I am in charge."

I was halfway down the stairs, but hastily turned about face. Lester covered the microphone. "I meant nothing by those words. I just said that to appease people."

I said, "This is neither the time nor the place for this twaddle. We will address this later. I must bury my father."

As I stepped off the platform, I told Tray, "Your betrayal will never be forgotten, as I know you are an intricate part of this conspiracy."

Lisa grabbed my arm to escort me from the sanctuary.

Tray said, "She's grieving, and I understand, as I lost my parents."

I countered, "I may be grieving, but it is a reality that you are a strong part of this conspiracy." Lisa hastily escorted me out the back door of the sanctuary.

"He's Dead, And There's A Grave for You Next To His Grave"

As I walked outside of the church, Mary -- three hundred and fifty pounds, tall, crippled, and husky -- walked up to me, "He's dead and you are next. There's a grave for you next to his. What are you gonna do now?"

Was this a horrible dream? No, it was a brutal reality. As Mary was speaking to me, Bernard walked up to add, "We always kill our leaders, and we will kill you, too."

I maintained my posture. No one dared touch me. I felt as if I were being watched over and protected.

Outside the Church

Lisa said, "Marci, you need some air," as we walked from the back to the front of the parking lot. I took long, deep breaths. Lisa held my hand as we walked to the end of the next block. A car honked, and a woman let down her window -- a dear friend of our family, Rose. Smiling, she asked, "Are you okay?"

Befuddled, I could not answer. Rose was not afraid of anyone or anything. She loved my father as well as my family. I knew Rose would do her best to protect me. I decided that it was best not to get any outsiders involved in this war.

I nodded my head, "Yes."

I did not wish for my mother to see me upset, so I sat inside my father's office for the entire service. As people paraded in and out of the office, I told myself, "I will get through this."

I again recalled my mother's prophecy about many adversaries and my dream of being locked out of the church. I remembered that I needed only to touch the locked doors and they would open.

At the end of the service, Clay came into my father's office, along with his supporters and their secretary. I requested the program for the funeral. There was so much confusion as Deb and Clay spoke while Clay's supporters shouted.

I demanded that the plaintiffs and their supporters give me time to speak about the details of the funeral and told them that I would speak with them after my father's burial.

Following the death of my father, the plaintiffs and their supporters stepped up their efforts to seize control of the corporation. As I waited to plan the funeral services, the plaintiffs became even more belligerent. We were taunted cruelly during our hours of grief. The members of the Board of Directors, as well as the members of the congregation who supported us were also taunted.

The First Telephone Call from Bishop Jerry

Immediately upon hearing the news of the death my father, Clay called Bishop Jerry, who was considered a great mediator. It later became clear that Clay was not asking for mediation but wanted Jerry to meet with me as the new President and ask me to step down.

Bishop Jerry was the Assistant Presiding Bishop of another organization, fully understood the dynamics of a fractured organization, and had weathered a difficult transition before becoming Pastor and President of his own corporation.

Bishop Jerry understood that his priority was a proper burial for my father.

I held an emergency meeting with the Board of Directors to determine our next steps. The board suggested that I inform Jim about my father's passing.

20
NO TIME TO MOURN

Withdrawal from The National Organization

"Jim, my father passed away last night."

ot only was Jim our counsel; he had also become our advisor as well and understood how the unconventional ecclesiastical structure of The National Organization meant that each church and Pastor was free to make decisions. A loose affiliation of different organizations, The National Organization was also an association freely entered into by the member churches under the direction of the Pastors in charge. The National Organization customarily allowed each independent church to withdraw whenever it decided to do so.

In the days of Mattie Poole, countless churches were a part of The National Organization. As recorded in the books and minutes of The National Organization, numerous churches had withdrawn following the death of Mattie Poole, thereafter Bishop Poole, and thereafter Bishop Richards. Following their withdrawal from The National Organization, the churches functioned independently of The National Organization.

Although The National Organization had previously been reorganized by Bishop Richards, Bethlehem withdrew its affiliation from that organization.

It was not unprecedented for locally incorporated bodies to withdraw from The National Organization. In fact, many had done so prior to our withdrawal. The litigation that ensued assumed that we were the first to withdraw and that we were prohibited from doing so.

Those who left The National Organization did so at no charge to them, their church, or the organization, since The National Organization was a fellowship of free and willing participants.

Based on this practice, the board of directors of Bethlehem agreed and decided to withdraw the church's fellowship from The National Organization. After the emergency board meeting and my conversation with Jim, we submitted a letter to The National Organization withdrawing our membership "effective immediately."

"You Have No Time to Mourn"

Following the initial conversation with Bishop Jerry, I was overtaken with the pending affairs of the organization. My life had come to a standstill. I did not know whether I should return to my job or continue as the President of our church's organization. I considered moving forward with my life and not returning to either position.

As I pondered the future, I could not see myself moving forward successfully without my father's spiritual counsel.

The plaintiffs took full advantage of my grief. There was no pause for me to bury my father.

My mother challenged me to remember my dream. As I sat at home overwhelmed by grief, my mother said, "Put on your sunglasses and get out of the house. I want to take you for a ride."

As I dressed, I wondered where my mother was preparing to drive me. I opened the door to my house and the light hit me in the eyes as a wake-up call. I realized the death of one person could bring important challenges for another.

My mother said, "You do not have time to mourn."

How could she have said those words when my heart was filled with so much pain?

Concerned, yet focused, my mother repeated, "You do not have time to mourn."

I stared straight ahead as my mother stopped to pick up Marie.

Bank Visits

I sat in silence while my mother and Marie held conversations as we drove. I was in such a state of grief that I was oblivious to my immediate surroundings. We drove until we reached the main bank of the corporation.

The funeral details dominated my mind. Within the next few days, there would be many activities and loose ends within the organizations. Tensions that existed prior to my father's death had heightened as the plaintiffs held many meetings outside and inside of the church, but I was in no mood to fight with anyone.

Each of the leaders within our corporation held the corporate funds at more than fifteen individual banks. During one of the committee meetings, the plaintiff's secretary became responsible for ensuring that most of the leaders placed their funds at one central location. Although she signed an affidavit and testified in court that she was not aware that our organization was incorporated, she typed a letter to the committee leaders stating, "Our church is a corporation, subject to being audited." She coordinated the efforts of the leaders to bring most of the accounts under a particular bank, given there were many different accounts within our ministry. There seemed to have been a plan to inform the leaders to withdraw all of the corporation's funds from the individual banks within the city.

My mother parked inside the main bank branch of the corporation and pointed to the plaintiffs and committee leaders standing inside the parking lot.

My mother said, "While you are mourning, evil does not stop. Evil only escalates." Tearfully I went inside the bank.

I was too late. Many of the leaders had already withdrawn the funds from the bank accounts. The corporation had given the leaders access to all the accounts, and the leaders apparently thought the corporation's funds were indeed their personal funds.

I did not have time to argue with the bank supervisors. When we left that bank, Marie asked if I was going to head to the next bank.

As I sat down in the car, my mother repeated, "I told you that you do not have time to mourn." This was worse than my dream – a great tribulation!

When we arrived at the next bank, Marie walked inside with me. When I met with the bank representative, I could hardly speak. My eyes were badly swollen, and my voice cracked with each word that I spoke. The banker recognized me, she had heard of my father's passing, and as she softly offered her condolences, Her words gave me courage. Once we provided the bank representative with the official documentation stating that I was the President of the corporation, she made it easy for me to complete the necessary paperwork.

I decided that there was no need to chase the other bank accounts and focused on the upcoming funeral plans instead.

"I Just Think It Would Be Better . . ."

Following the death of my father, I received more than my share of telephone calls and proposals, many of which concerned the future of the corporation. Several callers asked to meet with me to offer help as assistant or vice president of the corporation. I agreed to meet with some, but I was extremely careful to have someone accompany me to each meeting because there were so many people hoping to be the Pastor. The corporation was at tremendous risk. Having others present ensured support and provided me with witnesses.

During one meeting, a Pastor of another church proposed that he should be the Pastor of my church, while "allowing" me to be the President of the corporation.

"How is that possible?" I asked him. "I am the Pastor of the church and the President of the corporation. Are you asking me to resign as pastor?"

He responded with a statement so symbolic that it captured the issue that had sparked the holy war – namely, the sacrosanct traditional roles of men and women.

When I asked him whether he was urging me to resign as Pastor, he said, *"**No, I just think it would be better if a man was the Pastor and you worked in the background.**"*

The Funeral

Although the first court battle had been dismissed in our favor, there were many loose ends to tie up prior to my father's death.

The plaintiffs seemed to have taken my father's death as a sign of victory. Following Mary's statement, "He's dead, and you are next," I was determined to defend the corporation of Mattie. Whatever loose ends had not been addressed would have to wait. There were other priorities as we moved forward.

Bishop Jerry

Following the events of Sunday morning, I received a phone call from Bishop Jerry. Bishop Jerry was a dear friend to our organization who had counseled us and acted as liaison between the church and the Chicago political structure. He was a wise and prudent man as well as a strategic thinker.

He said, "Yes, Clay contacted me about the division. However, there will be plenty of time to address the war issues following the burial of your father, King Richards."

Bishop Jerry became the nucleus to ensure that my father's funeral would be conducted in a manner befitting a king.

An Assistant Presiding Bishop, Jerry not only understood the political structure of our city, but also understood the political structure of our religious community. We agreed to meet to discuss the funeral arrangements. He kept me and my family focused on the days ahead and kept the plaintiffs focused as well while we made funeral preparations.

Throughout the week, Bishop Jerry and I met at his church and made various plans for the funeral. My family and I listened carefully as Bishop Jerry precisely understood the smallest details of how Dad's funeral should proceed.

My father had been the Pastor of two churches as well as the Presiding Bishop of the organization. Whenever the organization needed political or religious authority, my father relied on Bishop Jerry. Following his death, all of the appointed leaders became involved in grappling for position.

Bishop Jerry had become so involved with every detail of the funeral preparations that my family and I were relieved. We were reassured that we could focus on the burial and related matters, as the Bishop spoke to each of the religious officials within our city. He also contacted those who were to be a part of the program from the political arena.

Friday Night Before the Funeral

All week, the environment was so volatile that I checked into a hotel to manage the affairs of the office, prepare for the burial, and safeguard my protection.

The comfort of the hotel provided me with serenity and tranquility. Scores of condolence calls are coming in from people offering their condolences. My voicemail boxes were filled with messages from all over the world. There was hardly time to grieve.

On the one hand, we were preparing for a burial; on the other hand, we were preparing for an ever-growing holy war.

I was so distressed that I missed my salon appointment. I had purchased a St. John suit several weeks earlier but had not yet worn it. It was the perfect outfit for my father's funeral. I knew a hat would go well with the outfit, but I had no time to shop. I went directly to Macy's in search of a hat.

Tears would not stop. Several of the salesmen asked if I needed assistance, but I waved them off. until I entered the millennial section.

I did not have to search long. There it sat, inside the counter, all alone, fit for a queen -- the hat I was to wear for my father's funeral!

I knew that this was the one. I made the purchase, flagged down a taxi, and headed back to the hotel to continue the funeral preparations.

I continued to remind myself of the way my father would have wanted me to behave, and so I decided to include the plaintiffs and some of their supporters on the funeral program because I did not wish to make a big deal of it, I did not inform my family of my decision to allow Deb, Lester, Lloyd, and Clay to speak. I called Deb and informed her that she and the three men would speak at the service.

Because my family would have been terribly disappointed with such a decision, I informed only my mother. She continued to maintain a sense of love and compassion for those who had wronged us.

Bishop Jerry asked me all day for a copy of the program, but a miscommunication meant that we still had not received any copies from the printer. At midnight, I left the hotel to go to the church to deal with the printing of the programs. Finally, my perfectionist brother, Arthur, left at 4:30am., and visited the printing shop to wait for the programs.

I took one last opportunity to look over the church for the final touches for the funeral. Lyndon, a florist whose late father had been one of my dad's best friends, had promised to handle the floral arrangements. As I walked through the entire church at 4:30 a.m., I saw that Lyndon had spent hours preparing the hallways and altar with glorious floral arrangements. An enormous picture of my father stood surrounded by the beautiful floral arrangement. It must have cost a fortune, but Lyndon told me that he did it as a gift to my father – a gift from his heart.

At six o'clock I decided to take a nap at the hotel. Arthur called an hour later to say that he had picked up the programs.

As the telephone continued to ring, I knew I would not be able to get any more rest, so I called Kelle to ask her to pick up the clothes that I would wear to the service. She replied that another printing company had called about the programs.

Kelle remained awake all night ensuring that the details of the funeral were properly coordinated. I knew I could count on her, but I was extremely anxious because she had not arrived with my clothes, and it was time to leave for the funeral.

My sister, Patricia, phoned me and said, "The limousine is downstairs at the hotel waiting to pick you up for the funeral." As I was attempting to explain that I was not dressed, she interrupted me. I could hear her talking to my mother. She said, "She sounds disturbed, and I wonder if she will be able to make it to the funeral." I asked to speak to my mother and assured her that I would meet them at the funeral.

When Kelle arrived, I hurried to get dressed while Kelle left to pick up the programs.

I said a prayer to ask God for strength.

The doorman said, "Madam, you look beautiful today. What gala affair could you be attending? Where to?"

"To bury my father," I replied.

He paused, whistled for a taxi, and said, "I'm sorry. But I hope you will be able to handle this tough time."

The cab driver said, "Good morning. You look fabulous today. This is your day. You must be the queen of the hour. Where to?"

Once again, my response was, "To bury my father."

This caught the taxicab driver completely off guard. He offered his condolences and was quiet for the rest of the trip.

A mile before arriving at the church there were people waiting. As I arrived at the church, I saw people lined up for blocks. There was very little place to stand.

Seeing all of the people waiting, the cab driver asked, "Who was your dad?"

I answered, "He was my father, my friend, my brother, my Pastor, my confidant, my caretaker, my provider, and my counselor."

My Arrival

Arthur greeted me and asked, "Did you put Lester, Clay, Lloyd, and Deb on the program to make remarks? I know you didn't put those people who are responsible for creating the lawsuit against dad on the program. I knew you were grieving but I know you aren't crazy."

As he was speaking to me, Lester walked up to me with the program for the service in his hand and interrupted him. "Am I on the program to make remarks?"

Positioning the hat on top of my head, I addressed both. "Lester is indeed on the program. Lester and some of the other plaintiffs will be speaking today on behalf of their individual committees."

Before Arthur could chastise me again for putting the plaintiffs on the program, some office staff interrupted.

Bobby hugged me and offered his condolences. He had such a pleasant face. It seemed that, amid all the confusion and during one of the most reflective moments of my life, there was always a pleasant face, a kind word, or a friendly reminder that hope was on my side. This time it was Bobby.

As I walked toward my father's office, there were so many people standing around that there was hardly enough room for me to get my mother's attention.

Once inside the office, I saw Dr. Arthur M. Griffin, the chaplain who represented the police department. He took me off to the side and shared a word of prayer, knowing that I would need the strength of God. There were many clergymen and politicians, but Reverend Griffin knew where my strength would come from.

"You Want Me to Take Over…"

I noticed Lloyd in the outside receptionist's office along with some of the supporters of the plaintiffs and Michael, who was one of the chairpersons in The National Organization. Michael asked Lloyd, "You want me to take over? Are you ready to take over this funeral?"

Before my family or I could respond, the funeral director came up to Lloyd. "Get your ass out of here." Grabbing Michael's arm, the funeral director dragged him out of the office and told Lloyd. "Don't make me put all of y'all out."

My brother Arthur warned me; "You had better make sure these people don't interrupt the funeral service of my dad. I will behave like you have never seen in your life."

"There is no need," I said. The wonderful reality was for every evil action there were hundreds and hundreds of kind acts from individuals who were genuinely concerned about my welfare as well as that of the church.

This was not a day for fighting. This was a day for celebrating my father and the good that he had provided to our community. This was a day to remember the way he had served his family, his church, his community, and those who were less fortunate. Dad had made his mark in history. Nothing and no one was going to interfere with his services.

The Funeral Service

Since the week of my father's death, I have felt disoriented. No one could speak to me without my becoming extremely animated. Knowing that it was impossible for me to attend my father's funeral in that state of mind. As I prayed for strength and peace, the power of the Holy Spirit overshadowed me and granted my wish.

As the clergy gathered to lead the funeral processional, my mother motioned for me to lead our family immediately following the clergy. I remember one smiling face in particular – Anna, Bishop Jerry's sister-in-law, a former classmate. Anna touched me, and as I turned to hug her, the look on her face assured me that I could get through this crushing moment. She whispered to me, "You are in my prayers. God is with you. You can make it."

I held on to those words. I would need them as I faced one of the most difficult moments of my life. I recalled contemplating how it was possible for someone to give his life for what he believed in and to serve, only to withstand the pressure that my father endured prior to his death.

I decided to focus on getting through the moment. Upon reaching the front of the sanctuary where the body lay, I refused to look at my father and walked to the second row of pews and could see that my father wore the robe that I had given Marie for his burial.

"Close the Casket"

The program was about to start, but the casket was not closed. I attempted to get the attention of Bishop Jerry, to have him tell the funeral directors to close the casket, but there were no funeral directors in sight.

The program started with the casket open. One hour into the program, I could not stand it any longer. I sent my sister to tell Bishop Jerry to close the casket, but. Bishop Jerry explained that he was waiting for my brother, Alvin, to arrive.

"What? Where is Alvin?" I asked my mother.

She said very softly, "He is running late."

As I sat there, my friend, Bishop Noel, greeted me with a hug and kiss. He whispered, "You are going to be fine."

I replied, "This seems like a dream. It doesn't seem real."

One of the artistic guys, Stan, who dearly loved my father, came to the front of the sanctuary, and lay across the front pew. He was overwhelmed with grief. He could not speak.

My brother, Arthur, who did not know of Stan's relationship with my father, looked at me and stated, "If you do not get someone to take care of this situation, I will remove him right now."

I tried to explain to Arthur the love Stan had for Dad. I could feel Stan's grief, but my brother would not hear of such a thing. I motioned for Henry to remove Stain from the seat. As Henry carried Stan away, he screamed and squirmed, displaying his heartfelt hurt at the passing of my father.

Finally, Alvin arrived. He went directly to the bier. He stood there for a moment. As I watched him, I wondered what he was thinking. Alvin later told me that he could hardly believe that my father was lying there lifeless. This was one of the most painful moments of his life.

It was as if we had been stung. I then understood the writing of the Apostle Paul in First Corinthians 15:55, "O death, where is thy sting? O grave, where is thy victory?" There existed such a sting -- piercing and heart-wrenching. The reality of death was confronting us, and we were compelled to accept what was happening.

I remember part of a prayer, "Lord, grant me the serenity to accept the things I cannot change." I continued to pray for strength. I did not shed another tear.

I, my mother, and several of my siblings were scheduled to share memories of my father. We loved our father and there was no doubt that our father loved us. Throughout his life our love for our father was uninhibited. I wish everyone could have an experience such as we had.

My sister, LaVena, and my brother, A.C., held hands as they approached the platform. A.C. My brother announced that he would allow my sister to share his time. After LaVena spoke, it was my turn. I would speak only what the Holy Spirit gave me.

I spoke with a heart of thanksgiving, "This is the Lord's doing and it is marvelous in our eyes." I continued, "My father often said, 'Once a person leaves this world, there is nothing you will say that can hurt or help that individual.' Now that he is in the presence of God, I say to you today that the glory of this latter house shall be greater than that of the former and there shall be peace in this house." Ending with those words, I heard a round of applause as I went to my seat and held my mother's hand.

There were many wonderful statements made about my father. There were many amazing remarks about the history of our ministry. We knew the clergy in attendance were aware of the warfare confronting us. However, those presiding over the service understood all too well the need to complete the ceremony.

We were confident that Bishop Jerry was familiar with the funeral service of a Presiding Bishop, and he monitored the microphone as he waited for Bishop Noel to officiate the service. We also knew he would not allow anything out of order to take place.

The next section of the program called for the plaintiffs, Clay, Deb, Lester, and Lloyd to make remarks. Although my family was concerned, I was not at all anxious. No one could distract me. I was there to bury my father, and whatever other details there were would wait until after Daddy's burial.

Clay's comments were brief, political, and cynical. He simply spoke of my father being a Pastor and his relationship with him as Chairman of the Deacon Board.

Lester spoke of my father being a Pastor and his relationship with him as an auxiliary leader.

Deb spoke of my father being a man of faith and attempted to cast aspersions on my father's character, but there were too many people listening who loved my father and saw through cynical remarks.

I stood to applaud and to thank them for their remarks as they exited the platform.

Lloyd was the final person to speak. He was angry and bitter. He made sardonic remarks and immediately left the service.

I realized that part of my life was over. There would never again be a time for any of these people to ever address our congregation or speak of my father from the platform he shared. The plaintiffs' assignment was complete. I would never again share a platform with them or their families.

The service was going on longer than planned. We should have known that there would be others who would attend unexpectedly.

We knew Bishop Noel was scheduled to catch a plane to return to California. I walked to the platform to request his patience. As we sat there, Bishop Noel placed his arms around me. I felt comforted. He again assured me that I would get through this moment. He was not concerned about any derogatory comments.

I convinced myself that with each passing moment, I could manage my father's funeral service.

I decided to eliminate several speakers from the program and asked Bishop Jerry to call for the eulogy. Bishop Noel addressed the audience. He also knew of the internal war, understood the political structure of Christianity, and did not hide it. As he eulogized my father, he alluded to warfare.

He was full of valor, exceptionally persuasive, and convincing. I had not spoken to him concerning the battle. However, it was as large a Christian community as it was small. There were those who kept their fingers to the wire informing the Christian community and others who spread the word about the battles.

Bishop Noel did not speak to me about the conflicts, but we had such a committed relationship that I was sure he understood that the future of the ministry was at stake. This historic ministry warranted preservation.

Riding to the gravesite reminded me of the times that I stopped to say a prayer, regardless of where I was or what I was engaged in, whenever I saw a funeral procession. I only hoped someone was praying for me as I traveled to the gravesite.

We arrived at the gravesite and noticed the lieutenants from the army who were present to give my father, a veteran, a 21-gun salute.

It was a remarkable gravesite ceremony. Bishop Jerry carried through his commitment to ensure us of a kingly burial. Another Bishop, Clay's brother, conducted the doxology.

We returned to the church for the repast and thanked those who provided us with such overwhelming support. My family and I spent the rest of the evening at my sister Patricia's home.

The service for my father was complete. I had successfully carried out the funeral service.

My mother's prophecies of the many adversaries had come to fruition.

21
WALKOUT, RIOT, GUNS, AND DOGS

The Staged Walkout

The Sunday morning following the funeral I did not go to church. I was in a deep sleep when the telephone rang. The voice on the other end said, "You need to get here now. The plaintiffs and their supporters are standing outside the church."

Apparently, some people were holding up placards reading "This church is closed, and services are being held elsewhere." The voice on the other end of the telephone explained that cars and the church vans were lined up to transport people from the church to a nearby hotel.

Perhaps I could have managed the staged walkout had the group only agreed to use their private vehicles, but there were designated drivers to transport others in the church vehicles.

Livid and frustrated, as I approached the church, I saw that the vans were preparing to drive away. I stood in front of the vans. The drivers could not drive off. "Get out! Park the vans and give me the keys," I insisted.

Without hesitation, as if they clearly understood they were acting inappropriately, the drivers parked the vans, handed me the keys, and drove away. It was one thing to continue their lies and stage a walkout. However, it was another thing to try and steal everything that was not bolted down.

Inside the church we learned that over the weekend the plaintiffs had informed their families and friends about the staged walkout.

I entered the building and noticed the two elderly twins, Mother Walker, and Mother Littlejohn. Mother Walker moved very slowly with her hands on her hips, saying, "Put your hands on your hips and let your backbone slip. They left."

Mother Littlejohn stared at me, waiting for answers. I asked, "What's going on?"

She said, "They tried to get us to leave with them."

"Who?"

"Clay and them," she said. "And your aunt is with them."

"My who? Never mind, there are friends who stick closer than a brother," I responded. "What happened"?

Mother Littlejohn explained, "When we arrived at church this morning, they had signs standing outside saying, the church is closed down."

"The church is closed down?" I asked.

"Yes madam. I read the sign and it said, 'This church is closed down' They tried to post the signs on the doors, and I stopped them. You aren't going to believe it. But they said they are having church someplace else, and they asked me and Walker to go with them. You need to go into the church. It's crazy there. That McDaze is talking under your clothes."

Another Pulpit Riot

Security and police officers were scattered throughout the entire building. I had noticed a police car in front of the parking lot as I surveyed the area. Why was the police car stationed there? I asked the officer inside the car if he thought he needed to accompany me inside. He replied that there was no need to assist me, but anticipating what was in front of me, I warned him to call for back-up.

This would not be a pretty picture. There was an outright war. Everyone entering the building could sense something unpleasant was about to happen.

The police officer continued to read his newspaper. I walked away, repeating, "You had better radio for back-up."

It was totally chaotic in the main sanctuary of the church.

Following my conversation with Mother Littlejohn, Clay followed me to what was now my new office.

"Do not go inside the sanctuary. It is a total mess."

I demanded, "Call off the charade because in less than five minutes I am going to enter the sanctuary."

He stuttered an emphatic, "No way."

As Clay and I were debating, Vince, who was my boss, entered my office and inquired about my well-being as Clay continued to stutter and dared me to enter the sanctuary.

Vince turned to me and said, "It is now time for you to change seats. You are the Pastor and President of this organization and that is your seat." He pointed to my father's chair, which appeared large and empty to me. "Go and sit in that chair without fear of their threats."

It was wonderful having Vince around. The wolves backed off as I took my seat in Daddy's chair. It had such a high and round back I felt as if it fit me perfectly. I was now officially performing my responsibilities as Pastor and President of our organization.

I realized that some people should make a hasty exit to avoid becoming involved in this war, and Vince was one of those people. I explained, "We don't want to put our jobs in danger. This is not a good time for us to interrupt our responsibilities with the city as a result of my internal war. I think it would be better that you exit the premises rather than jeopardize your position as Director." I stood, hugged Vince, and prepared to enter the sanctuary.

With my mother's encouragement, I began walking down the center of the aisle in the overflowing sanctuary. I turned and noticed several police officers were following me inside of the sanctuary. It was obvious that the policeman had heard the noise and decided to call for backup.

McDaze, who was one of the more contentious plaintiffs, and several other supporters of the plaintiffs were stationed at the microphones. McDaze said, "Marci, the Pastor, is a ho. She isn't a godly woman. She ain't saved."

Someone shouted, "You the ho!"

Everyone stood gasping for breath, as McDaze continued to slander me. I stood there thinking time would prove my character. This was not an issue to be addressed before the audience. I positioned myself closer to the microphone as she continued to shift her statements from me to my deceased father.

I went up to her and whispered, "When you have finished, I will take over."

Following my whispering in her ear, she immediately coughed and spat into the microphone. Unable to continue her remarks because of coughing, she was escorted away.

Cindy, the notorious convicted felon, took the microphone out of McDaze's hand.

As I began to approach the microphone, she began to sing loudly. I was not going to allow her to take over the service. The audience was going to be in for some drama!

Before I could get to the microphone, other supporters of the plaintiffs moved toward the microphone in support of Cindy. Kelle, standing on the floor of the sanctuary, looked over at me on the pulpit and asked if I wanted her to unplug the microphone. I nodded my head.

As Cindy's voice rose with the unplugged microphone in her hands, Kelle rushed onto the pulpit and snatched the microphone.

As Cindy and Kelle fought for control of the microphone, I asked the organist not to play the organ. Kelle then snatched the microphone, and people started coming to the platform to intervene.

There were more than thirty officers on the platform -- the City of Chicago Police Officers, the security firm officers that we had retained, and the security firm officers that the plaintiffs had hired to oust me.

There was absolutely no room for anyone else to approach the stage. We were standing shoulder to shoulder. The plaintiffs and their security on one side, the Chicago Police Officers in the middle, and the officers that we had retained shield me on the other side.

Security and policemen spread throughout the entire assembly now flooding the front of the platform.

There was utter pandemonium. Some people were raising their voices and others were confused. There was complete turmoil. The police approached me and said that it was perhaps best to officially close the service for that day. We complied.

As Lester and Jimmy, Deb's husband, were leaving, Jimmy started screaming, "Everybody, go home. Go home. There is not going to be any service today!"

Following Jimmy's outburst, I stepped toward him and said, "I will take over from here."

Jimmy screamed, "Y'all go home!"

I came up behind him and said to the audience, "There will be a meeting tomorrow night for those who are interested in hearing the truth."

There was a quick exodus by the plaintiffs and their supporters. Those who came late to the service missed the action.

Neither our opponents nor their witnesses and supporters could deny their actions. Everything had been video recorded.

"She Put Us Out with Guns and Dogs"

If I had not been an eyewitness, I would not have believed the chain of events which were happening directly before my eyes. As I filed through the court documents, I saw hundreds of sworn affidavits.

There were sworn affidavits from individuals who were not members of our church, people who had never been members of our church, and people who had not been members in over thirty, even fifty years, and there were even affidavits from deceased individuals. I was absolutely certain that most of those individuals signing those sworn affidavits did not know of me. Therefore, they could not have known the details concerning the litigation.

As I continued filing through the affidavits, there was one sworn affidavit in particular which struck me. It was from my aunt, Maye, one of the last people to leave the church that morning of the staged walk-out. Following the plaintiffs and their family members, Aunt Maye remained behind to talk to Mothers Walker and Littlejohn. She reminded both of them of a previous dream she'd had.

Mother Littlejohn shared with me Aunt Maye's story. "I had a dream where there was nobody in the church but y'all two." Mother Littlejohn stated that she could not believe what was happening and refused to comment on Maye's dream. Mother Littlejohn said that, following her refusal to continue her conversation with Maye, she had left.

I did not put Maye out of the church, just as I had not put any of those individuals out.

Several of the supporters of the plaintiffs were standing outside in front of one of the corporation's properties. Two of them, Leroy, and Mac, watched as my sister, Gwendolyn, drove up and parked her truck.

Leroy immediately screamed at Gwendolyn, shouting loud enough for the residents to hear. "She put us out with guns and dogs! We left. But we are going to get y'all."

Gwendolyn, having no idea why Leroy was making such horrible accusations, stepped out of her truck, and stood up on its running board. "You have no idea what you are saying. You have no clue as to what is happening. You have some nerves. After all that, my father contributed to you and your family, and now he is dead."

Mac yelled, "I loved your father."

The residents from the community watched as Gwendolyn defended us against the slander by the plaintiffs and their supporters. By the time Gwendolyn had finished her defense, the supporters of the plaintiffs left.

Following their staged walkout, I explained to Gwendolyn the misconception brought on by the pending litigation. "The Sunday following Dad's funeral, Deacon Clay hired security. Tuesday, when he and his supporters arrived at church, we had hired security as well. When that group discovered that we had, in fact, hired a licensed and professional security firm to maintain peace, they became outraged. There were many threats to my life, including the bomb threat.

Leroy was not at all present that night. Like all the others who swore in their affidavits, he continued to accuse me of throwing them out with guns and dogs."

"Have you shared publicly that they killed Dad?" she asked.

"Killed Dad?"

"Yes, just as if they are reporting publicly that you personally put them out with guns and dogs, did you report that they stressed our father so much that he died? While Dad shielded their dishonesty and immorality, he prayed day and night that each of them would be transformed from notorious drug addicts, prostitutes, and worse to become decent citizens of society?"

"I am so glad that Dad didn't have to witness this horrible masquerade," I said. "May his soul rest in peace."

When she nodded, I cautioned her, "We must not become distracted by the loud noises. That's one of the opposition's objectives – to distract and to veer from the facts and laws supporting this case. There is a lot of truth to be revealed and that cry, my sister, will far exceed the screams and distractions from the plaintiffs, their supporters, and the Giant law firm."

Pimp turned Preacher –

The Monday following the pulpit incident, Clay and a group of his supporters met in the church sanctuary, where I overheard him say, "We should not have done what we did."

Threatening shots rang out, "We will destroy you!"

Amidst the shouts there were others who walked up to me to express their condolences. Turning my attention to the clamor outside, I noticed fights in the parking lot. One fight involved Kelle and Mary. Someone said that there were gang members outside, but I noticed that they were friends of my brothers, not gang leaders.

Tray's wife, a short and stocky woman, began pointing her fingers in my mother's face and verbally abusing her. "Your daughter isn't going to be a pastor here. We are going to do whatever we need to stop her from being Pastor."

As my mother walked away, one of my brother's friends, Manning, a former pimp turned preacher, asked Tray, "Is that your wife pointing her fingers in Bishop Richards' wife's face?"

Tray responded, "Yes."

Manning offered to see Tray outside in the parking lot.

I started walking toward Tray's wife, Linda, but Manning turned to me and said, "I got this."

I walked outside to determine whether my mother was okay.

Outside I overheard Manning speaking to Tray. "I watched as you allowed your rude children to disrespect Bishop Richards the Friday y'all called that so-called meeting. At that time, Bishop asked that I not say anything to y'all because I would have started a war. I respected his decision and dropped it. But now that he has passed, you may not like Mother Richards, and you may not agree with the Bishop's choice for Pastor, but you and your wife and children had better respect Mother Richards. You had better teach that respect or else someone else will. Mother Richards has been nothing but kind to y'all. And since she didn't respond to that dumb witch, I'm addressing you – now."

Tray responded, "I'll talk to her."

"Yeah, you better talk to her and your children. And I mean, you better talk to them quickly."

As I was searching for Linda to confront her, someone else met me and said, "We got this. You do not have to worry your pretty little self about that ignorant wench. We got this. This is crazy. They won't even let the man's wife grieve for her husband."

I soon discovered that there were others standing around who had witnessed Linda's actions.

At the other end of the parking lot, I noticed several of our friends speaking to the supporters of the plaintiffs and their family members. LaVena was arguing with one of Tray's daughters. Tray was getting into his vehicle, along with his fifteen children.

Derrick looked at Tray and said, "Aren't you the one who sat up in that church while all of these others disrespected the Bishop before he died?"

As Tray was threatening Derrick, I heard glass breaking. I turned to see a van window burst and blood running from faces as someone said, "We gotta get you out of here right now."

Someone yelled; "She put us out with guns and dogs!"

Derrick T, one of the guys from the neighborhood, yelled, "I was there, she didn't. Yall do not have to like her, but you are going to respect her!"

As I was leaving, I heard someone scream, "Call the police!"

Warfare

We knew there would be an uphill battle, but we did not anticipate the intensity of the warfare immediately following my father's burial. of my father. The following Tuesday, we planned to have Bible study as usual. The Board of Directors and I were also planning to excommunicate several individuals who would be attending.

Two hours prior to Bible study, the plaintiffs and their supporters started gathering outside of the church, causing a mob scene. I decided to call a professional security firm. One hour prior to Bible study, Clay arrived with his security officer

The professional security firm I had called was available, and the president of the company, Deputy Chief Brown, looked as if he bench-pressed three hundred pounds daily. Following him was Chief Rasul, who looked as if he bench-pressed four hundred pounds daily. There were two other gentlemen, one who positively looked as if he could have bench-pressed 1,000 pounds!

Deputy Chief Brown introduced himself, and I explained, "My father passed, and we buried him Saturday. Now we are experiencing a battle."

Deputy Chief Brown was amazed, "Are you saying he's only been in the ground two days?"

"Yes. We have *just* buried my father."

"This is unbelievable. Even crooks allow time for people to bury their loved ones. What is wrong with these people?" he replied.

"This all seems like a dream," I replied.

"It may seem like a dream, but it's real. We are here and there is a mob going crazy outside," he stated.

"I really need you to ensure our safety."

Deputy Chief Brown said, "We are here to provide for your safety." And he turned to instruct his team.

As we stood there, Lisa said, "The Robocops have arrived. We will wait and see what the toy cops will do now." Deputy Chief Brown's security team was familiar with managing crises. They also knew the rules of the law to administer proper solutions.

As the Board of Directors met in my office, Mike was sitting in the banquet hall holding a private meeting with some of the plaintiffs' supporters. When we requested his presence in the Board of Directors meeting, Mike refused to meet with us.

Chief Rasul asked Mike several times to come downstairs to meet with us. When Mike continued to refuse, the Board requested that he leave the property. Mike again refused.

Chief Rasul calmly informed me that they would arrest Mike for trespassing.

Even though we had no idea of the authority of this security firm, we gave our approval, and Chief Rasul returned to the banquet hall to bring Mike downstairs.

As we continued our Board of Directors meeting, Lisa informed us that the police were outside to arrest Mike. The security cameras showed Mike being escorted outside in handcuffs.

Suddenly Marie remembered that Mike had not received his excommunication letter, left to give him his letter, and as I watched her on the cameras, I noticed her speaking to the police officer, who nodded. Marie then placed an envelope inside Mike's shirt pocket. Mike was taken to jail.

Yes, Daddy had passed and there was no need to pretend any longer. Everyone took off their gloves and prepared to take the war to another level.

We were determined not to submit to the threats and the antics of the plaintiffs and their supporters.

As the crowd started to gather for Bible study, Chief Rasul asked for the list of those whom we would serve with excommunication letters.

A group of rowdy individuals incited those arriving for Bible study. The Board of Directors agreed that it would be best to give those who were inciting the riot excommunication letters as well. They included Cindy, the felon, Mary; the lady who threw Marie off the stage; and Gene, the one who had snatched the microphone from my father. As Chief Rasul spoke to Marie, Gene interrupted to demand a letter of excommunication.

When I called Jim for advice, he calmly informed me that as Pastor and Board of Directors, we could call the police and have the others escorted from the property.

Lloyd arrived at the church, along with Clay and Lester, and all entered my office. Several police officers arrived as Lester was addressing me. When I asked Lester to step outside my office, he replied, "This is not your office."

I asked again, "Will you kindly step outside my office as I speak with Lloyd and Clay?"

Then one of the police officers said, "Step outside. While we are here, this is her office."

As Lester and the others left, we closed the door.

There were numerous conversations among Bishop Jerry, the Board of Directors, deacons, trustees, and others to offer mediation, but the disgruntled people were not interested in mediations.

After Lester left, I called Jim, who said that we would petition the court the following day to have a restraining order issued against anyone who continued to disrupt.

As the police officers stood and listened to Jim on the speakerphone, we informed the police officers that we would carry out this precaution and that they could leave.

While the commotion was still going on outside, people were still gathering for Bible Class. Other police officers arrived on the scene. After speaking to the supporters of the plaintiffs, one of the officers asked me who I thought I was.

"What do you mean by that?" I asked.

"Do you think you are the king who sits on the throne?"

I told him, "There is no way I could be the king. However, I am the queen, and I am asking you to leave my office immediately."

As that officer stepped outside, I asked Lloyd and Clay to stay and talk. There were others present as the three of us sat down to meditate.

I began by asking Lloyd for his advice to settle the confusion and whether he had a proposal to resolve the problem. He said that it might be an idea to have a vote for the Pastor.

Knowing that the group was divided, I asked Lloyd who the candidates should be. He responded by saying he did not know. I then turned to Clay, as the chairman of the Deacon's Board, and asked who he thought would be a good Pastor for the ministry. I named those who were working together, Lester, Jimmy, and Gene.

Clay emphatically replied that he thought none of those men was qualified to be Pastor. I then asked him if he desired Lloyd to become his Pastor, to which he responded "no."

The three of us talked for nearly an hour-and-a-half. There was no resolution. Each of the men suing me wanted to be Pastor, and there was no way to resolve this volatile situation.

As we were preparing to leave the meeting, Bishop Jerry arrived and asked to speak with Lloyd and Clay, but neither man was amenable.

Lloyd looked at Bishop Jerry and said, "I won't be back no more."

Clay entered a dialogue with Lester in the back of the sanctuary. As I monitored the security cameras, I saw the plaintiffs gathered in the back of the sanctuary.

When I opened the office to walk into the sanctuary, Lester shouted, "Bible study is canceled -- everyone go home!" Then he motioned the plaintiffs to follow him as he walked out.

22

SABOTAGE

o serious warfare would be complete without sabotage, and our conflict with the plaintiffs supplied a prime example of deliberate subterfuge.

It was 9:30 a.m., Monday morning, the day following the staged walkout by the plaintiffs and their supporters. I received a telephone call from Kelle, my administrative assistant. Noticing her cell number, I asked, "Why aren't you in the office?"

"I am! I'm in the office. They disconnected all of the utilities."

"What are you saying?"

"Lady Bishop, upon my arrival at the church, the entire staff was standing outside. When I asked why, Sam, the custodian, told me that there was no electricity. When I tried to call the electric company, I couldn't get a dial tone. The telephone lines were all disconnected. The custodians turned on the water, which was all cold, and discovered our gas was disconnected as well."

"Call the utility companies and have them reconnect everything."

"Before I called you, I phoned each of the utility companies. All of them said that our services had been disconnected." Kelle sounded so upset she could hardly speak.

"Calm down and ask them to reconnect the services."

You don't understand. We can't get any information on our accounts. Someone put a secret passcode on each one of them."

After hours of trying to have our services restored, speaking with supervisor after supervisor, we were unsuccessful. This would be an additional legal expense.

Jim wrote letters to each of the utility companies informing them of their obligation to remove the blocks and restore our services. After several hours, we were back in business.

We realized that this was not going to be a fair fight. It was an undying war, "a game," as the plaintiffs' counsel called it, a game with no rules.

We had to prepare ourselves for everything. My father's former attorney told me, "Prepare for war in the time of peace." We were certainly not fully prepared.

Figuring it out while "up there"

I was still grieving the death of Eric and of my father, and the stunts of the plaintiffs intensified my grief. As I stood in the sanctuary wondering whether I should continue, Mother Littlejohn jerked me from my daze. Pushing me down the long aisle onto the platform she ordered, "Teach right now, girl."

"I am filled with so much grief. I don't know what to say. What am I supposed to say?"

"Figure it out when you get up there. But for right now, get up there and teach." She continued pushing me with as much strength as her frail body could manage. Nearly tripping onto the stage, I stood there frozen as I tried to find the proper words.

Breaking what seemed to be hours of silence, Mother Littlejohn shouted, "Speak!"

That word exploded through my head and body. I had to obey.

Literally shaking as I spoke from the platform, I began by saying, "Praise the Lord, everyone. Thank you all for coming out tonight. There is a lot to address, and I realize that there are many questions. However, I'd like to thank each of you for your support. Please bear with me as I get myself together. My heart is overwhelmed with the death of my father and the activities of the events surrounding us. I am here to answer any questions you may have. No question is too personal. The floor is open."

Someone positioned a microphone in the middle of the floor and proceeded to tape the meeting.

The flood of questions raised many concerns:

"How did you guys pay for your father's funeral given the allegations that the plaintiffs took all of the money from the different accounts?"

"How did all the confusion come about?"

"Who is primarily responsible for this turmoil?"

"What should we say to those from the plaintiffs' and their supporters who are trying to persuade us to leave the church?"

"Who masterminded this conspiracy?"

"Are we going to just sit and do nothing?"

"Why don't we fight back?"

"How is it that deacons can try and be the Pastor?"

"What is it that you want us to do?"

"Can you inform the authorities about the threats we are receiving?"

"We know all of those people are divided. How is it that they are pretending to be together now?"

"We can fight just like them. Let's get our large families and parade like a circus just as they are doing."

As the questions and suggestions continued, I responded as best as I could. After nearly three hours, I concluded the session by announcing that we would be open to answer more questions later.

As I prepared to close the meeting, I noticed the leading plaintiff, Rogers, sitting at the back of the room. Rogers had come from Mississippi and listened attentively as I answered question after question.

Before closing the meeting, I asked Rogers if he would offer insight on the issues. As Rogers prepared to address the audience, the crowd started shouting out in protest. Someone shouted out, "Does he think we are fools?"

"God will work everything out according to His divine plan," Rogers began. He quoted a familiar Bible verse from Acts 5:39 -- "If this thing be of God, ye cannot overthrow it, lest happily ye be found even to fight against God." He ended his statement by looking at me and saying, "No one can stop you no matter how hard they try."

Threats Increased

The threats were growing so rapidly that we needed additional security. It was clear that the proper course for our organization was sound leadership and guidance.

As I took office, I decided to maintain the focus of the organization and its primary purpose. Although the conspiracy opposing my leadership as the new President was increasing, it would have been a disservice to the corporation and to those who desired me to be Pastor to submit to the opposition.

The emotional dynamism that surrounds the responsibility of leading these great historical Pentecostal organizations ran deep. Under my leadership, we were becoming part of something greater than ourselves. This board decided to do this for the generations who would follow.

By staying focused, we had hoped to strike a smooth transition. But this was not to be. The plaintiffs and their supporters threw out many more threats.

After several board meetings, we started developing strategies to become an intricate part of the revitalization of the community. We were aware that whatever decisions we made in the present would have to address the challenges ahead. Those suing us were attempting to keep us and our corporation buried in the past under leadership which no longer existed.

Evictions

Several of our properties were occupied by tenants from the plaintiffs' supporters. Those tenants did not pay rent. Before we began the tedious eviction process, we discovered that we did not have new sets of keys to any of the properties because the plaintiffs and their supporters had changed all of the locks.

As Kelle and I prepared to change the locks we traveled throughout the properties with the locksmiths, amidst threats, serving five-day notices to tenants who were not paying rent. After delivering the notices, when we attempted to change locks, we were held off by men who appeared to be notorious street guys.

One of the men standing guard for the plaintiffs told Kelle, "Bitch, we own this MF."

Kelle immediately phoned Manning, the pimp turned preacher, who arrived at the property within twenty minutes. As he stepped out of his vehicle, the notorious individual started yelling, "We own this mutha--." but before he could complete his obscenity Manning wrestled him into a headlock.

With the man's feet dangling in mid-air, Kelle turned to the locksmith and said, "You can now change the lock."

The locksmith, a short Hispanic man, named Ernesto, was shaking. He looked at me and said, "I ain't never seen anything like this. Am I going to get paid?"

I replied, "Yes. We need keys to the property, and I must teach Bible study tonight."

Once we began the eviction process, the court informed us that as a corporation, we needed legal representation. Therefore, we returned to Jim's office for assistance -- yet another unexpected legal expense.

This war was becoming unbelievably expensive. But the financial burden did not compare to the transition we faced as employees of the corporation and tenants of the properties of the corporation.

His Baby Mama Evicted

As I taught Bible study, I noticed a gentleman sitting in the audience that I did not recognize who appeared to be another notorious guy from the community. After Bible study, he followed me to my office. "I want to have a conversation with you."

"A conversation? About what? For what?"

"That was my baby mama you evicted, and I got something for your black ass."

"You don't scare me. If that's your baby's mama, then you need to support her and your children by either paying their rent or finding a place for them to live. And whatever you have, please don't be so gullible as to believe that the law does not have something for you as well. Get out of my office and do us both a favor." I walked away.

He started screaming threats. "I got something for your ass!"

I turned around and heard Kelle, who was standing nearby, repeat his words to him. "I got something for your ass as well."

As we filed several police reports, I had to park several blocks away from my home until a district police officer escorted me home. I was so tired of calling the police that one day, I arrived home to find several of the plaintiffs' supporters standing outside my door. When I tried to enter, I discovered that my door locks had been changed.

I left and returned with the locksmith, only to find that someone was inside the house. Kelle again telephoned Manning, who accompanied the locksmith. When the man opened the door, Manning grabbed him and pinned him to the ground while someone called the police.

When I went to the police district to file more reports, the officers were laughing and joking about our war, as if the filing of the report were trivial. I interrupted the officers and asked them to speak with their lieutenant.

I asked; "Does something fatal have to happen to someone before you guys take this seriously? Should the headline read, City Employee Killed Immediately Leaving the Police Station?

The lieutenant replied, "Madam, I understand." And he sent several officers to escort me home again.

When two police officers and I arrived at my home, the officers knocked on the door. No one answered.

I noticed a new doorknob. As I tried to open the front door, my keys didn't work. My locks had been changed. When the female officer knocked on the door again and said, "Police, open up," a man opened the door. The officer looked at me and asked; "Do you know this man"? I shook my head, no.

The officer placed the man in handcuffs. As she took him to the squad car, the male officer searched the house. As he opened the door to my bedroom, we heard a loud bang. The male officer stepped inside. Hiding behind the door of my bedroom stood a totally naked man. I gasped. The officer pointed his club at the man and said, "Get your clothes now. You and your partner are going to jail."

As my head buzzed with adrenaline, I stepped outside for some fresh air.

The female police officer followed me and asked if I was okay. Before I could answer someone driving down the street shouted; "Hey, Marci, you alright?"

I nodded my head, yes.

The officer asked; "Do you know those guys"?

I shook my head, no.

She replied, "Well, they know you. Those guys are some of the drug lords in the neighborhood. And since they know you, you should get them to help you. I bet you won't have any more trouble from these people."

I could not believe the officer suggested that I enlist drug lords to help me. Instead, I phoned the locksmith and asked if he would come to change the locks of my home.

Bullet Holes

In our community, where drugs and violence existed side by side, I was a community liaison and a sponsor of many youth activities. I had earned the respect of community leaders as well as the street gangs.

One day I arrived home to notice my house surrounded by supporters of the plaintiffs. Leaving my house again, I went to the police station and asked them to escort me home.

Several days later when Kelle, Frank, and I were cleaning my home I noticed broken windows. There were also shells from bullets. As we continued to clean, we discovered bullet holes in the walls.

My place had never been a target for the gangs.

Frank said, "To ensure your safety, we should hire additional security." Although the staff feared that my life was in danger, we could not afford additional security. I assured them that I would be careful.

Reports and Letters

We were consumed with filing police reports. There were police officers and fire marshals at our corporation daily to investigate the numerous complaints received from anonymous callers.

Whatever it took, those who were attempting to cause our demise increased their anonymous letter writing, including to Pastors within and beyond the city.

The reputation of the corporation was at great risk. I received numerous calls informing me of anonymous letters challenging my position as Pastor and praising the lawsuits attempting to prevent our success. The continued harassing letters to others, including clergy and city officials, were soon widespread.

As a liaison for the city, my position included interacting with pastors, not only within the church, but in the community as well. I had established an excellent rapport with a number of those pastors and received several telephone calls about the anonymous letters they had received.

A pastor friend for more than twenty-five years read the anonymous letter he had received. The phrases were familiar:

She has a staff that puts people out of church.

Dr. Janell had done that.

Since our Pastor passed, we are asking you not to support her until (the) Mayor has heard our plea to fire Dr. Janell.

After reading me the letter, the pastor assured me of his support. "Marci, I just wanted you to know that there could never be anything that could make me question my support for you." That pastor remained constant during those challenging times. Several other pastors telephoned the church to inform me of the letters that they had received.

Soon after receiving those telephone calls, my employer, Vince, called me into his office to tell me that a copy of the letter had been sent to the mayor's office and the Police Department as well.

Vince asked if I had any idea who was behind the anonymous letters.

I could only speculate.

I trusted that my previous relationships would outshine the slander and lies confronting me, including the anonymous letters to the pastors.

Fire Marshals

Each day for months, we had been receiving visits and telephone calls from the city's fire marshals. The fire marshals searched our facilities looking for circumstances that might warrant citations. Although Bishop Jerry was an Assistant Commissioner of the fire department, who volunteered to assist us. We maintained a clean environment in the church. After we made countless repairs and improvements, the fire marshals stopped visiting our facilities.

Services in the Cold

The winter months were upon us, and we were without gas. We were holding our worship services in the cold church. Individuals sat through our services wearing their coats. A few people in the audience had colds. Young children stood to clap with their gloves and hats on. We danced more often to help generate a little body warmth. No one complained. It was amazing to witness the commitment and the dedication of those worshiping with us. No one asked why we did not have gas. Week after week, we just held our services in the cold.

We were using propane tanks in the back of the sanctuary to keep the room warm. Whenever the members arrived, we removed the propane tanks. However, the stench from the propane lingered in the church. Our congregation endured the weekly smell of the propane tanks and never once complained. We were constantly seeking new scents to offset the smell of the propane tanks.

The fire marshals returned to our facilities. An anonymous call to the fire marshals said that we were holding services with propane tanks. The fire marshals took a tour of the building. There were no propane tanks. They continued to visit us but were unable to find any violations involving the propane tanks.

Each week, I wondered how many members would stop attending our ministry because of the cold and the smell from the propane tanks, but instead of losing attendees, we gained members.

We hoped that Jim would develop a strategy to bring an end to the lawsuit. Instead, we were served a new lawsuit.

23

THE NEW LAWSUIT

ne week after I buried my father, Jim called to say, "Marci, we have been served with a new lawsuit by the plaintiffs."

"What is the lawsuit for this time?" I asked.

The new lawsuit -- filed two days after my father's death – targeted me, the members of the Board of Directors, and the corporation. Since we were still in the appeals court for the first lawsuit, I could not understand the purpose.

Jim explained it to me. "The plaintiffs have filed a lawsuit for the only original living director of the corporation, named Rogers."

"Jim, that man lives in Mississippi. He left the church nearly twenty years ago to become pastor of his own church."

"Well, he is now a part of the lawsuit, Rogers versus Richards."

The Only Original Living Director?

Rogers was one of the original five members of the Board of Directors of our corporation. All of the other original directors of the corporation were deceased.

Rogers would return to the city and stop by the church, bringing a large van loaded with items for sale. He would set up shop directly outside the church, selling mops, brooms, Mississippi Polish sausages, and Mississippi pecans from long lines of tables spreading from the door all along the sidewalk, ending at the parking lot. During the growing conspiracy within the church, more and more regularly I noticed the tables outside the church filled with items for sale.

One day I approached him, "Why are you frequenting the city?" Rogers informed me that he was in the city to watch.

"What are you watching?" I asked. I remembered walking in unannounced to my father's office where Rogers was huddled in a corner talking to him. Upon my unannounced arrival, Rogers rushed out of the office.

"Do you recall the day that I walked into my father's office, and you were huddled in a corner?" I asked.

"Yes," he responded.

"Why did you rush out so quickly?"

"I don't remember."

"That's strange because with all of the watching you've been doing lately; it seems you'd recall why you were huddled in the pastor's office and ran out when I arrived."

"I'm just here to sell my stuff," he said.

The day following my conversation with Rogers, I walked into the financial secretary, Rubi's, office. "Who were the initial primary signatures on the church's building fund accounts?"

"Rogers and Clay, the Chairman of the Deacon Board," she replied.

"It's no guess why he's visiting the city more and more."

In the days following, Rubi provided me with the checks adding into the thousands, payable to Rogers and Clay. Rubi also provided me with thousands of dollars in NSF checks from Rogers payable to the corporation.

That week, Rubi came to my office. "Rogers and Clay have been getting' and taking the money for a long time. Rogers owes the church almost $90,000.00," she stated.

I gasped. "Ninety thousand dollars? What?"

"Along with some other documents, here are the minutes from the meeting with Bishop Poole, the Board of Directors, and Rogers. These minutes are from the board meeting with Bishop Poole in May 1977. We were all in the meeting when Bishop Poole appointed your father as Pastor of this church. We all signed it. Here are all of their signatures and my signature to prove it," she explained.

Rubi was correct. The document bore the signatures of Rogers and each of the signatures of the Board of Deacons, Trustees, and Directors.

"I want to give you the rest of the stuff," she said.

"What stuff might that be?"

"The records and letters showing where Clay and Lloyd met with attorney Arnold, acting on behalf of the corporation. Also, there are records showing that Lester agreed to be on the board of directors, in his personal handwriting," Rubi had been the financial secretary for the corporation for nearly forty years. I was sure that the documents she provided me would prove useful.

After reading the copy of the minutes from the meeting with Bishop Poole appointing my father as his successor, I read Bishop Poole's remarks stating there was $90,000.00 owed to the church by the only living original director, Rogers.

Could Rogers have been in search of the minutes from the meeting with Bishop Poole decades before, when he was huddled in the corner of my father's office?

24
THE GIANT

"It's Like A Divorce ..."

I t's like a divorce, you get half and we get half and I'm here to take my half now," said Margie, the senior citizen who had voluntarily left the church with those who staged a walkout and then sued us, claiming that we had driven them from the church with guns and dogs.

Standing inside the corridor of the church, grandmother Margie walked directly up to me and stated that she had returned to the church to take our personal property.

I was trying to formulate my response to Margie's comparison of the pending litigation to a divorce when the doors of the sanctuary swung open.

I watched as two other senior citizen members came storming into the corridor -- Mother Walker and Mother Littlejohn, the fearless pillars of the church for more than 50 years, two members held in the highest esteem.

Both Mother Walker and Mother Littlejohn immediately objected. Mother Walker said, "This isn't a divorce! Get out of here. You got some nerve showing up in this place after y'all lied and tricked those po' people into leaving this church. God is going to get y'all. Now get out of here!"

I stood in amazement as Mother Littlejohn added, "Well, if it's a divorce, we get everything, since y'all is lying and left the church. What are you here for anyway? More lies and more lies. God will have the last say."

Mother Walker, who was legally blind, added, "I have been here way before y'all. You don't know what you are talking about. I was here with Mother Mattie, and I will be here long after y'all gone. They did not want Mother Mattie because she was a woman and now all these years later, they have come against this po' girl. I know y'all. I know that y'all made this up. But God is going to get y'all. Get out of here."

Mother Littlejohn continued, "Pastor, don't give her anything." Then she addressed Margie. "It's a shame what y'all did. Leave now!"

Margie interjected, "It's just like a divorce and …."

As both sides continued to argue, verging on physical contact, I was speechless. Margie's voice escalated, as did Mother Walker's and Mother Littlejohn's. Back and forth, Mother Walker and Mother Littlejohn insisted that Margie did not know the truth behind the staged walkout.

These seniors continued their heated debate until I had to step in between them.

"It is not worth it," I said. "Enough is enough. This is exactly what those who are suing us want. They want you to fight. This is crazy."

Mother Littlejohn turned toward the door and demanded that Margie leave the property. As Mother Littlejohn pointed to the door, Margie resisted my asking her to leave. She repeated, "It's like a divorce, you get half, and we get half."

Mother Littlejohn shouted over Margie's voice, "Y'all don't get anything!" She demanded that Margie exit the property immediately, but as Mother Littlejohn pointed toward the door, Margie continued to argue with Mother Walker.

Divorce

Margie's takeover of the corporation's property set the stage for others to return and do the same. A few days later, when Kelle and I arrived at the church, we noticed that the doors were open. Equipment had been taken, the marble floors were stripped, and pictures were missing from the walls.

Unfortunately, that incident turned out to be minor compared to the roller-coaster adventure upon which we were about to embark. We had no idea that what was about to happen would perhaps change the course of religious history, governing, and corporate laws forever.

The split turned out to be much like the worst sort of divorce. Margie's thought-provoking words proved to be true as we ended up witnessing one of the most infamous and revolting splits in church history.

Quite often, the results of a bitter divorce change people's names. However, the plaintiffs decided to incorporate themselves under a similar name.

"The plaintiffs began their own church, calling it Greater, something," Jean stated. "Greater, Who, Greater, What?" I asked.

"It's the same name as Bethlehem Healing Temple, just with the word Greater in front," she explained. According to any church organizational process, the separation from the original church meant that they could not lay claim to any part of the previous organization. Therefore, the decision of the court to insist that the plaintiffs were members of our church seemed downright bizarre.

The Plaintiffs and Their Supporters Meet in a Gym

Once the plaintiffs and their supporters staged their walkout, they held their initial meeting at a hotel. It seemed that the group was too rowdy for the hotel, and they were asked to leave, according to the hotel's clerk, when we telephoned them. After being booted from the hotel, the group began services in the chapel of a nearby hospital, but the hospital could not tolerate the uncontrollable noise of the group either. The group then met at another location.

As they continued to wander around the city, I received a telephone call from someone who worked for the public school system. He had heard we were searching for space to hold our services because we had closed the church. It turned out that the plaintiffs began holding services in the public-school gym.

Take the Church By Any Means

Should we have been surprised at the events taking place around us? Perhaps not, given the plaintiffs' primary goal was to gain corporate control of our organization and throw me out as the Pastor. The surprise was the response of justice to their preposterous claims. There were other courtrooms, which did not allow the plaintiffs to engage in legal actions against the former church. However, one judge allowed those who had left the church to try to decide how our church should operate.

Looking at the affidavits and misrepresentation of the plaintiffs and their witnesses, it would be naïve to trust that justice would see through the lies.

We became familiar with a similar case, "Christian Love Tabernacle of Holiness vs. Christian Love Tabernacle." When one group changed their name and started their church, the court immediately threw the case out, stating that the latter group had ceased to be a part of Christian Love Tabernacle of Holiness.

Because of the dismissal of the first lawsuit, which did not provide the answers, the plaintiffs went in search of a Giant law firm, which soon commenced a new lawsuit against us.

David and Goliath

As children, we were often told the Biblical story of David and Goliath.

David was a shepherd boy who tended his father's sheep. He protected the sheep by striking predators with stones hurled from his sling.

Goliath was a Giant, a strong warrior experienced in warfare. Goliath's army was at war with King Saul's army -- the army of God. Goliath had many more skilled men and more resources, more influence, plus a larger and more powerful army.

The law firm taking the case for the plaintiffs reminded us of the Giant Goliath.

In the Biblical tale, David slays Goliath by striking him in the head with a stone flung from his sling.

The "Giant" New Law Firm

Following the initial dismissal, the plaintiff's second counsel withdrew. The plaintiffs returned to court represented by this large, renowned law firm, by the name of SNARE, known as "the Giant," located in the heart of our city in one of the tallest buildings in the world.

The law firm had more than a thousand counsels and unlimited resources. Its client list included some of the most prestigious companies. There seemed to be no limit to their access legally, financially, and politically. Their size did not intimidate us, however, for we were fighting for and defending the rights of our corporation.

The law firm represented the Giant Goliath, and we were like David. In our hand was only a sling -- the truth behind the case against us.

The faith of David becomes the sustaining power for those who fight Giants. Just as firefighters run toward a fire rather than away from it, this faith drives fighters toward the Giants and not away from a frightening confrontation.

Like David, we were taught to run toward the Giants and not away from them, because, sooner or later, Giants do fall.

The Giant soared above David in stature and physique; however, David had a greater awareness of survival. Giants do not have to learn the art of survival, as they are constantly taking from those who are smaller than themselves. People like David in their faith will often be able to conquer the Goliaths.

Pro Bono

The plaintiffs had convinced the counsels from the law firm that we were the bad guys. Therefore, the Giant agreed to represent the plaintiffs' *pro bono* -- "for the good," usually meaning that legal services are provided for a case that is potentially regarded as needing to be decided for the general good of the greater society. In this case, of course, it also meant that such a huge, renowned legal firm was representing our opponents for free. While the plaintiffs were no longer required to pay for their legal services, the Giant spared no expense to represent their clients' obtuse lawsuit.

Several members of our church were employees of the GIANT law firm; there were also family members who were employees. We knew that this could be considered a conflict of interests for the law firm to represent the plaintiffs; however, struggling to maintain legal counsel we did not embrace the challenge of confronting them over these conflicts.

The Internet included records from one of the Giant's board meetings in which one board member stated that those who represented the losing party should be responsible for paying the fees of the defendants. At that point I realized that the law firm was prepared to win at any cost.

There was too much evidence pointing to the truth of this case; there were too many facts supporting the conspiracy of those suing us. However, we seemed to be at a total disadvantage. We were incurring legal fees daily, while the plaintiffs' law firm represented them for free.

Upon visiting the law firm's office, I read a copy of its internal monthly magazine, which included a piece about the company representing the plaintiffs' *pro bono*.

The article cited very demeaning remarks about my character while stating that it represented the majority of those who staged the walk out from our church. The counsels of the Giant law firm had no true idea about us or what was the character of those they were representing. For the time being, the remarks I read were not important, as we had bigger fish to fry.

The law firm seemed to frivolously waste its resources. Time after time, their counsels served us with duplicate motions. Most often, if we did receive their motions, it was six or seven of the same documents.

Perhaps if the law firm had taken the time to thoroughly investigate their own clients it might have had second thoughts about representing such an unprincipled group.

As the Giant law firm prepared to provide the plaintiff with unlimited resources, we found ourselves in a battle to retain our counsel. Yet we were determined to maintain our faith and dispel the false claims the plaintiffs and their supporters made against us.

Although the law firm was the Giant, we believed that there existed a greater cause. That cause was to stand against injustice, even if such a position meant standing against the law firm. While there were countless individuals and counsels advising us that we could never win against such a connected and huge opponent, we continued to state the truth.

The Giant amended their complaint to include the only living original director, Rogers, as being a holdover director. The complaint was based on the plaintiffs' theory that Rogers was a holdover director of the corporation even though the truth was that Rogers had not served on the corporations' board for more than twenty years and had ceased to be a member of the church.

As the only original living director of the Board, Rogers was now the central focus of the litigation.

25

INVESTIGATION

The Attorney General Dismissed the Plaintiffs' Complaint

Among other suits, there was also a complaint filed by the plaintiffs with the Attorney General's office, accusing the organization of misappropriating funds. Jim explained what had happened.

"Marci, the Attorney General dismissed the complaint of the plaintiffs," he said.

"What complaint?"

"Don't worry about it. It was dismissed."

As the Attorney General dismissed the plaintiffs' claims, I struggled to maintain my employment with the city (directly as a result of the pending litigation), while the letters poured into the mayor's office and my place of employment demanding my termination.

One of my greatest challenges was that of my former employer and friend, Vince, who was caught up in city and government politics.

Vince asked me to apply for a managerial position in the city. At first, I was reluctant because of my ongoing responsibilities within the corporation, but also because he was a dear and close friend.

Vince and I shared a common interest. Our relationship was that of minister and minister, employer, and employee.

It was when Vince first applied for his position as Commissioner that we talked through the possibilities of my working within his department. We were cognizant of the reality that this position would be very high-profile and that, as the Director, his life could possibly always be under scrutiny. However, because the two of us shared a common goal for developing strategies for a better community, we thought we could be an effective team and overcome any difficulties together.

Upon my agreement to accept the position, Vince and I worked well together on the complex issues that came before us. The Sunday following my father's funeral, Vince's presence in the church office during the riot caused resentment to the plaintiffs and their supporters. Thereafter someone wrote an anonymous letter to the Police Superintendent, as well as the Mayor and I was told by inside sources; "You should consider resigning… or else you're going to be fired."

Letters to the Mayor and to City Officials

The anonymous letters sent to the office of the mayor, and to my immediate employment supervisor, and his superiors, requested my immediate termination.

One of the letters written to the Internal Affairs of my department was copied and returned to me stamped by the department. The letter accused me of throwing individuals out of the church.

When called into my employer's office, I sat there in disbelief. Aside from other accusations, the letter accused my employer of hiring me because of my personal relationship.

At the same time this letter was sent to the Mayor, Bishop Jerry, the assistant fire commissioner, called to share the awful backlash he was experiencing as a result of his being the overseer of our church. The commissioner of the fire department had received an anonymous letter regarding Bishop Jerry's relationship with me. The letter sent to the Fire Commissioner was sent to the Internal Affairs Department and Bishop Jerry was investigated as a direct result of his support of me.

Bishop Jerry was compelled to decide. If he would continue to support me, his position would continue to be jeopardized. "My being the overseer of the church caused adverse attention within the department. As a result, I am now under investigation by Internal Affairs."

I had many conversations with Jim about these new dilemmas. However, he convinced me that I had a lawsuit in front of me that demanded my immediate attention. It was not our sole responsibility to try and respond to every letter that some raging pit bull had sent. There were just too many accusations to manage, as our country was reeling from the 9/11 attacks.

As our country reeled from the attacks of 9-1-1, the letters regarding my position as Pastor flooded throughout many of the churches surrounding our city. This was not the time for our city's political and religious leaders to be distracted with these letters and the harassment from those suing us. Therefore, the pressure increased for me to withdraw from major activities within my department.

My father loved the Twin Towers. He would spend hours talking about the World Trade Center. He made certain that we would visit New York annually to visit the World Trade Center.

As I reflected on the country my father was privileged to have been a citizen of, and what would happen next, Bertha, an elderly lady who had left with the plaintiffs and their supporters, walked inside the church office appearing very agitated. I spoke first. "Praise the Lord, Mother Bertha, how are you?"

"Are you going to put me in jail? I just came here to get my choir robe," she asked.

"Mother, I am not responsible for putting anyone in jail. I did not ask you to leave, and you are welcome to have anything you desire," I replied.

The conversation with Mother Bertha reminded me of the war between nations. Why was our country being attacked? Then, again, why was I going through the pending litigation?

Working Relations Were No Longer the Same

The communication between Vince, the director of the department, and me was disrupted. Our working relationship had taken a turn for the worse. As the pressure from the scandal increased, he distanced himself from me. It seemed as if I could no longer manage my outside responsibilities and remain Pastor.

The events that had occurred, including the letter to the mayor, the letters to the department, the letters to the Pastors, and all of the negative attention brought on by the lawsuits meant that I was called into Vince's office more frequently. My assignments were now being intensely monitored and scrutinized. Walking into an executive meeting, Adrienne, who was also a manager within the Director's office, asked if she could speak with me outside. "You will be docked on your next paycheck," she said.

"For what?" I asked.

"I overheard the Director say that he is going to make an example out of you because you were late," she replied.

"Are you sure? I was not late on the day he questioned me about it. Phil sent me on an assignment in the neighborhood," I said.

"Who would know better than I?" she countered.

After my conversation with Adrienne, there was so much tension that I thought it would be in the interest of everyone for me to resign. It was now the end of the year, and I thought a good time to resign would be after the holidays. With a few days of vacation left, the decision was made for me to take a vacation and report back to work for two weeks in January, give my two weeks' notice, and then resign.

The time between my decision to resign and the pressure that Vince experienced ultimately affected the decision. After a few days of vacation, I reported back to work to discover that I was on probation. I never did find out what had occurred between the few days of vacation and my return to the office.

Upon approaching me to inform me of the probation status, the assistant director, Phil, was gracious to me. Very apologetically, he expressed his genuine concern about my welfare. At the same time, the flurry of internal meetings dictated that I leave the department.

The Internal Affairs Investigation

Vince told me that he had received a call from his various superiors and that the matter of the internal war with me and the ongoing litigation had been taken up with the city's office of Internal Affairs. Following his meeting with the Office of Internal Affairs, Vince and Bishop Jerry met with the mayor regarding the war at our church. I was certain that Vince was experiencing the pressure of having me as an employee.

As the Internal Affairs Department conducted its investigation, Vince called me into his office.

Vince wasted no time in telling me that I must immediately choose between being Pastor of the church and working as a manager within the city department. The meeting was candid. "Because of the city's attention to the fallout from 9/11, I cannot afford any distractions from my official duties."

"Are you implying that the tension growing from the war at the church is threatening your position?"

"You must make an immediate choice!" he declared.

"What choice might that be?"

"The choice between continuing as Pastor or holding down this position."

"Since I was divinely appointed to be Pastor, there really is no choice."

To attempt such a choice would be like telling Oprah, "You must make a choice either to be who you are or become a secretary."

'This is not like choosing between brands of toothpaste, "I explained.

Following our conversation, I had to decide on what date I would render my resignation.

The tension and apprehension between Vince and me increased, and it was difficult for me not to be the central focus at major events. I was now compelled to work additional hours, and during one of our major events where the city officials and other important guests were present, I was forced to sit in the back room and clean the trash.

I also received telephone calls from other city officials inquiring about the church conflict. One of the city officials working within the mayor's office explained that if I did not submit to the plaintiffs, it would jeopardize the church's receiving of city services such as garbage removal.

Time to Resign

There was too much negative and suspicious attention drawn to the department. There was hardly anything that I did that was not heavily scrutinized.

The city could not afford a needless distraction. I knew that it was time to resign.

In a meeting with my supervisor, I was told, "Marci, there is an internal war within our department coming from higher up to get rid of you."

I replied, "It's time for me to resign, for the health of the department. There is too much attention focused on my position with my church, and it has become a terrible disruption to the department."

Our department had a wonderful team. I reported to my supervisor, Phil, who said, "You do not have to resign. We will find a way for you to maintain your position by keeping on track."

But realistically, we knew that this could not happen.

After several conversations with Phil, he agreed with my decision to resign.

26
ARUBA

I had not taken a vacation in years. My only thought was to take a vacation far away, or not to take a vacation, but instead make a permanent move. I decided to travel to Aruba and not return to the States. If Aruba were not my destination, I would travel elsewhere and start my life over.

Without informing anyone of my decision, I made my travel plans for Aruba. I recall thinking that I did not have to tolerate insults, lies, and slander.

Upon my arrival in Aruba, I met Sammy, the taxicab driver. My life was in such turmoil that Sammy's smile seemed to have confirmed that I should not return to the States. Sammy was fluent in nine languages and was one of the kindest people that I have ever met. As I sat on the beach at the Marriott Resorts, I relaxed and read books.

I did not want to think of events back in the States, much less the litigation. Sammy took me to the best restaurants in Aruba and gave me a tour of the entire island. I was at total peace.

After one week in Aruba, I decided to call the office. Kelle answered the telephone and said, "You are greatly missed. But we want you to get some much-needed rest. I hate to mention it, but the brown envelopes have been pouring in from SNARE."

I did not respond. I refused to allow anything to interfere with my stay in Aruba. Kelle's statement confirmed that I should not return to the States.

However, there was one additional telephone call that I needed to make. That telephone call was to my mother.

That long-distance phone call was another life-changing incident. Prior to making the call, I was prepared to abandon the incessant battles against the Giant law firm and its unscrupulous, downright evil clients – my former flock as Pastor. Because I was no longer active in my former job with the City of Chicago and was instead totally absorbed and overwhelmed by open warfare, I looked forward to launching a new, independent life elsewhere.

My conversation with my mother totally reversed my ambitious plan as she reminded me of my lifelong commitment to the church, to my family, to my distressed community, and to my destiny as Pastor of Bethlehem Healing Temple – a destiny formally bequeathed by my late father, Bishop Arcenia Richards.

Following that existential conversation with my mother, I decided to return to the States and continue fighting for justice.

Lawsuits

In addition to the plaintiff's lawsuit, I was served with a lawsuit from another state, brought by Gabe and his father, Stanlie, who had previously given the speech announcing his desire to be Pastor upon the passing of my father.

I was forced to choose my battles. I determined that Stanlie's lawsuits and his son's presence at the church were both inconsequential. They were not individuals to consider being a part of our corporation. I continued to receive numerous letters and court documents threatening that if we did not position Stanlie as the President and Pastor and Gabe as the assistant, they would initiate a lawsuit against me and the corporation.

Stanlie and Gabe made good on their threat. As Gabe continued traveling to church with the threats, I continued to encourage myself to stay focused. Stanlie's lawsuit was only classified as a mere distraction.

Stanlie's Death

One day Kelle called to tell me that all the phone lines were lit up informing us of Stanlie's death. She asked whether that would bring an end to Stanlie's lawsuit.

I replied, "It does not matter."

Of course, Gabe continued his father's lawsuit. Week after week, Gabe attended our services and attempted to harass me. One Sunday, as I prepared to teach, he asked if he could speak with me in private.

"Where have I heard those words before?" my brother A. C. asked.

I interrupted and said, "I have no problems speaking to Gabe in private. However, whatever you have to say to me can be shared in the presence of my family."

Following Stanlie's death, Gabe had his hands full defending his father's corporation. There were rumors that there were fights among Stanlie's sons and Stanlie's corporation about who would be the successor. Following months of litigation, the Stanley lawsuit was dismissed in its entirety.

Gabe's travels became less frequent, and eventually he never returned to our church.

My Neighbor's Lawsuit

Amid the ongoing conflict, I left the church, arriving home only to notice my gate wide open. Voices were coming from within my storage space. What in the world is going on? I ran around to the storage space just in time to encounter people leaving my garbage area.

I inquired, "How may I assist you?" With spiteful looks, a man, and a woman, along with four other individuals looked at me, said nothing, and walked back into my storage space.

I repeated, "How may I assist you?"

The man said, "We are looking into our storage space. I am an attorney, and you are on part of my property, and I will sue you for my portion of this land."

"Is this some kind of joke? Are you part of the lawsuits?"

He refused to answer. I threatened him. "If you do not get off my property, you are trespassing, and I will call the police."

He dared me to telephone the police, and soon two police officers responded to my call. After hearing what the commotion was all about, they said, "This is a legal matter. We can't handle it."

I grew more and more frustrated. He continued to threaten me and insisted he was a lawyer. I shouted, "You had better get off my property now."

The group turned to leave and got inside a church van.

I read the name of the church on the side of the van, First Church. I had been a guest speaker there several times, and my former employer was a member of that church.

Armed with this information, I telephoned him and shared what had happened. He informed me that the gentleman who had trespassed on my property was a member of First Church. His name was David and he had recently married my neighbor.

In just a few days, the church was served with a lawsuit from David and his wife, claiming possession to our property. Our corporation had previously owned their property. However, it had been quickly deeded to a former member of the church.

We turned this lawsuit over to our attorney.

We were in and out of court so many times that we needed to determine which court appearances were most important. It no longer mattered what transpired or who initiated another lawsuit, I could not make every court appearance.

Jim's office began sending us the documents from all of the pending lawsuits.

One lawsuit involved the city. The city informed us that our property was on three feet of the city's property. After more than forty years, the city stated that we must consider how we were going to close up an alley located by our parking lot. There was no way we were convinced that the alley had not been closed forty years earlier. No one had ever approached us before informing us of the need to close the three feet of space. I refused to argue or fight with the city over three feet of an alley. I placed that concern in the file with the other city lawsuits.

Courtroom after Courtroom

When Jim told me about an upcoming court date during the Christmas holiday, I asked why there was a court date scheduled during the holidays. He explained that the counsels from the Giant law firm had filed their lawsuit in a different courtroom, hoping to have another judge hear their complaint.

We were forced to make an appearance in court. They traveled from one courtroom to another in search of someone who would grant them a hearing to their motions.

"This is another one of their designs -- dragging us from courtroom to courtroom. This is more than an inconvenience, it is harassment, because it is one of our busiest times at the church," I argued.

The new judge agreed with me.

Bark, the counsel from the Giant law firm, reminded me of the character in the movie, "Anger Management," portrayed by Jack Nicholson.

When Bark presented his motion, the judge asked, "Why dig up the plaintiff Rogers to have him return from Mississippi to be a party to your frivolous lawsuit?"

As Bark attempted to explain the complaint to the court, the judge rose from his seat, said he'd hear no such ridiculous motion, turned his back, and proceeded to his chambers.

Bark began to shout at the judge. "What about my clients?"

The judge continued to walk.

The plaintiff's counsel continued to file motions in courtroom after courtroom. It took the law firm numerous other filings to locate a judge who was willing to listen to its complaint. Finally, they found one.

I asked Jim why the judge in Courtroom 4210 would provide an audience to the plaintiffs' complaint when the other courtrooms had vigorously refused to listen to their claims. Jim responded, "The plaintiffs have filed a motion to freeze your bank accounts."

Amid the daily struggles to manage the affairs of the corporation and pay our astronomical legal bills, I received an alarming telephone call from Jim. "Marci, all your bank accounts have been frozen, and you have to open a new account. The plaintiffs filed a motion asking the court to freeze the bank accounts. The court granted them an order."

"This is lunacy. How does the court expect us to operate, much less, pay our bills?" I asked.

Jim continued, "Once you open up a new account, one that the plaintiffs have mutually agreed upon, you must add them as signers on your accounts."

"Jim, if I understand you correctly, are you saying that we cannot sign our checks without the plaintiffs' signatures?" I asked.

"You cannot sign your checks or pay any bills without the signature of the plaintiffs."

Upon adhering to the court's order, we placed the plaintiffs as signees upon our bank accounts.

The required signature of the plaintiffs placed us in a dire position. There was no approval for employees' salaries. There were outstanding bills, which the plaintiffs refused to pay. The utility bills were left unpaid. The insurance bill was not paid. The plaintiffs and their supporters had previously returned and destroyed much of the property. There was no approval for much-needed repairs to the facilities.

The signer for the plaintiffs, Gene, did not cooperate with us. At the time he was supposed to meet us at the bank for his signature to pay the bills, Marie and I were left sitting there waiting for him. Only once did he appear to sign checks. He then refused to sign the checks for the employees, so the employees worked without any pay.

We barely survived. Daily, I encouraged our staff to be patient as we navigate our way through the apparently biased judicial system. The employees of their support assured me. The faith and support of our staff provided the strength we needed to endure the challenges of dealing with situations while our assets were frozen.

Jim filed an appeal to the lower court's rulings. We waited for the appellate court to rule on our appeal.

Miracles Do Happen

The court ordered our personal assets frozen without inquiring about the details of the litigation. When the plaintiffs and their supporters staged their walkout, they left us with outstanding utility bills. For example, the energy bill was in arrears for more than $25,000. Each day, as the weather changed, we wondered how we were going to make it through the winter months.

One day, as we were seeking methods to secure the funds to pay the outstanding energy bill, an elderly lady walked into the church seeking to speak with me. She was confident as she informed me that God had instructed her to pay the church's energy bill.

I smiled and suggested that she should return and seek God for further directions. She had no idea of the cost of our energy bill, yet she insisted that I accompany her to the energy company.

However, I did not go with her to the energy company, because I could not imagine this lady had produced the funds for the outstanding $25,000 energy bill.

In two weeks, she visited my office repeating her request, insisting that she would pay our energy bill. Finally, I caved in and provided her with the church's energy account number. While the offer was a kind gesture, I still did not believe she could afford to pay such a large bill.

At the end of the day the lady returned and handed me a receipt proving that our energy bill was paid in full.

This was one of the most incredible miracles we have ever witnessed, We would no longer have to use propane tanks.

27

IN HIGH PRAISE

Appeal

Two months following my father's death, the plaintiffs petitioned the Appellate Court to hear its complaint. The Appellate Court remanded the case back to the trial court. The Appellate Court mistakenly thought the organization possessed an original constitution. The court therefore requested the trial court to refer to the corporation's original constitution, which had never existed.

This was not a case of who the lawful Board of Directors were, but rather a case of what governs the church polity and the religious practices and beliefs of that organization. That burdening truth was lost amidst the distraction and faulty misrepresentation of the corporation's accounting system, along with the emotional antics of the plaintiffs and their witnesses.

The stage had been set for a battle in the lower court. We were then confronted with the reality that the law is often misinterpreted and sometimes even overlooked. It seemed that the Appellate Court had made its decision without having thoroughly read the corporation's Articles of Incorporation and by presuming that the corporation had corporate members.

The court combined the two existing separate lawsuits, and the case then became Rogers vs. Richards.

Our First Supreme Court Appeal

After the Appellate Court sent our case back to the trial court, we petitioned the State Supreme Court. Jim informed us that the Supreme Court did not hear all the cases presented to it and that our chance of being granted a hearing was slender.

Jim's voicemail message sounded as if he was walking down the street. Jim said, "Marci, this is Jim. The Supreme Court will not hear our appeal."

Our case was remanded back to the trial court.

While we waited to begin the trial, we continued major renovations of the church. The church was beginning to look new again.

The First Renovations

In the fall, the first consensus of the Board was to purchase a new fence to put around the parking lot area. We also did a complete makeover on the inside of the church. We painted every place within the church, put in new sets of pews, and added an overall more contemporary feel.

The local Christian television station contacted us to be on one of its programs. We were delighted that a Christian television station wanted to feature our ministry. We were prepared to make our debut on television.

The renovation process was thoroughly underway as we prepared for a great revival. We stayed up all night working hard, averaging three hours of sleep nightly. The volunteers, along with my siblings, were worn out. Feet were swollen as people stood working for hours. Some slept on the floors.

A day prior to our revival, the pews were not yet installed in the sanctuary. We were behind our scheduled deadline. It looked as if the renovations were not going to be completed. We found ourselves in a quandary.

As we walked into the main sanctuary, the owner of the painting company assured me that the painting job would be complete. The guys laying the carpet assured me that the job would be completed prior to the installation of the pews. Oh, the pews, I forgot. I telephoned the owner, who assured me that the company would deliver the pews the morning of the event.

"No way," I responded, "We have gone far beyond the deadline, and we need the pews installed today."

The owner replied, "We will have your pews with you today."

As promised, the company arrived with the pews.

One of the volunteers came to inform me that I should look at what the guys were doing in the sanctuary. As I walked into the sanctuary, I noticed parts of pews on the new carpet. The guys had in their hammers, saws, and other tools, as if they were going to complete the job of making the pews inside the sanctuary.

I was horrified. The guys who were painting had not completed their job either. The guys who were installing the carpet stood there in amazement. The place was in total disarray as these guys were bringing in more unfinished pews, more tools, and more workers.

I hurried back to the office to summon Joe, the owner of the pew company.

Joe rushed over to the church. His first statement was, "I know, madam, but we will finish this job in a little while."

I asked, "How is it possible for your company to bring unfinished pews into this place and place them before the carpeting is installed?"

I did not wait for him to respond. I insisted that he have those guys immediately remove the unfinished pews. We were one day away from organizing a week-long revival and there were no seats. How could there be a revival with no seats?

It was the day of the scheduled Great Revival. The painters were still painting, and the carpet installers had not yet finished their work. We rented 2,000 chairs, but who would be responsible for placing all of the chairs in position? We had many volunteers, but each of them was already occupied, assisting in every area of the renovation.

It was nearly 5:00 p.m. The painters were still painting, the carpet installers were working feverishly to install the carpet, and the fence had not yet been completely installed. Amidst all the noise, I ran into the sanctuary and shouted, "Gentlemen, you must stop painting. The carpet must be completed now. We are scheduled to begin our program in an hour."

As the painters were moving out their equipment, the carpet installers were working in another area. Without delay, we summoned other volunteers as we started to place the chairs in the sanctuary.

Amazingly, at 6:00 p.m., the sanctuary was ready for our evening service. All the rental seats were in place. The main section of the sanctuary carpet was complete. The audio was installed. The floral arrangements were set in place. It had been a long time and the battle had been intense, but we were ready to have a good time.

The service kicked off with a bang. We were in high praise. The music was great, the people were excited, and our friends were with us. We had a hallelujah good time. This was a celebration.

The hard work of reconstructing the church had paid off.

28

BLOODY WARFARE

"They Are Taking the Fence"

t 6:00 a.m., the Saturday morning following the revival, we heard a clanging sound. The loud noise persisted for at least two hours. Sam, one of the custodians, telephoned to warn me there was a continuous banging sound in the back of the church. Opening the back door, he said there were men working on the fence.

We had not hired any contractors, nor was there any work to be completed around the building. I asked Sam to step outside to see what was happening. It was the heart of winter. We were busy organizing our programs and decided we would resume more renovations during the spring season.

Nearly out of breath, Sam called me back to report that a group of Mexicans removed our newly installed fence. Despite the winter cold, I ran out of the house in my pajamas to see why they were removing our fence.

"What happened? What's going on?"

The worker told me that the fence company had ordered the crew to remove our fence. Sam insisted that the men leave the property. As they exited, I stood there in shock because the fence surrounding the back area of the church was completely missing. Where would we locate a company to replace the missing fence?

I was scheduled to speak at a conference that morning. I could not spend the entire morning searching for a company to replace the missing fence. My mobile telephone rang nonstop as callers reported seeing someone stealing part of the church's fence. Others asked whether we were moving and had decided to take the fence with us.

After spending two days searching for a company, we were able to locate a small company who repaired the missing part of the fence.

If I thought the removal of the fence was bad, I was not prepared for what would happen next. It confirmed that there are some things you just can't make up!

Blood Spilled in Warfare

Opening the door of my house, I noticed something which appeared to be blood at the front of my yard. Upon closer examination, I could see that my front lawn was covered with this substance.

I stepped outside to take a closer look. At first, I could not determine what the substance was or what the thing was in the middle of the yard. I proceeded to walk down the stairs. Moving closer toward the yard, I walked cautiously.

In the middle of the yard was a dead animal surrounded by blood. Enormous flies and other insects swarmed around the dead animal. Moving slightly closer, I saw that it was a chicken. Parts of the animal were cut off. The head was cut just enough in order that it could barely hang on. Feathers were scattered all around the lawn.

As I stepped back, I felt something squishy underneath my heel. I screamed!

It was an organ of yet another animal.

I went inside the house to call my mother. She immediately declared it to be witchcraft. She said she would come right over to survey the site.

We were always taught of the beliefs and workings of witchcraft. With all my heart I believed in the power of God being greater than the powers of evil. Therefore, I did not panic at the gruesome sight of the animal surrounded by blood.

 phoned Kelle to request that she contact the city. "Tell them that they must remove the animals immediately. The stench is terrible."

"Who could have done such a hideous act?" she asked.

"No doubt this is connected to the war we are in. Blood is drawn in every war."

The Lady with Blood in the Black Bag

The following Sunday, Marie and I were discussing the dead animals when Marie said, "You think that's strange. There is another strange thing happening in the church."

"Now what?"

"The lady who comes every Sunday is here." She replied.

"Excuse me? We are connected to a church; everyone comes every Sunday! What do you mean, the lady who comes every Sunday?"

Marie explained. "Sunday after Sunday, Danny and I watched a lady enter the church with a colossal black garbage bag. During the 8:00 a.m., this lady traveled to the church with this big black bag. She was never late. Her routine was always the same.

"She would arrive and go upstairs to the cafeteria. She walked around, chanting something and would take items from her black bag and scatter them around the cafeteria. She would leave the black bag near one of the garbage cans. Later the custodians would throw the bag away.

"Last Sunday, I asked the custodians to look inside of the bag to see what this lady was dropping off every week. They opened it up and saw bloody animal parts."

"Marie, how long has this been going on?" I asked.

"Nearly two months."

"Why didn't you tell me about it?"

"I didn't want to worry you."

I said, "Now I know this is related to the war we face. Does anyone know who she is or has anyone ever seen her prior to the last few weeks? Has she ever attended our worship services? Does anyone know anything about her?"

"No, she just appeared, and this is what she does every week."

I was totally dismayed. Indeed, these were two experienced individuals who were familiar with the threats and litigation confronting us.

I said, "Marie, if you see her again, have security throw her out and lock the doors to the banquet hall."

Sure enough, the next Sunday the strange lady came back, only to discover the doors were locked. After two weeks of confronting locked doors, she did not return for a while.

When she did return, I noticed my sister, Gwendolyn, speaking to her. As I walked toward them, Marie told me that this was the lady who had visited us weekly.

Gwen confronted the lady walking from the ladies' bathroom to the front door and demanded that she pick up her black garbage bag and get out of the church. As the two of them argued back and forth loudly, Gwendolyn backed the lady and her black bag up toward the front door and ordered her to leave the premises.

The lady continued to chant as she took her black bag and left.

We never saw or heard from that lady again.

Black Grease Surrounds the Entire Church

As was our custom, we believed in the power of the pouring of oil. As a sacred act, we customarily anointed ourselves for blessings and protection. Often, we poured oil upon leaders, anointing them to be prepared for special assignments.

One day I noticed enormous black grease spots surrounding the church. As I took a walk around the entire building, I noticed the black spots continued across the entire front of the church. I nearly slipped as I followed the trail. Around the entire church, around the parking lot, around the back of the church, and to the adjacent alley, I found that the entire area was covered with lots of dark and dirty oil. I knew the cost to clean up the oil spill was going to be astronomical if we were even able to locate a company to remove it.

When I reported this incident to my mother, she said, "Some people will stop at nothing. Your father said we can rehabilitate some people spiritually, but whose responsibility is it to rehabilitate them mentally?"

"Mother, some people have never been rehabilitated spiritually; true spirituality does not reflect the character of some people."

My mother replied, "The Bible teaches us that the wheat and the tare grow together. It is not our job to separate the two. There is good among the bad. Besides, you must become laser focused."

My mother was referring to my upcoming installation services.

The Ceremony

Despite the tumultuous litigation, we continued to carry out our responsibilities. The board members continued to meet with community leaders and liaisons. We introduced programs which would revitalize the community, including establishing computer literacy courses.

After many celebrations and official ceremonies, it was time for my official installation as Pastor. While we did not think that it would draw as much attention as it did, it caused much stir among the plaintiffs in their efforts to halt the ceremony. We were informed by the bishops, pastors, and ministers of numerous telephone calls and threats they were receiving if they supported my installation as Pastor.

The depositions and trial continued as we prepared to celebrate an open, public event -- one of the most celebrated occasions within our organization. Although some of the supporters of the plaintiffs were present, we celebrated, we danced, and we rejoiced. We refused to allow them to intrude.

During the celebration, the bishops and the officials of the ceremony assured our hearts that God was with us. The bishops were in place, and the installation message was from the book of Esther. Bishop James looked at me as he preached, "Queen Esther, you have come to the kingdom for such a time as this."

We celebrated. As there had never been an election for the Board of Directors for the corporation, it was following my communion celebration that Bishop Eskine stood before the crowd and asked me to turn to the celebrating audience.

Catching everyone off guard, he stated, "You want the vote, you got the vote."

His words sent waves of electricity coursing throughout the audience. With a thunderous round of applause, the cheering audience celebrated my inauguration as Pastor and President.

Although we had never discussed the litigation, Bishop Chambers was aware of the lawsuit against us and the accusations concerning the election.

The lawsuit did not matter to the thunderous audience. We danced. We celebrated and stayed in the celebratory moment. The place was lit up as if this time were prepared for us in advance. No one could have spoiled that evening.

Surely, my father was watching as we celebrated. That night, I believed, he was smiling.

Pastor Larry

One of the people I invited to the installation services was Pastor Larry Martin, who was an ordained Elder and had been the Assistant Pastor of one of the renowned Pentecostal churches in the city for more than thirty years. Larry also served as the Facilities Manager of the more than 130,000 square foot edifices of his church. His experience, skills, and expertise in management and supervision prepared him for his position as Pastor.

I informed the Board of Directors of my desire to invite Pastor Larry to join our organization. I would ask him to join if he accepted the invitation to attend the installation services. I was not certain if Pastor Larry had accepted my invitation.

Two days after my installation, my brother A. C. and I were reminiscing about the success of the services when he mentioned that Larry had been in attendance. I questioned that because Pastor Larry had not made himself known to us. A. C. explained to me that Pastor Larry had sat at the back of the sanctuary and had left prior to the dismissal of the services. I reviewed the videotape of the services, and, sure enough, there sitting in the back of the sanctuary I saw Pastor Larry. I immediately called him to inquire why he had not spoken to anyone. Pastor Larry told me he had attended three events that evening.

I decided to ask him to join us and become the Pastor of our church.

Pastor Larry and I spoke for nearly three hours. I told him the details of the pending litigation and invited him for a scheduled meeting with the Board of Directors. He laughed as I said that it was time for him to become a part of something bigger than himself, as well as a part of history in the making.

After nearly a week of conversations, Larry agreed to meet with our Board of Directors. Following the meeting with our Board, Larry shared with me that he had been attending a focus group and the individuals in the group were sharing ideas of his pastoring. We decided to petition God for further direction and have more discussions concerning the possibility of Larry joining our church family.

Following our conversations, the Board of Directors had additional meetings concerning Larry joining our ministry. The Board agreed that Larry would indeed be an asset to our ministry. We introduced the concept to the leaders, who immediately agreed that a person of Larry's caliber would be an asset to our organization.

Then we held a church meeting where members were eager for someone to assist us as we continued to rebuild.

The transition was set. I phoned Bishop Jerry, who was the acting overseer of the church, and asked him about the possibility of Larry joining our ministry. After several meetings with Bishop Jerry, he stated he would meet with Larry's Pastor, Bishop Arthur, to begin dialogue. After several meetings between the two, Bishop Jerry initiated a meeting between Bishop Arthur and me. The meeting was successful, as Bishop Jerry and I explained the necessity in rebuilding such a historic ministry and having such skilled people as Larry become an integral part of our rebuilding.

Bishop Arthur agreed, and the transition was confirmed that Larry had his Pastor's full support to leave and come to join our ministry. With Larry's background in management and theology, we were set to rise to another level in our organization, especially considering Larry's compassion for the youth and senior citizens. Larry was deliberately chosen to bring critical analysis to help our organization as we moved forward. Larry became the nucleus to our corporation's survival throughout the trial, as we prepared for the pending litigation.

Jim, Our Counsel, Withdraws

Soon after Pastor Larry agreed to serve as Pastor of the church, I had a terrible dream.

We were in the courtroom, where it was extremely crowded. But where was Jim? As I looked around, the plaintiffs and their supporters were present. I searched the entire building, but there was no sign of Jim anywhere. I saw a member of the Board of Directors, Mother Walker, had arrived. As she entered, I looked around to see if Jim was behind her. In the dream, I became very flustered, as we never concerned ourselves with the particulars of the legal aspect of the litigation confronting us. We were inside the courtroom, and it appeared that we were heading into the trial.

I knew we could not begin without Jim's representation. Finally, I returned to the courtroom and sat down. It was time to begin the trial. As I looked up again to determine if Jim would appear, I noticed him walking through the door with a smile on his face. I took a deep breath, so relieved that he had appeared.

I woke up and called Marie, informing her of the dream. I told her that Jim had disappeared for a while, but in the end had reappeared. Marie asked me for my interpretation of the meaning of the dream.

I said, "Whatever the interpretation is, should Jim disappear, we may have to search for him. However, he will reappear. So, it really does not matter. He will return."

Preparations for Jim's Withdrawal

The dream came true all too soon. Jim called me to reluctantly give me notice that he could not continue to represent us unless the past legal bills were paid. Our legal bills were growing. But sadly, after spending hundreds of thousands of dollars on legal fees, we were out of funds.

We were busy raising the finances to retain his services, and it had been an arduous task. The day finally came when Jim did not return my telephone calls as quickly as he did in the past. The trial was approaching, and Jim informed me that his firm would not represent us during the trial if we did not pay our outstanding bill.

Jim will not be present for the trial. This was unimaginable. We knew without a doubt that this case was close to Jim's heart, for he believed in us. His commitment was as strong as if he were one of the defendants. Jim's expertise provided us with essential responses to motions prior to the plaintiffs presenting their motions. Furthermore, Jim was astute. His familiarity and knowledge of the laws governing our case assisted us in not having to appear in court each time the plaintiff's counsel presented one of their motions. He managed the tedious legal matters and informed us of the decisions via follow-up calls.

How were we going to make it without Jim's representation?

The board looked to the pastors for the next step to secure counsel. There was no way we could have been prepared for Jim to withdraw, especially immediately prior to trial. Marie reminded me of my dream when Jim disappeared. Was the interpretation of the dream supposed to be that Jim would have to withdraw? However, I knew we must locate and secure counsel for the trial. Perhaps in the end, Jim would come back.

The Court Allows Jim's Withdrawal

Each law office we visited said it was impossible for the court to allow our attorney to withdraw directly before a trial. We received a letter, along with a copy of a motion in the mail, from one of the partners of the law firm informing us of the firm's decision to withdraw. The signature on the motion was not Jim's signature. I telephoned Jim but was unsuccessful in my attempts to reach him. He was apparently out of the country. We did not believe it was Jim's desire or design to withdraw from our case. This must have been a very hard decision for him.

We believed that the court, by allowing our firm to withdraw directly before the trial, prevented us from introducing proper evidence in our defense. This evidence would have clearly exposed the plaintiffs and their witnesses' deliberate conspiracy over an extended period.

Jim provided a wealth of legal knowledge, expertise, and wisdom in managing the antics presented by the Giant law firm. Now we would become responsible for representing ourselves. The thought of having to do that was certainly intimidating; managing the details and concerns of the lawsuits would undoubtedly interfere with the responsibilities of carrying out the mission of the corporation.

How were we to enter a battle without Jim and tackle the lawsuits confronting the corporation? This was hard enough to fight, but we also had to decide whether to actively contest Jim's firm's withdrawal. That was a swift and easy choice. We chose not to engage in a battle with the counsel who had previously represented us so well. However, following our counsel's withdrawal, we would meet with many legal issues we were not aware of until after the Giant law firm's motions were granted.

Day-After-Day Court Appearances

The counsels from the law firm demanded our daily appearances in court immediately following Jim's withdrawal. The Board and I were informed that this law firm was notorious for its abundance of paperwork. I often wondered how many trees were destroyed on a daily basis as a result of the firm's practice of executing numerous motions. We received thousands of legal documents from the firm representing the plaintiffs. One of the offices within our corporation was labeled "the war room." We further referred to the plaintiff's motions and notices as "the Brown envelopes."

The war room was filled with the Brown envelopes. Most of the envelopes were never opened and contained numerous copies of the same motions. As often as three times a week, we were running in and out of court to appear before the judge or to file our responses to the plaintiff's motions.

The Blessing - the Trial Copier

Facing the court without the presence of a counsel, it was a severe strain for us to contend with the law firm's motions. However, we were determined.

Prior to Jim's withdrawal, we petitioned the court to order the plaintiffs to return documents and items they took from our corporation. Instead, the court ordered us to provide the law firm with copies of the records from our corporation.

All our records had been given to our former counsels, and we had no idea where to begin organizing our records. Jim assured us that his firm would send copies of the documents to the Giant law firm but added that the cost of copying the documents would be astronomical.

It seemed impossible for us to generate the revenue for copying within the time frame the court had ordered.

One week prior to the deadline for the records to be produced, a sales representative walked into our office, inquiring if we would like to purchase a copier. Larry told him that we were not interested. The sales representative insisted and, as a motivation for us to purchase the copier, he stated, "We will leave the copier at your place of business for two weeks, and your company is free to make all the copies that you so desire."

We could hardly believe our ears. "Are you saying that there is no limit to the copies we can make?" we asked.

When the sales representative assured us that there would be no limit to the copies we were allowed to make, we were ecstatic. We agreed to take the copier on a trial basis. We only needed the copier to help meet the necessary court order.

I asked Jim to send the documents to our office. Two days prior to the deadline, the company delivered a copier to us for a demo. Jim sent us the documents. Due to the large capacity of the copier, we were able to meet the deadline by staying up for two nights to copy the documents.

In our hearts, we believed the trial use of the copier was indeed an act of God's mercy. We could not have raised the funds to copy those documents.

A Pot of Gold

The court ordered an inspection of all our properties. Since we believed it was not justified, we vigorously fought to prevent the plaintiffs from entering our property. We were successful in raising nearly $15,000 in order for our law firm to fight this court-ordered inspection, but we lost this battle. There was no way for us to escape the inspection.

We had been working to have the place perfectly clean the day before the inspection. This meant that we had to get rid of a lot of old furniture. We decided to order a dumpster. The dumpster we received was huge. Taking shifts, volunteers threw old furniture out of the windows.

Along with volunteers at the church there were volunteers at my house with me, painting and plastering the areas which needed repairs. We worked earnestly to ensure that we would pass the inspection. We knew it did not matter how beautiful the property was; the group suing us would search for the smallest detail to point out to the court and accuse us of neglecting our property. The reality was that we invested all of our resources in renovating the properties.

A week following Jim's withdrawal, a friend of ours, Aaron, an attorney, agreed to represent us during the inspection. Aaron assured us that he would arrive on time.

That morning, the plaintiffs arrived with their attorney, an architect, and other individuals. We did not trust this group entering our property for an inspection, so we instructed them that there would be no inspection until we heard from our attorney.

When Aaron arrived, the group started the inspection on the first floor and went through the entire building. The plaintiffs searched for areas which they thought appeared to be damaged or out of the ordinary, taking many pictures. They searched for any flaws they could find.

The plaintiffs were aware that we had no heat at one time. Therefore, they searched diligently for the heaters we previously used.

In the boiler room sat the propane heaters the plaintiffs were searching for. It was no secret that we did not have any heating gas. However, we certainly did not wish for the heaters to be noticed. The group lingered in the area, gleeful that they had found the heaters. Clay let out a sigh of relief as he sat down on top of one of them. He said, "Yes. Yes. Well, well we got them now." It was as if they had discovered a pot of gold.

After the all-day inspection, the group left the church to head over to our other properties.

There were tenants in each property. The tenants were not as flexible as we were. Kelle informed the group that only one person was allowed to enter the property, as she had not taken her prescription for Prozac or any of her other medications. The visit to that house was short. The group came up short when they demanded entry to another private property that held my personal belongings. Upon the plaintiffs' arrival at my private property, Larry stood outside, along with Aaron, and said, "This is the end of the inspection."

Clay said, "We are supposed to go into Marci's place."

Larry repeated, "This is the end of the inspection." The plaintiffs stood there in amazement – waiting for an explanation -- as Larry and the attorney got into their cars and drove away.

The inspection was exceedingly arduous and monotonous. It had been a long time since those who staged their walkout had entered our property. Aside from a few funerals, they did not visit us, nor did we visit with them. They appeared to be like hungry wolves entering the building. Clay approached me and requested a hug.

Each time Clay visited the property for a funeral, we were served with a motion stating that we "did something to alter the church."

The "something" that we did was to renovate the property!

29

PRO SE-- ON OUR OWN

The Second Annual Report Filing

The counsels from the Giant law firm perceived that we were vulnerable without counsel. They and their clients became increasingly aggressive.

Prior to his withdrawal, Jim had warned the plaintiffs along with their corporate secretary, concerning their previous attempts to file the annual report with the Secretary of State. The plaintiffs attempted to file an annual report on behalf of our corporation once again. This time, however, it was with the assistance from the counsels of the law firm.

We knew it was time to file our annual report. Two months earlier, I had told the Board of Directors that we must not take anything for granted, as we were without counsel, and we must file our annual report prior to the deadline. However, as the motions came in from the law firm, we were compelled to make more appearances in court. We were not accustomed to having to make all these court appearances.

When we approached the deadline for filing our report. I asked Marie if she would file our Annual Report in person. When Marie attempted to do so, she was given a report by the clerk stating that someone had already filed documents representing the Board of Directors of our corporation.

When I reviewed the documents, I noticed they had been filed by the Giant law firm, bearing the signature of their secretary. We were stunned as it appeared that the law firm was now encouraging the behavior of their clients.

We called the Secretary of State's office and explained the entire situation. The clerk there informed us of the necessary steps to correct this idiocy. However, it was the holiday weekend, and many people were on vacation.

The Visit to the Secretary of State

The due date for the Annual Report was the day after our initial telephone call to the Secretary of State. We were in a race against time and the workings of the plaintiffs and the law firm.

It took us all day to contact the Board of Directors to call an emergency meeting to inform them of what had taken place. We needed a resolution signed by all of the members of the Board of Directors.

Once we received all the signatures, Kelle drove to the Secretary of State's office to file the corrections in person. The drive was four hours downstate to Springfield. Kelle was a fast driver and we believed we would make it on time for us to correct the faulty information of our opponents.

But Kelle's arrival as the Secretary of State was not met without challenges.

One of the clerks did not wish to assist us. We were given the run-around.

"Do not be distracted," I said to myself and to Kelle. "God will give us favor with someone inside the office who will make the corrections."

Kelle and I spoke with several individuals prior to the drive to the Secretary of State's office. We took down the names of the people we spoke to. Kelle went from one building to the next in search of justice against the actions of the plaintiffs.

Although clerks gave us the run-around, Kelle had repeatedly heard me say, "There is always someone who will listen to the truth."

As Kelle entered one building after another, she requested Samuel, the supervisor who had provided us with the information over the telephone.

The clerk responded, "He is in the administrative building."

After three hours, we located Samuel, who said, "I have been in this business long enough to recognize companies attempting to seize other companies." He looked through the records for the last several years, noticed that we were the legal Board of Directors for our corporation and made the necessary corrections.

As Kelle drove back to the city smiling, she said, "Doc, you're right. There is always someone who will assist us."

I responded, "Yes. But it's only when we refuse to give up – it is then – and only then that we find those who are willing to help."

It was a very long day. Kelle and I were grateful for the imminent holiday weekend. We needed the rest, as there were more upcoming court appearances and additional motions to answer over the coming week.

With Jim's withdrawal as our counsel, we needed to prepare ourselves to find another counsel, or we would be forced to move forward as *pro se* litigants. I could not imagine us representing ourselves *pro se* against the law firm.

Pro Se

Latin "for himself" "on one's own behalf" "A person who represents himself in court." The Lectric Law Library Lexicon.

We Represent Ourselves

Being represented by counsel afforded us the luxury of not having to make court appearances. The court refused to allow us time to locate counsel for the trial. Therefore, we were compelled to act on behalf of the corporation. Representing ourselves this way proved to be time-consuming. Marie took advantage of her lunch hour to represent our side in court.

The primary existing challenge was that, prior to Jim's withdrawal, there was no discovery for our case, no depositions taken on the plaintiffs or their witnesses. There was no witness list submitted for us. There was no evidence submitted on our part. We were heading for an uphill battle.

Hannah's Poem

Counting the times on the one hand that I appeared in court when Jim represented us, I was never apprehensive. Although Marie was able to make appearances in my absence, my employment forbade me from running to the courtroom each time the law firm filed its monotonous motions. I recalled speaking with Jim after his court appearances, sometimes four times a week. I was not prepared to run to the court daily.

What would I say to the judge? As my thoughts wandered, Marie's voice interrupted, "It's almost time to head over to the courtroom."

"Marie, I really do not feel prepared to stand before the judge. Jim has all the information we need to intelligently speak to the judge."

"Whatever the case, you have got to make your appearance today," she insisted.

Sitting in my office on the couch was my nine-year-old niece, Hannah. Although she did not fully understand what was happening, she was aware that I was under a great deal of stress. Rising from the couch, she walked over to my computer, which was behind me.

"Auntie, may I use your computer?" she asked.

"Yes," I said.

As I continued to read the documents Marie handed to me, Hannah handed me a piece of paper. Looking down at the words on the paper brought tears to my eyes.

Hannah had typed a poem.

"God is on your side. It is He who is your guide. It is through Him, you shall stride. You will make it through this difficult time. Wherever you go, whatever you do, trust that God has angels by your side to lead you every step of the way. Do not be afraid. I love you and I am praying for you this very day. Go in peace and God shall go with you."

Hannah's poem awakened me out of my daze and provided me with the grace that I needed to take my first step into the courtroom.

I Did Not Initiate the Lawsuit

The entire lawsuit seemed to have been personal. This lawsuit was about truth and facts vs. lies and distortion. It was about ethics, integrity, morals, and justice. Jim, our former attorney informed me, "Marci, this lawsuit is a personal vendetta against you as Pastor and no negotiations will work as long as you maintain your position as Pastor."

I was the Pastor. I did not initiate a lawsuit. Our choices had run their course. We prepared ourselves to report to the Giant law firm for depositions, with no legal counsel.

Our Deposition

The court ordered us to report to the Giant law firm.

The counsels from the law firm requested that I be the first of the defendants to be deposed. When my schedule did not meet the demands of the counsels from the law firm, I received a telephone call from one of the counsels, Terri, threatening me. Terri informed me that if I were not available at the time he requested, he would file a motion and bring me before the judge.

I responded by informing Terri that I had a speaking engagement and was not available on the date and time that he had requested. Terri warned me that he would file a motion and allow the court to determine my availability. I made one final remark before hanging up the telephone, "You have to do what you have to do, Counsel."

Terri's statement to me was not just a threat. Because my schedule did not permit me to appear for deposition at the requested time, a motion was filed by the law firm demanding my appearance before the court. Walking to the courtroom, I thanked God for people who had paved the path before me, in the fight against injustice. Reflecting on those who stood for their rights and their principles provided me with great comfort as I opened the door to the courtroom.

My presence in court seemed to have startled the court. Approaching the bench, the judge held his head down. As I walked up, I greeted the judge, "Good morning, Your Honor. I am Dr. Janell the defendant."

The judge immediately looked up from his desk as if to say, "I wondered what you looked like and what sort of character you were." The judge put his head down and slowly looked up at me again. He was all too familiar with our case. However, he was not familiar with my presence or my personality.

Without waiting for the counsel from the law firm to speak, I spoke first. "Your Honor, my schedule does not allow me to meet the demanded deposition dates of the plaintiffs' counsel."

The counsels from the law firm side argued their position. The judge asked when I could make the appearance, and I provided the court with a copy of my itinerary.

The dates for the depositions were set.

Our Depositions at the Giant Law Firm

Since we were without legal counsel, we decided it was best to record our depositions.

My brother, A.C., was the first one to be deposed. Following his deposition, he returned to my office, where I sat working at the computer. "We need legal counsel. Those men do not play fair. If Mother Walker is going to be deposed, she needs to have a lawyer."

"Those lawyers are as unscrupulous as the clients they represent. However, the court has demanded that we proceed without counsel, representing a corporation, and that is the way it is. Let's just get this over with and do our best to have a lawyer during the trial," I said.

Marie was the next person to be deposed. Marie and I entered one of the large conference rooms of the law firm. There sat each of the plaintiffs along with some of their supporters. With smirking looks on their faces, each of them moved their chairs aside as we looked around the room for seating.

At first sight, Marie and I were not sure if the plaintiffs and their supporters' presence was some kind of a practical joke. Therefore, Marie whispered to me, "Are they allowed to sit here during my deposition?"

I replied, "Are we personally allowed and able to represent a corporation? Are we not allowed the privilege of due process? Has our counsel been allowed to withdraw directly before the trial? Are we being ordered to proceed without having legal counsel present? Who knows what's allowed when one does not have counsel?"

After a few minutes, we realized that they were indeed going to sit in on Marie's deposition.

Marie's deposition was rather lengthy, given she was not only a Board of Directors member of the church, but was also the General Secretary of The National Organization. Without taking a break, Marie refuted all of the untruths presented by the plaintiffs and their witnesses to their counsels. As we left the law firm's office, Marie said, "Mother Walker needs to have a lawyer present during her deposition."

"A.C. shares the same sentiment," I said.

Although Larry was not a named defendant, he was also required to be deposed by the law firm's counsel. I had hoped that Larry would not have to be involved in this war, especially as a witness, given he was not a party to this litigation. I asked his thoughts on being deposed. "Are you okay being called upon for a deposition?"

"We have to move forward. This is a part of the process," he replied.

Although none of us accompanied Larry during his deposition, Larry informed me that the plaintiffs and their supporters were present during his deposition. We listened to Larry's recording of his deposition from the tape recorder. The counsels from the GIANT law firm grilled Larry on his position and his support from the previous church that he had attended. Larry shared his testimony relating to his position with his former church and how he became a part of our church.

A few days after Larry's deposition, I appeared at the law firm for my deposition. There again sat the plaintiffs, some of their supporters, and -- wouldn't you know it! -- Rogers.

After I greeted everyone in the room, I turned to Rogers. "I feel so privileged that you drove hundreds of miles to sit in on my deposition. How long did it take you to drive here?"

My deposition was excruciatingly long. However, I was able to hold my own. The questions posed to me were bizarre. Whatever the plaintiffs and their supporters had told the counsels from the law firm, it appeared that firm was prepared to build their case against us, and the corporation based upon hearsay and lies.

An Existential Meeting

Following my deposition, one of the counsels, Albert, asked if he could meet privately with me. Stepping into the back office, he asked what it would take for me to forget about the others involved in the lawsuit and simply walk away.

I have often reflected carefully about that face-to-face meeting. I realized that instead of unethically trying to manipulate me, Albert was sympathetic, personally identifying with my dilemma.

He was telling me that if he were in my shoes, he would walk away.

Albert was presenting me with an existential decision – the option to abandon my current mission to start a brand-new life.

As I had to make a life-changing choice during that phone conversation with my mother on my vacation in Aruba, I faced another crucial decision: I could change my life forever in a brief instant and agree to walk away.

But at that point I did not share Albert's perspective. I was too immersed in moment-by-moment warfare.

I responded with a counterproposal, reminding him that it was his clients who were suing me. Therefore, I suggested to him, since we did not have legal counsel, I was not even certain how to take a private meeting with him. Furthermore, I suggested, Albert should speak with his clients and ask them what it would take for them to admit their lies and drop the lawsuit that they had brought against us.

Albert walked me back to the room where I was being deposed and never spoke to me again about walking away from the lawsuit. I had made my decision to stay the course and pursue the cause of justice, no matter what.

Our Need for Counsel

Throughout our depositions, it was consistently clear that we desperately needed counsel for the trial. However, the last deposition proved it more clearly. The last defendant to be deposed was Mother Walker, who was nearly ninety years of age. Marie and I picked up Mother Walker, along with her twin, Mother Littlejohn. Mother Walker was severely visually impaired and handicapped. With much trepidation, Mother Walker held on to my arm as tightly as she could. Rubbing her hand, I attempted to assure her as best I could, "Mother Walker, it's going to be okay. This should not take too long. Following your deposition, I will take you and Mother Littlejohn to get a wonderful dinner." Mother Walker simply nodded her head.

As Marie and I led Mother Walker into the conference room of the GIANT law firm for her deposition, we heard familiar voices. Mother Walker whispered to me, "Is that who I think it is?"

"Yes, Mother, it is who you think it is. It is the plaintiffs and their family members," I replied.

"What are they doing here?" she asked.

"I am not sure. However, it's okay. They were present during our depositions as well. All you have to do is answer the questions to the best of your ability and we should be out of here in no time," I assured her.

As we took our seats inside the conference room, Mother Walker asked if I would sit on her left side, as she sat directly next to the court reporter. Jon was the council responsible for deposing Mother Walker. Jon's first question was striking. He asked Mother Walker if she understood and agreed to the documents in front of her.

I immediately attempted to inform Jon that Mother Walker was legally blind. However, Jon started shouting at me demanding that I be quiet. Mother Walker slowly started to speak. Her voice was as soft as a whisper. "I cannot see."

I responded, "That is what I was trying to tell you. Jon, please do not take advantage of us because we do not have legal counsel."

Mother Walker's deposition was very taxing. She was harassed so badly during her deposition that she nearly lost control of her bladder. I interrupted Mother Walker's deposition and requested a break. Upon taking a break, she spent more than a half an hour in the ladies' room, breaking down in hysterics.

Following the continued harassment by the counsels from the law firm and with the trial's being but a few days away, we made hundreds of telephone calls in search of counsel for the trial, with no success. We prepared to defend ourselves to "fight on the lie."

"Fighting On the Lie"

My mother taught her children not to tell lies. Mother's philosophy was that if you tell one lie, you must continue to lie to support the first lie, and this will ultimately lead to more lies. She would often say, "One lie doesn't end with one lie; then you must tell lies after lies."

At the age of five, my niece Vickie was sitting in a hair salon chair waiting to have her hair styled. The salon had a very strict policy of not servicing children under the age of seven. Vickie was aware of this policy. However, she desired to have her hair styled. Therefore, when the stylist asked her age, she responded, "I'm seven."

"When is your birthday?" the stylist inquired.

"Tomorrow," Vickie replied.

"What grade are you in at school?" the stylist asked.

Vickie replied, "Second."

We were quite amazed that Vickie was able to continue building her story. However, when we questioned Vickie she responded, "I wanted to get my hair styled and they wouldn't have let me, if I didn't say that."

"How were you able to arrive at your story?" I asked.

"The lady asked me about my birthday. I didn't know what to say. But I knew that I needed to be seven. So, I just told her that my birthday is tomorrow," she explained.

"How did you come up with the answer regarding second grade?" I inquired.

"I remember seven-year-olds are in second grade."

No one had coerced Vickie into telling that story. She started down that path and became trapped.

It was a very simple rule, if you tell one lie, you must tell another lie. Perhaps the law firm was in too deep. Like a child, to obtain a win, the law firm must build its entire case upon lies. No doubt pride and the lies had such counsel running in and out of the court. The counsels continued to fight one lie after another until there was no turning back.

I vividly recalled having had a conversation with my brother about a program of some alleged drug and gang leaders who reported that one of their members committed an act of violence and the leaders subsequently prepared themselves to go to war.

The leaders later discovered that the member had lied concerning the details of the events. Although the leaders knew that the members had lied, they explained to the reporter covering the story that their gang was bound to fight, even though it meant the gang had to "fight on the lie."

The gang leaders realized they were getting ready for war on faulty information. Even though they knew this, they were willing to carry out hideous acts of brutality, at the possible expense of their lives, just to support the lie.

Amidst all the lies, the gang's "General" insisted, "It doesn't matter if it is a lie, or it doesn't matter if we fight on the lie. We know that it is a lie, but we are constrained to fight on the lie in the name of our gang. No matter whether it is true or not, we still must fight."

Remarkably, the report confirmed that the leaders knew that they were defending a lie. However, the commitment to win and not suffer embarrassment or irreparable harm to the gang outweighed the commitment to truth. The lie caused those leaders to prepare for war, inspiring and obliging the gang to continue the war.

Could it often be the same with attorneys and their clients? Such was the case, in the movie, "The Lincoln Lawyer," starring Matthew McConaughey, a criminal defense attorney, who thought his client was innocent. After discovering the truth concerning his client, in the movie, the attorney continued to defend his client, who was indeed guilty.

Attorneys can start out believing their clients are innocent. However, throughout the discovery, when the truth is revealed, they conceal the truth and continue to fight and defend lies. Although the attorneys instinctively and distinctively can be aware that their clients are perjuring themselves and have based their case on outlandish lies, the attorney's commitment to the deceptive, destructive practice of "fighting on a lie" can often prevail over justice.

I believe that this is a rather frightening reality for a judicial system which has sworn to promote justice.

Some attorneys know categorically that their clients have engaged in conspiracies and committed crimes. Yet the law firm is bound to represent their clients willingly and knowingly. Even as truths unfold, the attorneys must continue to hide their client's lies and misrepresent the truth. Truth can end up a casualty to blindness, passion, and greed.

One must seek, find, and defend the truth to confront injustice. Searching for proper justice and relief is supposedly the task or the duty of the justice system. Justice must not allow itself to be manipulated by those seeking to hide the truth by outlandish claims of conspiracy. It must also stand in the way of those who conspire for the purpose of litigation compelled by attorneys whose primary purpose is to "fight on the lie" for money, achievement, or reputation.

If I were not the one experiencing this horrific ordeal, no one could have convinced me of the reality of the proceedings against us. Yet, on the other hand, if I were not the leading defendant in the case and personally witnessing the actions of the plaintiffs, their witnesses, and the counsels from the law firm, I would no doubt, perhaps, have sided with them in their quest to dethrone me, as they and their counsels were quite convincing in their testimonies. In the plaintiffs' and their counsels' painted picture of us, we were the villains and needed immediate execution.

The Courtroom Fight for Justice

Those swearing to uphold the justice system have a solemn responsibility to maintain the integrity and trust of that system. In the words of John D. Hutson, a former Navy judge advocate general and President of New Hampshire's Franklin Pierce Law Center, "The honorable thing is not to 'protect' your subordinates. The honorable thing is to look above that and realize they have a greater responsibility to the justice system." Hutson said officers played an integral role in the way crimes were reported and how justice was handled. He further stated that if the officers did fail to properly investigate those below them, their failures may well be more enduring "than these guys who allegedly murdered people". We believed this statement applied to legal counsel as well.

In our efforts to obtain justice, and to fight against the lies, we continued to search out the governing laws that we hoped would not support the behavior, character, and malevolence of those opposing true justice.

Standing Against a Flood of Motions

The counsels from the law firm cranked out and amended motions daily as we were denied the rights of due process prior to and during the trial proceedings. The courts denied our motions to produce certain critical material and substantial evidence, which we were sure would have enabled this case to be properly tried and properly adjudicated.

Our sole reliance upon our previous counsel's expertise and proficiency left us defenseless and, again, at risk to supplementary conspiracy and discrimination. I feel that one writer has succinctly articulated the issue: "In the face of accusation, an accused has but one person in whom he can confide, his counsel, whose allegiance shall be undivided, his trust uncompromising, and his efforts tireless."

We had invested our resources and explicit trust in our former attorney to present all necessary facts and legal documents for this outlandish litigation. We attempted to share with the courts the critical documents as evidence, but we were unsuccessful in our defense.

The court denied our motions to depose the plaintiffs. The court denied our motions to perform discovery. Over and over, we were sidelined by the court. The Giants and the court emphatically knew the absence of counsel severely jeopardized proper litigation of the case. Notwithstanding, we were not given time to locate any counsel.

What about the Corporation's Counsel?

The law is clear. Counsel must represent a corporation. However, by demanding that we represent the corporation in lieu of counsel, the court broke all its own rules.

The court was fully aware that we were forced to search for new counsel midstream that would be unfamiliar with the four years of history of the case. There was no reputable counsel who would make an appearance on our behalf without sufficient time to prepare for the case. We did not choose to represent our corporation but were forced to do so by the rigid stance of the court. This severely prejudiced our opportunity for a proper legal brief.

Jim's absence impacted several deadlines, from evidence to trial witnesses. Finally, the absence of counsel caused a failure to adequately recover the direction of the trial and severely prejudiced us in filing a proper brief to the court.

So, we explicitly trusted in the judicial system to allow us to present all necessary facts and legal documents for such an outlandish litigation but were betrayed by the misrepresentation of the false claims of the conspirators.

Motions Denied to Secure Counsel for the Corporation

While each motion from the law firm was granted by the court, our motions were consistently denied. We motioned the court to allow us to depose the plaintiffs, as well as to file our witness list and to subpoena witnesses. Each of those motions was denied.

In addition, the counsels from the law firm failed to respond to our various requests to return all assets, our request for discovery and depositions, and all other requests which were pertinent to the case. On numerous occasions, we petitioned the court for the discovery of the plaintiffs and were denied.

When we appeared before the court, we stated, "Your Honor, as defendants, we do not have counsel, there has been no discovery, and there have been no depositions by the plaintiffs and their witnesses. Our witness list is included in this motion. We request that the motion for discovery, to depose the plaintiffs and their witnesses, as well as the opportunity to file our witness list be granted."

The court was emphatic about all its rulings. We were not allowed to produce evidence of any kind.

What a way to prepare for a full-blown trial! Nevertheless, without discovery, any evidence, or any depositions from the plaintiffs, we headed into the

30

AN ELECTION IS INEVITABLE

Counsel Rosenthal

ne week before the trial, we were able to retain the services of Counsel Rosenthal. We successfully paid the retainer fee and were prepared to proceed with much confidence. We knew that Counsel Rosenthal had his work cut out for him, but we believed he could properly represent us.

We arrived at his office with the essential documents. Following his one and only appearance for us in court and upon reviewing the documents, he immediately informed us that he would have to withdraw, stating the court refused to allow him time to prepare for the trial.

The motion to withdraw submitted by Counsel Rosenthal pointed out to the court that there was no discovery completed by our former attorney of record and that if he did not immediately withdraw, he would place himself in a position of a potential professional malpractice suit. He further criticized the court on its position to proceed in such a critical trial without allowing us time to search for proper counsel.

The court immediately allowed him to withdraw and scheduled the trial within days after his withdrawal.

Counsel Rosenthal informed us that he thought we would have a very difficult time going into a full-blown trial without discovery. He further explained to us that not being allowed to produce any evidence confirmed that the system was prejudiced against us.

Two Days Prior To the Trial

Two days before the trial, someone recommended an attorney to us by the name of William Brooks. We had no history or previous information concerning this counsel. However, we were in desperate need of counsel and agreed to meet with him. A day prior to the trial we retained William's services.

We were not certain of William's expertise as a trial lawyer, in litigations, or with corporate and religious law, but we secured him as counsel, nonetheless. After briefing him as much as possible, we were desperate and reduced to merely hoping for the best.

William was assured that the court would provide him with time to review the files and records. Upon arriving at the courthouse, William informed the court that he was retained the day before and requested time to review the files. The court would hear no such thing.

We did not appear for the first day of the trial. Following the court's decision, we determined that justice had been decided. The trial would proceed with or without our being represented by counsel.

Our new counsel, William, respectfully and strongly addressed the court about our lack of access to information and about his need to take some time to review the material and get up to speed on everything. But the judge, apparently, did not think this was necessary or important.

Mr. Brooks said, "Your Honor, respectfully, I'm requesting that we reconvene next Tuesday or whatever day, the earliest the Court has. I am not prepared. My clients aren't prepared. I can't do adequate preparation. Your Honor, I know that I would only need one day. I have not reviewed their documents. I'm asking if I can be allowed Wednesday, Thursday, and Friday to study the documents. I got to the office, and I found out that my clients don't have discovery. I'm asking if I can be allowed to personally get the discovery into them no later than 5:00p.m. I want to do my duty, your Honor. I need that time for discovery. I'm also asking if my discovery could be admitted. I'm overwhelmed. I can't do it. I can't do it, your Honor."

The Court responded, "But that's the reason your predecessor, who I guess never filed an appearance, that's why he came in one day and came out a week later."

Bark corrected, "Two days, your Honor."

Mr. Brooks replied, "It's a one shot, but I want to make it the best shot, your Honor. I'm really up against it. I'm not going to withdraw. I am just overwhelmed because I have not read through the documents, and you've seen it, the volumes. There are thousands. It's not twenty and thirty pages and what have you. Judge, I'm not prepared. I'm just asking you. I'm not going to ask you for anything else."

The Court decided, "I have to deny your request, Mr. Brooks."

Mr. Brooks asked, "Your Honor, may we approach the bench?"

The Court answered, "Sure."

Mr. Brooks started over, "Good Morning, your Honor, William B. Brooks. Your Honor, I'm asking if we can reconvene in your chambers instantly. I must draw the Court's attention to something."

The Court responded, "Okay. Fine. Do you want the court reporter?"

Mr. Brooks replied, "The court reporter, yes. Your Honor, respectfully, I know -- I said I would do it because I thought that this was a hearing, not a full-blown trial against the biggest law firm in the city."

The Court reminded him, "When you were coming into the case, I told you that this case had a long history."

Mr. Brooks agreed, "And I want to put it to bed. I want to do my duty, your Honor. I need that time for discovery. I need ---- and I was going to ---- and I'm also asking if my discovery could be admitted. I'm overwhelmed. I can't do it. I can't do it, your Honor…That is why I'm saying that I can get what they need, and I know that I would have to get everything done, all my witnesses, in one day. It's one shot, but I wanted to make it the best shot, your Honor. I'm really up against it, and I can do it. I'm not going to withdraw."

The Court answered, "Well, I don't think you can withdraw during the trial."

Mr. Brooks replied, "And I've come to you. I've worked with you. My relationship with you really means a lot to me, as well as the whole jurisprudence. I want to do a good, adequate, thorough job. I'm not going to ask you for any more dates. I'm not asking to withdraw. I am just overwhelmed because I have not reviewed anything, and you've seen them, the volumes. There are thousands. It's not twenty or thirty pages, Judge, I'm not prepared."

The Court responded, "They're just going to tell their story. You know, I guess what I'm saying is off the cuff, but a lot of the stuff, I don't even think it's really that important to the decision."

Mr. Brooks stated, "Judge, I don't even have my notes. Your Honor, I just can't do it. I'm overburdened. I've got a dying wife at home, and I got a boy that I just put into school this week. If there was any way I could do it, I would."

The Court reiterated, "I really can't continue it, but let's take a fifteen-minute break, okay, so you can try to compose yourself."

Mr. Brooks replied, "I've got to have a fighting chance. I've got to, at least, I've been asking for discovery every day. That's how bad things are."

The Court again stated, "Do you want to take ten minutes? I think we have to continue, so I'll have to deny your request for a continuance. Do you want to take ten?"

Mr. Brooks pleaded, "Judge."

The Court answered, "I have to rule one way or the other."

Mr. Brooks requested, "I haven't reviewed them. But I'm not prepared. I'm just asking you. I'm not going to ask you for anything else. I just want that. Can I ask you? Can I ask you, could you give the defendants until Friday?"

The Court stated, "I have to deny your request, Mr. Brooks."

Mr. Brooks begged, "Judge, Judge, Judge, and everybody here, please, I have an idea of what I want if I can just get it in. I can come to your office on Thursday, 1:00 to 4:00. Can we do it from 1:00 to 4:00 on Thursday? Is that possible? I want to go over the documents."

The Court responded, "We can't waste today."

Mr. Brooks replied, "I'm not wasting today. I'm just trying to get up to speed."

The Court offered, "I'm willing to go as long as we can today."

Mr. Brooks stated, "I might not want any of them to testify. I don't know because I haven't gone through the documents."

The Court let on, "I was impressed with Larry. I was impressed with Larry, but, I mean, they're very sharp people. Marcenia Richards is extremely sharp. I'm sure you could probably put Marcenia on and say just tell your story and she'd have a great testimony."

Counsel Brooks continued to plead with the court as he would throughout the entire trial. "This is their opportunity to present the truth."

The Court reiterated, "I've got to deny your request."

This was more than just a story or a simple testimony. This was about the law and what the truth was.

We thought it was astounding that the judge did not think our attorney needed time to become properly prepared and that he didn't seem to think the facts and evidence would have much to do with the eventual decision.

In retrospect, proceeding without counsel may have been the best decision, rather than proceeding with improper counsel and putting him through such a horrific ordeal. It was apparent that the court had already reached a decision about this lawsuit prior to any of the proceedings, discovery, or trial.

An Election

Following Mr. Brooks' first appearance in the court, the day before the scheduled date of the trial, he returned from the court and said to us, "There will be an election. The court has made up its mind. None of you stand a chance. I am not sure that you have to proceed with the trial. The court has established a predisposition for an election."

I asked, "What happened to equity? What happened to due process? What about the evidence? What about the laws governing the facts relating to this case? What about justice? What about the truth? What about proven, long-established practice?"

He responded, "The reality was that truth, evidence, justice, and even the pertaining laws are apparently not relevant issues in this case. It is what the court wanted, and it is what the court decided will happen."

I asked him, "How will the court determine the membership status of the church and which members are entitled to participate in such an election?"

Walk Away?

The attorney looked at me with a dismal expression and simply said, "Walk away, Doctor Richards. All of your questions are irrelevant, and you can cross that bridge when you get there. Prepare yourself how to respond to the court's predisposition for an election."

"What do you mean walk away?" I replied, "This is a divine call from God. If it were up to me personally, I would have walked away a long time before this."

And at that moment I realized that I had declared in only a simple sentence the difference between my values and theirs – between the values that I had absorbed from childhood and that I had lived by to that very moment as sharply opposed to the value shared throughout that courtroom.

The attorney explained why I should walk away. "You can do better than this. You can have any position you desire,"

"What do you mean by that?" I asked. I was daring him to explain what he meant by "better than this."

"You should accept another position outside of the office of Pastor, and that position would be granted, if you simply walk away."

There it was – that existential choice repeated in virtually the same words that the younger attorney, Albert, had used in his face-to-face meeting with me.

Our principal concern was the position of the court to have an election.

One of the primary decisions remaining was to determine how to maintain our Religious Freedom Rights while the court determined how the election would be carried out.

31

OPENING STATEMENT

The Grand Entrance

The trial was a mere formality. I could hardly believe my eyes. I stopped counting the number of counsels from the law firm after five of them entered the courtroom. The counsels made their grand entrance into the courtroom, slowly rolling in carts with volumes of documents on them, the boxes echoing throughout the courtroom. As we sat in the courtroom, they reminded me of the movie, "The Firm." At the end of the movie, the character played by Tom Cruise walked into a room alone…then a large crowd of opposing attorneys entered with masses of books, records, documents, and exhibits. "Run Away Jury," starring Gene Hackman and others and "The Devil's Advocate" starring Al Pacino.

In each of these movies there were scenes where the underdog faced giants who controlled the law through manipulation, influence, and dollars, without respect for the truth.

As defendants, we walked into the courtroom empty-handed, slowly leading Mother Walker. Furthermore, we had no counsel walking alongside us. The courtroom was filled with the senior citizens who were forced to leave our church along with a few of the plaintiffs. As the counsels sat in the section they were supposed to sit in, we took our seats off to the side, along with the plaintiffs' supporters. I sat between Mother Walker and Mother Littlejohn, holding each of their hands as I waited for my mother.

In one of her hands, Mother Littlejohn held a "prayer cloth" (one of the ones that Mattie Poole was summoned to court for in the early 50's) towards me as I held each of the seniors' hands. Marie sat directly behind me with a Bible in her hand. Marie immediately opened the Bible and began reading scriptures aloud. As Marie read the Bible verses aloud, you could hear a pin drop. Larry and A.C. entered the courtroom and everyone's heads slowly turned.

Larry walked directly towards me and asked, "What is Marie doing?"

I responded, "Reading scriptures."

Larry shook his head, turned to Marie, and said, "Marie read silently."

As Marie stopped reading out loud, the silence in the courtroom broke. There were conversations throughout the courtroom.

My mother arrived, along with my sisters, Mildred, and Gwendolyn. I motioned for my mother to come up to the front of the courtroom to sit beside me.

Looking around the courtroom, I sat with my hands folded. I did not see the leading plaintiffs, Rogers, Lester, Lloyd, and Deb inside of the courtroom.

I took inventory as I remembered the words, "throwing rocks, hiding their hands." Sooner or later, they would have to appear. I reflected on the prophetic words of our founder, Mattie B. Poole, "Those who are a part of this church will come against this church to destroy it."

No Opening Statement

William was not in court for the beginning of the trial. We needed an opening statement on record. Had we known we would be responsible for the opening statement, we would have certainly prepared for such a statement. Given William's lack of knowledge of the case, we were apparently to conduct ourselves as counsel throughout the trial. William merely laid the foundation for the questioning. Each of the questions posed to the plaintiffs was constructed by me and given to William.

The beginning of the trial was crucial to establishing a foundation for our organization. The law firm's counsel's opening statement focused on the accounting methods of the organization and included faulty information.

One can always look back and project the way an event should have been conducted or what could have been accomplished. For us, perhaps it would have been a good decision to request a trial by jury. We could not understand why we were compelled to participate in such a trial, given the court's position.

As we waited for the arrival of our counsel, an individual from his office arrived to inform the court that the counsel would be an hour or two late -- not a good way to begin a trial.

The court would not hear of any delays and demanded that we proceed without counsel.

Proceed Without Counsel

At the beginning of the trial, the counsels from the law firm presented two motions, which we were unclear about. We could not confirm if we had received the motions. The court, however, allowed the motions to be entered, and the trial began.

The leading counsel from the law firm, Bark, stood reading his prepared opening statement for nearly forty-five minutes. There was much faulty information, misrepresentation of facts, distortion of facts, and outright lies shared with the court. We came to understand later that it did not matter because the court had already reached a verdict for an election, without ever going to trial.

Relying Upon the History, the Truth, and the Facts

We were completely stunned when the court insisted that we proceed without the presence of our counsel.

Following the reading of the Opening Statement by the opposing counsel, Bark, it became our responsibility to make an Opening Statement.

I could hardly believe this was happening. It was not as if we did not obtain counsel. But William had only one day to readjust his schedule.

As I stood to speak, the Judge stated that we could take our seats in the attorney's section of the courtroom. Walking over to this area, I mustered the courage to face what would follow -- days of shear anguish.

This would perhaps be the only time we were given an opportunity to set the platform for the record to fight for justice. Relying on the history of the organization and the genesis of this litigation, I prepared to inform the uninformed.

My Opening Statement

Given time to prepare the opening statement, I would have shared the following with the court.

"Your Honor, given this court has denied all of the defendant's motions to present evidence, failed to allow us to bring any witnesses, denied our motions to depose the plaintiffs, denied our motions to present any evidence, allowed our counsel to withdraw prior to trial (and not given our new counsel time to become familiar with the case), have allowed the evidence which is available to not only be inadmissible, but have concealed the truth, laws, and facts relating to this case, I can only offer the following:

"Never in the history of the Bethlehem Healing Temple has there ever been an election for the Board of Directors of this corporation; never, never, never. For more than seventy years, it has been the policy and the church practice of this corporation to appoint its directors. Each of the plaintiffs was appointed to the Board of Directors and each of them represented the corporation on behalf of the Board of Directors. While the plaintiffs have already perjured themselves inside this courtroom, as well as on their affidavits, it is they who have conducted themselves as criminals.

"You, Your Honor have already stated that 'the stuff is not important.' Well, the one thing that we have to say to that is this: It is very important. You will take the law into your own hands by not allowing evidence to be submitted. It is very important, Your Honor. It will always be important. And if you have already made your decision regarding your verdict, we request a trial by jury.

"Further, everything that we have done for the last seventy years has been a waste of time, money, and energy, as well as allocating the taxpayers' money to cover your salary for the law you swore to uphold. It is important.

"Finally, Your Honor, again there has never been an election for the Board of Directors of our corporation. Rogers is not a holdover director. He has been in another state for more than twenty years. Each of the plaintiffs and their witnesses is aware of the polity of our church. It is those individuals who are now using the policy that was instituted years ago, as their own.

"So, I submit to this court – given those facts and that established history, the court cannot determine who the members of our church are.

"Our by-laws are written, and this is the truth of the case before you. Whether you choose to determine who the members of our corporation are, it does not nullify our seventy years of prior practice, or the truth or law related to this case.

"However, that did not happen as I desired. Not having time to prepare for an opening statement, I took my time to speak about the history of the corporation and the actions of those attempting to control the corporation. As the plaintiffs' counsel objected to nearly everything I said, it did not matter. I continued to speak about the facts surrounding the lawsuit."

With no notes in front of me, I spoke for nearly half an hour, forgetting the fact that our attorney was not present.

Things were established and rolling. Now, finally, the trial was set to begin.

32

THE TRIAL BEGINS

To begin, I reached back to the days of Mattie B. Poole to draw out the path that led to the founding of the church. I talked about her and Bishop Poole and about her prayerful nature and her holy healing power. Then came the establishment of Bethlehem Tabernacle, and, later, because of her God-given healing gift, the renaming of it to Bethlehem Healing Temple. And, of course, as I talked about the flowing history of the Pooles' and their church, I kept mentioning how all of this was recorded and that we had records pertaining to every step of the way.

For the period after Mattie passed away, I focused on the more modern era of the church and its corporation. Yes, back then the plaintiffs were on the Board of Directors as the appointed Directors, by Bishop Poole and Bishop Richards. Everyone knew that each of these appointments and many others were the decision of the presiding Pastor. There had never been any doubt or any past protest about that. That was how the church operated, survived, and thrived. In fact, following Bishop Poole's appointment of Bishop A. C. Richards as his successor, the Board of Directors and the Board of Deacons signed a letter stating, "We, the Board have selected our new Pastor, Bishop A. C. Richards." And, in fact, that document has the signatures of plaintiffs Rodgers and Clay!

I also talked about the auxiliaries established within the structure of the church and its corporation and how each of these operated independently of Bishop Richards, and how each had their own bank accounts that each auxiliary head managed and signed off on.

I noted that everything seemed to come to a point of change when my father decided that the church needed to start progressing. We had been talking about how the church needed to start doing something differently, as the community was changing, and was facing different needs. We decided as a board, as a group, that we needed to move up and keep up with the community. At that time, our Christian Education Department was not moving with these changes and Bishop Richards decided to change the Sunday School Director from Mike to Lisa.

The Beginning of the Riots

I informed the court how Mike, the plaintiffs, and their supporters had risen and threatened us that if Bishop Richards did not return Mike to his position that he would pay for the change he had made. From that point on, the plaintiffs began to make all kinds of threats and started promoting their meetings.

Once they started having these meetings and plotting against the church's established leadership, we began to try to have some dialogues with them. But that did not work.

The plaintiffs and their supporters started galvanizing individuals, some through exaggerations or outright lies, and others through confusion, to sign petitions against the Bishop.

Afterwards they attempted to take control of the pulpit in the church. That never happened. Bishop Richards continued pastoring until his death, when, as appointed and agreed, I took over as Pastor. Then came the legal action and the initial dismissal from the first judge, who said it was not the court's or the government's place to tell a church how it should run itself. Of course, we could not have agreed more!

I also mentioned the claims that I had put people out of the church. I let them know that those who threatened me, the church, our employees, our family members, and our loyal congregants had chosen to leave the church themselves. Yes, we agreed to issue excommunication letters, but only because of the threats issued by those individuals and their subsequent actions.

Then came the staged walkout. Unable to accept the course of how things were or to discuss compromises even possibly with us, they willfully exited the church. They did not want problems solved; they wanted me out; they wanted control of the church and everything to which it was connected.

I also told the presiding judge that, while I may not have known all the potential legalities involved, I certainly did have factual history on my side. I did have documentation that supported this case. No case, no rule will ever change the fact that this had always been a traditional organization that had built its history on its appointed leaders.

I concluded by telling the judge about the threats on my life, that the conflict had already cost me my job, and a lot of other things that had occurred within our formerly tight-knit community.

I stood strongly, saying that I was not crying about those things. Things happen in life, and you must deal with them. However, what I was most concerned about was the fact that we were standing there before the judge as a group of God-fearing people coming forward because we had not been able to settle our differences.

And even though there were firm feelings on both sides, I let the judge know how I felt, that once we were provided with an opportunity to fully present evidence and prove our case, this lawsuit would be dismissed as well as the first one with Judge Madden.

Spent, but proud, I completed my statement and took my seat.

The Plaintiffs' Counsel Reacts

There was no doubt that no one in the courtroom had been prepared for my statement. I could not take my seat before Terri, the plaintiff's counsel, jumped up. "We'd like to call Marcenia Richards to the witness stand."

The judge called for an immediate recess.

Once the court reconvened, I took the stand. I testified to my background. The law firm's counsel asked me about our corporation and how and when it withdrew from The National Organization, as well as our tax-exempt status and our overall financial management. I answered as best as I could.

Then they asked me about my history with the church. I was also questioned about the excommunication letters that were issued to the most rabble-rousing plaintiffs and their supporters. I truthfully said that I had not issued or even signed those letters.

The counsel who was questioning me became confused because my answers to his questions contradicted his clients' claims. Therefore, he withdrew further questioning. The court directed me to step down from the stand. Following the intermission, the counsels from the law firm called their first witness.

Mike, Former Director of Christian Education

The counsels from the law firm attempted to set the stage for this trial by calling their first witness, Mike.

He testified about having grown up in the church and having become a leader there. Of course, he also had to admit that my father had removed him from his Sunday School position. He also stated that he blamed me for his dismissal.

During my cross-examination without counsel, he again claimed that I had put him out of the church – even though he had just testified that he and others had left the church.

He was making little sense, and I was growing fatigued at these round-about answers to my questions. On that note I ended my questioning.

Where in the World Was Our Counsel?

This was our counsel's first day in court. If he did not appear, I would be responsible for cross-examining the other witnesses. We learned that he was in another courtroom. We did not understand why he agreed to take this case with the pending caseloads prior to our trial.

Since our attorney was not present, I began preparing the questions to cross-examine each of the plaintiffs and their witnesses. If it were to go anything like Mike's cross-examination went, this was going to be a full-blown circus trial. For now, I sat back and watched the counsels from the law firm demean our characters as leaders of the church.

Just when the judge asked if I desired to cross-examine another witness, William rushed through the doors of the courtroom. He had neither a briefcase nor papers in his hand. We knew we had to request his withdrawal as quickly as we had retained his services. Yet, we were caught by the need for representation. So, it was agreed that William would stay.

Custodian Over The Vending Machine Elevated to Bishop

The day arrived when the missing plaintiffs were scheduled to testify against me as the Pastor.

The counsels from the law firm set the stage for their case against us. One of the first witnesses was Lloyd. Following my father's death, Lloyd became the "self-appointed" Presiding Bishop of The National Organization.

Lloyd was asked how he became Bishop. "What did you say? Did you say you supervised the vending machine? – Then you were elevated to Bishop?"

Lloyd's primary statement concerning his elevation to the office of Bishop left us stunned, "Well, to be frank, I held the vending machine down until I was asked to be elevated."

Lloyd had stated earlier that he left to go to the suburbs to pastor there. He was also asked to define the role and responsibilities of a bishop. Was the inference of the qualifications for Bishopric to manage the organization's "vending machine" and then be elevated to a Bishop? Not one of the clients of the law firm could adequately define the qualifications or elevations for that of a Bishop because one was appointed Minister, Elder, Pastor, or Bishop.

We dared not demean or make light of the title or office of a Bishop. A Bishop held the highest office within the organization. Therefore, each of us kept our heads bowed as the Presiding Bishop spoke. However, for the court records, the office of a Bishop was to be addressed to shed light on the authority of a Bishop. But for Plaintiff Lloyd to state he was supervising and manager of the vending machines and from there to be elevated to the position of a Bishop was beyond belief.

Although Lloyd, in his sworn affidavits, stated that The National Organization had no power to govern the local churches, his testimony offered no credibility to the responsibilities of a Bishop's authority or the role of a Bishop in the governing affairs of a local church.

During Lloyd's testimony, he admitted that I had not sent him the excommunication letter. He also testified that other churches had left The National Organization and that he was subservient in his roles to Bishop Richards while my father was still alive.

More testimony from Lloyd ensued that showed he had little or no interest in remaining involved in the church when I became the Pastor.

Mr. Brooks: Q. Did you receive a letter from Marcenia asking you not to come back?

Plaintiff Lloyd: A. I did not receive a letter… So, when I got to the door, she asked me to go into the office along with Clay. She asked us to come in. She says, "Bishop, what do you think I should do because I'm the pastor?" I said, "…If you choose to be a pastor, fine. I wouldn't stay. So, when I got outside the door, I said these words, I said, "I will not be coming back no more." There is - somebody says, "Bishop, if we get a place somewhere, will you come and be with us"? I told them, "Yes, you get a place, I will come to you."

As Mr. Brooks held in his hand a copy of the letter sent to Lloyd, he shook his head in disbelief.

Former Bishops of The National Organization

Most of the Bishops formally connected to The National Organization sought the title of a Bishop without carrying out or fulfilling the responsibilities of the position of Bishop. Although the qualifications for Bishops were clearly defined and outlined; several of those carrying the title of Bishop were "self-made, self-appointed" Bishops.

Actually, there were no educational criteria given; there were no authorities which governed this self-appointed office that the plaintiffs "held;" neither were there written evaluations to be appointed to the office of a Bishop. Each Bishop simply promoted himself to that position.

The evidence neglected to show that it was my father who made the recommendation for the plaintiffs to be Pastors. While Lloyd stated there was an election for him to be Pastor, he could not cite any evidence of such an election, for there had never been one.

The appointment of each plaintiff as Pastor, Board of Director, and any other office was recorded in the minutes of Board of Directors meetings. Those minutes, however, were not deemed admissible in court.

The Presiding Bishop at the time of Lloyd's appointment announced the appointment of Lloyd as the Assistant Presiding Bishop. Lloyd neither challenged nor disagreed with his appointment as assistant.

Each of the plaintiffs undeniably knew the former Presiding Bishop was Bishop Poole's successor, solely by appointment, and that there was no election of that Bishop for Presiding Bishop of The National Organization. Furthermore, they were aware that it was the former Bishop who reinstated the corporation of The National Organization after its dissolution.

Lester's Testimony

Along with the other self-appointed Bishop, next to testify was Lester, who reminded me of the crafty character of Laurence Fishburne in the movie, "Hoodlum."

Lester was the former treasurer and on the board of directors of The National Organization. He too had been appointed by my father. He admitted leaving the church and going elsewhere when the plaintiffs and their supporters became disgruntled and started their lawsuit.

Under cross-examination, Lester admitted that his "Bishop" title had been bestowed upon him by Lloyd and, although he described himself as an "elder...a Bishop...an associate minister...a preacher," he admitted that he was not a Pastor either at our church or at any church at all.

Clay's Testimony

The law firm and its clients made startling accusations against our corporation regarding its financial affairs.

Clay testified about taking four thousand dollars from the church collection and giving it to Lloyd with only Rubi's knowledge. He also testified that he was never a member of the church's Board of Directors, even though he had been a member for over twenty years. He further claimed that he did not know there were articles of incorporation for the church and that he had never received a tax-exempt letter from the Bethlehem Healing Temple -- a direct contradiction because he had signed documents on behalf of the corporation using the tax-exempt letter.

Although Clay also testified to the court that he did not remember what he had signed, records showed that he had signed as a participant to the selection of Bishop Richards as Pastor following the appointment by Bishop Charles Poole.

Clay, whose wife had been excommunicated by Mattie decades ago, had walked into my office and said, "Just you wait. I know Bishop Poole appointed your father. I don't care 'bout no election. We all signed a letter for your father when he became Pastor. But when I get to court, I will swear on the Holy Bible that there was an election."

It was widely known that Clay never favored female Pastors.

As Mother Walker took the witness stand, she testified that she had sat in various meetings for over forty years with Clay and his supporters. She stated, "he said he did not want a female leader. Clay often said, 'I have always been a bad child. I disobeyed Mattie Poole. I disobeyed Bishop

Poole, and I disobeyed Bishop Richards. Bad, bad, bad. Yep, that is me – a bad, disobedient child.'

The Plaintiffs' Secretary's Testimony

As each of the plaintiffs and their witnesses expressed their desire to control Bethlehem, we sat in amazement as we witnessed the avaricious motives of those seeking to gain control of our corporation. The plaintiffs' secretary stated her motives this way; "Because I feel that's our church…We left, but that's our church. That's just the way I see it. I looked around and saw my people, and I tried to remember as many as I could…"

She further stated that she told her people to leave with her. When the judge asked how she determined members as there had never existed a membership roster, she repeated, "I looked around and saw my people."

In her pre-trial affidavit, the plaintiff's secretary stated, "I had never heard that the church was incorporated, nor did I ever learn any facts that caused me to wonder whether it might be incorporated." Yet, in a letter dated years earlier, on the organization's letterhead, she had typed a letter stating, "The church is incorporated within the content of the letter suggesting to the letters that the corporation is subject to audit," and she signed it with her initials, DLM.

She then told the court that Rogers returned because he had discovered that he was the only living member of the Board of Directors. Did that matter? He had been living out of Illinois for years. The plaintiffs and their witnesses knew they had no way to substantiate their claims; therefore, someone had called Plaintiff Rogers and advised him to travel from Mississippi.

She continued with various confusing parts of her testimony regarding her membership. She was not a member of our church; rather, she was a member of the plaintiffs' church.

Our lawyer asked her why they staged a walk-out, organized under a similar name, and then returned to sue us. She answered, "We left, and we started another corporation because we did not wish to have Marcenia as the Pastor."

As the plaintiffs' secretary continued to testify regarding the membership list of her church, where the lists came from, and how she managed to choose who or who would not be included on her list, she emphatically declared that it was her decision to determine who the members were. During the trial, even the judge stated that the list for membership of Bethlehem Healing Temple was presented solely by the plaintiff's secretary.

She also testified that her mother was the former secretary of the corporation and the church. No documents or information pertaining to the organization or corporation were returned to the corporation following her mother's passing. She alone possessed all the documents and information about the organization.

33

THE LAW FIRM FOCUSES

The counsels from the law firm used the entire trial to divert the focus of the court by placing the financial affairs of the church at the center of the trial. The trial barely addressed the issues of the lawsuit: "Was Rogers a holdover board member?" and "Given that there had never been an election for the Board of Directors for this organization, how would the court determine membership for the organization and deliver its opinion to justify an election?"

Throughout the trial, we were constrained by the need to consistently address the plaintiffs' misrepresentation of financial affairs.

As the counsels from the law firm were successfully distracting the court with the financial affairs of the organization, they further attempted to distract the court with the physical condition of the property.

The reality was that physical evidence revealed that the property had deteriorated during a period when some of the plaintiffs were responsible for its maintenance.

Checks and Balances

Failing to support their claims regarding the election process for the board of directors, the counsels from the law firm centered their focus on the financial affairs of the corporation. The strategy was to distract the court from the present and overriding legal issues. Therefore, the accounting system of the organization served as an enormous distraction.

The counsels from the law firm presented to the court a series of checks from the corporation. Terri, one of the plaintiffs' counsels, spent nearly forty-five minutes questioning one of their witnesses, McDaze, about the accounting system of the corporation, although she was never privy to any information regarding the accounting system. Despite McDaze not being a credible witness, the court seemed to take her testimony into serious consideration to solidify the court's position to order an election.

While the court denied us the opportunity to present any evidence of the plaintiffs' deliberate thievery of funds from the corporation, we had in our possession hundreds of copies of paperwork about loans and financial records and insufficient fund checks from both plaintiffs, Clay, and Rogers. The corporation also possessed canceled checks from loans written to each plaintiff as well as to their corporate secretary, Deb. As overwhelming as the evidence against the plaintiffs would have been, we were at a severe disadvantage, not being able to present any of the evidence.

Others among the plaintiffs' witnesses who had no knowledge of financial affairs were questioned about the financial affairs of the organization. We requested that the court allow us to respond.

That request too, was denied.

When McDaze was cross-examined about her knowledge of financial affairs, she started hysterically crying and throwing a tantrum. As she stepped off the witness stand, Terri applauded her efforts. "Your performance was outstanding."

We shook our heads in amazement. Even the judge shook his head in disbelief.

One of the primary reasons that injustice persists is because the truth remains concealed among the overt actions of those who are attempting to cover up previous lies. The trial constantly provided dramatic examples of that root cause of injustice.

Our Response

According to their admissions, it was the plaintiffs, as deacons and trustees of the church, who were primarily responsible for the financial affairs of the corporation. Each department within the corporation was responsible for the individual department's finances and accounting methods.

Not having proper counsel, we knew that we must somehow find a path that would allow the court records to reflect the behavior and character of the plaintiffs' indebtedness to the corporation for thousands of dollars. Therefore, when the plaintiffs and their witnesses made such outrageous accusations, we questioned them about their outstanding debts and checks with insufficient funds to the corporation.

The court also asked that our questions be stricken from the records.

To bolster their claims, they presented into evidence a series of checks purported to be made out to me. As a full-time employee of the corporation, my weekly salary from the church was two hundred dollars. I was a full-time employee with the city and owner of several businesses and pieces of real estate. From my government salary, I invested money in the church by making loans. A generous amount of my resources were filtered into building the organization. However, the plaintiffs along with the counsels from the law firm used the financial records as a way to misrepresent the evidence and cast aspersions on the character of the former President, the corporation, and all of the rest of us.

Perjury?

In each of their affidavits represented to the court, the plaintiffs and their witnesses accused me of expelling them from the church. Yet when asked if I had expelled them or asked them to leave the church, each of them responded, "No." Following these admissions, William asked several of them if they were thrown out or if they were asked to leave the organization. Each of the plaintiffs responded according to the following court transcripts.

Plaintiff Lloyd: "I wouldn't stay. So, when I got outside the door, I said these words, I said, 'I will not be coming back any more.' There is somebody who says, 'If we get a place somewhere, will you come and be with us?' I told them, 'Yes, you get a place, I come to you.'"

Plaintiff witness Mike: "We left in August, this month."

Plaintiff Clay: "I was not put out; we left."

Witness Deb was asked: "Did Dr. Janel personally ask you to leave the Bethlehem Healing Temple?"

"No, she didn't."

Plaintiff Lester: "We started our church. We left."

Filing off of the witness stand were individuals with notorious criminal backgrounds as pimps, prostitutes, drug lords, robbers, and worse, whom my father had prayed for, petitioned God for, and asked Him to make them better citizens to society, but more importantly, to accept them into His kingdom and give them eternal life, if they would only receive Jesus into their hearts as their Lord and Savior. And most of those witnesses stated they had confessed Jesus as their personal Lord and Savior. Only God could reveal the heart of everyone leaving that stand.

Following the plaintiffs' and their witnesses' testimonies, I felt completely numb! Then – within a matter of seconds – my faith increased even more! How merciful was my God! Only a true, merciful God could accept any of us and love us despite our faults, weaknesses, and sins.

At that moment, it did not matter to me what the plaintiffs or their witnesses testified. What was significant was that Jesus Christ died for the sins of humanity and whosoever would call upon his name would be saved from their sins.

I exited the courtroom with this thought in mind.

34

SAVING THE BEST FOR LAST

nyone who witnessed the Rogers vs. Richards's trial would have to reevaluate the rule of thumb to save the best for last.

Following Rogers's departure to another state, there had no longer existed a corporate relationship between Rogers and our church for nearly twenty years. It was not until we discovered the law firm's prerequisite to continue the preposterous claims of their clients that we fully realized Rogers's agreement to return to the state for the litigation.

On the stand, Rogers stated, "A member is not supposed to have but one church." He went on to state that a person is a robber and thief if that person does not pay tithes and attends services at another church. While the court waited to determine if Rogers was a member of the church, Rogers seemed to have already answered for himself. He could not be a member in good standing or a faithful member because of his absence from the church.

During examination by the counsel from the law firm, Rogers was asked if someone is a pastor at one church and a member at some other church if that person is considered a faithful member. Rogers answered, "A member is not supposed to have but one church."

Counsel continued, "And if a person attends your church in Mississippi, and does not tithe, would you consider that member a faithful member?"

Rogers answered, "No, sir. No sir because he's a robber and a thief."

"Mr. Rogers, are you referring to yourself as a robber and a thief?"

$90,000

The minutes read: "Finance: Ninety thousand dollars of the church's money is tied up by Brother Rogers…"

During Rogers's testimony, the court ordered certain parts of his testimony restricted as questions related to Rogers being indebted to the corporation for more than $90,000. However, we were compelled to mention Rogers's indebtedness to the corporation.

As we sat in the courtroom, our counsel and I entered a heated discussion about the evidence which had been ruled inadmissible in court. I stated, "We must devise a strategy to have the information shared about Rogers, who has been in another state for more than 20 years but is indebted to our corporation." Because William was so adamant concerning the evidence, each of us was shouting. It did not matter that the counsels from the law firm or anyone else could hear our conversation.

I was resolute in having the records reflect the actions of the plaintiffs. Following a thirty-minute debate, I said to William, "You are the attorney, figure it out." Later, during Marie's testimony, our Defense Counsel successfully brought Rogers's indebtedness to the court's attention:

Q. As a member of the finance committee and after reviewing the various documents regarding Rogers, do you know if Rogers owes the Bethlehem Healing Temple any money?

A. Based on the ---

Plaintiffs' Counsel: Objection. Foundation.

The Court: Overruled. Yes, or no?

The Witness: Yes.

Mr. Brooks: How much money does he owe the Bethlehem Healing Temple?

The Witness: The records state ninety thousand dollars.

Rogers continued to borrow thousands of dollars during subsequent years. Was he, along with others, ashamed that their loans would no longer be available once I became Pastor?

It was time for our defense witnesses. We had not adequately prepared our defense.

Our Witnesses

We did the best we could under the strenuous conditions surrounding the trial with no discovery, no depositions of the plaintiffs, no witnesses, and no evidence being allowed in court on our part.

Day after day, we sat in the courtroom transfixed by the on-goings of the trial. Often, we desired to speak out at the injustice, but remained silent, as there was no platform for justice within the judicial system, where we sat as defendants. Sitting directly in front of us were the volumes of books with all our evidence in them. Each time the plaintiffs and their witnesses perjured on the witness stand, we referred to our evidence books, which had been disallowed by the court.

During a brief court recess, Pastor Larry said, "I hope that the court will allow us to present the truth. However, we must do the best we can."

I agreed. "That's all we can do. Besides, William has not been able to set up a good defense, given the court denied his request for time to prepare for a full-blown trial. If it were not happening to me personally, I would not believe it."

"We can only hope for the best," he replied.

"Since we have not been allowed to share our story here, we will need to find another platform to share our story after this is over," I insisted.

"And we shall."

"I'm sorry that you must go through this. You had nothing to do with this war. Since you are so close to us, this is just another way for them to get back at us," I continued.

When Pastor Larry took the stand, he was asked about his historical connection with our church. On the stand he described how his grandmother's uncle had been healed from an incurable condition because of Mattie Poole's prayer. When asked about his thoughts on coming to a church that was under the cloud of litigation, he gave the great answer that summed up the man and his humble passions and commitment, "I didn't come to fight a lawsuit. I came to pastor a church."

During his testimony he was able to describe what it took to be a member of a church. It was important because it shored up our point that Rogers had not been a member for the last twenty years.

It was clear that Larry made a favorable impression on the judge, "I think Larry Martin has a good testimony. I am impressed with the defendant's witness, Martin."

He was also strong about what it took to be a member of our church: regular attendance, tithing, a full commitment to our goals, and being filled with the Holy Spirit. He had joined us after the plaintiffs and their supporters had left, so there had been no excommunications, no major disruptions, and no staged walkouts since he had been there. Pastor Larry's position was very strong. Anyone was welcome to attend the services at the church, even if they may have been suing the corporation.

"They Do Not Want a Woman"

The next person to testify was Mother Lela Walker. She was nearly ninety years of age. Due to her lack of vision, she slowly felt her way toward the witness stand, escorted by Larry. Sensing the difficulty that Mother Walker was experiencing, the judge stopped her in the middle of the courtroom and instructed the bailiff to bring her a chair. Mother Walker sat in the middle of the courtroom to give her testimony.

In recounting the many years she had been with the church, she described the tension that existed among the Board of Directors, deacons, and trustees.

She stated this tension had grown over the years because of the role of women in the church, which dated back to when Mattie Poole founded and presided over the church. She testified as to the content of the weekly meetings, saying that the attitude was always extremely hostile to the thought of a female pastor. "They did not want a woman."

Mother Walker's testimony became extremely emotional as it appeared that the plaintiff's counsel Jon was harassing her. The judge immediately admonished Jon and directed Mother Walker to return to her seat.

There was no need to continue with our witness. The court had reached its decision but insisted that I testify.

My Testimony

During the trial, our counsel was frequently tardy. On the day of my testimony, he was not present for the beginning of the trial. The courtroom was packed to capacity. I was scheduled to be the first witness. When the court noticed our counsel's absence again, the Judge said to me, "Start talking."

I was compelled to take the witness stand. I asked the court what I should say. The judge simply said, "Start talking."

The judge had previously said, "I'm sure you could probably put Marcenia on (the stand) and say, 'Just tell your story, and she'd have a great testimony."

I decided to start with the Pooles' and continue on with the appointment of my father by Bishop Poole. As I spoke, Mary, the three-hundred-and-fifty-pound lady who had thrown Marie off the pulpit, sat in the juror's seat directly next to me, breathing threatening statements. I smiled at her and said, "God bless you."

I ended my testimony as I had started, without legal counsel present and with the facts surrounding the lawsuit.

The End of the Trial

Following my testimony, I took a deep breath and stepped down from the witness stand. I wondered why we were forced to go through the formality of a trial and endure the hellacious torment.

Each of us has a journey upon which we embark. Some journeys are greater than others. Some journeys are small. However, they are nonetheless our journeys. I decided that the trial in the Rogers vs. Richards's case was simply a part of my journey.

Walking off the witness stand, I reminded myself, "For me, this part of the nightmare is over."

There on the witness stand was Jimmy, Deb's husband. Our counsel questioned Jimmy: "Who gave you the authority to dismiss the service following the death of Bishop Richards?"

"Bishop Richards gave me the authority," Jimmy replied.

"Are you saying Bishop Richards gave you the authority from the grave?" William inquired. How is it possible for one to communicate with you at church during Sunday morning worship when he has been deceased for nearly five years? Perhaps we can see if Bishop Richards can appear in this courtroom, from the dead, of course, and direct this trial which seems to put everyone in here in a state of amnesia."

Everyone inside of the courtroom laughed loudly.

Our defense counsel did the best he could under the unorthodox circumstances. There existed much confusion throughout the trial. With nothing to work with, William was not successful in developing a legal defensive strategy for our case.

The Odor of Food

There were many odors permeating the courtroom, including the smell of soul food, including collard greens, pork chops, chitterlings, and other food.

There were also body odors as there were senior citizens with different illnesses. The court proceedings were very lengthy because we often did not break for lunch.

This posed challenges for some of the senior citizens with health concerns, who needed to eat at certain times of the day. The senior citizens often reached into their bags and pulled out whatever foods were piled inside of the aluminum foil and ate directly in front of the judge.

Additionally, during the trial, I overheard one senior citizen state he needed to take his medication because his blood sugar level was rising. Another senior citizen said she forgot to take her high blood pressure medication.

There were overwhelming body odors as there were other senior citizens with bladder and related challenges. However, the plaintiffs demanded that these senior citizens board buses and cars daily to be driven to the courthouse as they built their case against me, stating that I put each of the senior citizens out of the church with guns and dogs.

To watch the plaintiffs and their counsels was like observing children play hide and seek or waiting for a magician to pull another rabbit out of his bag of tricks. Every moment of the entire trial was like being in a movie full of drama.

The actions of the plaintiffs and their counsels, however, were not a game or entertainment. These were real live events occurring within an unhealthy organization with a very powerful history.

35
IS JUSTICE A GAME?

In a case that would set precedence for religious and corporate law, Terri referred to the trial and the litigation against us and our corporation as "a game."

At the end of the trial, I asked the plaintiffs' counsel, "Why are you so hostile?" Terri responded, "This is a game." No doubt, I should not have been surprised, but his statement startled me.

"Who spends hundreds of thousands of dollars, engages in a trial, the litigation process, and the challenges that arise from such litigation, and considers it merely a game?" Unbelievable! "A game?" I inquired, anxiously. "Is this what this litigation is all about to you and your law firm? Is that why your firm is representing the plaintiff's *pro bono* in this conspiracy -- because this is a game to you?"

While the life of our corporation, as well as the life of our historical ministry, was on the line, those words proved staggeringly true to those opposing the truth. We watched as those suing us made a mockery of the trial, which became one of the most historic religious lawsuits, potentially setting precedence for cases nationally. Ego, corruption, and perversion overtook justice.

The laws were very clear, and it seemed to us that even those who were not educated in the law could seek interpretation and know that the trial was based on faulty information and a misrepresentation of facts. What we read and saw assured us of the miscarriage of justice.

We speculated that if the counsel from the law firm considered the overall wrongness and mistakenness of their clients and their perjury, including their apparent acts of conspiracy and other outlandish acts, he would certainly not categorize such activities as a game.

I often wondered why the legal system did not compel counsels and law firms to revisit the laws which each swore to uphold. It seemed clear that if counsels believed their clients' games and lie-supporting arguments, it did not say much for the firm they represented. We often wondered who, if anyone, might be working behind the scenes against us and, if so, what were they doing to influence things? It appeared that individuals were permitted to conspire with witnesses, tamper with evidence, hide evidence, present false evidence, and distort the truth during the litigation process.

We witnessed the facts being manipulated and distorted. We often cringed as we saw laws pertinent to our case entirely ignored or dismissed while other laws not relating to the case were cited if they seemed likely to help assure a win for those opposing us. We observed the strategic processes of injustice only to discover that the evidence produced by those suing us was completely misrepresented to give an appearance of notorious criminality on our part. It was not surprising that the counsels from the law firm did not look at the truth. What was surprising was the apparent refusal of the court to consider the facts objectively.

To those who suffer from its miscarriage, justice is not a game. How could it be a game when individual lives are at stake and more than seventy years of community service are in jeopardy?

The mission requirement of our church is the "Introduction of Christ to lost souls and societal transformation." Thus, this Christ, who can transform an individual from existential hopelessness to a purpose-filled life and can change a dilapidated community into a thriving, progressive, and successful environment, is the primary focus of the corporation's mission.

These matters relate not to individual careers, but to our mission. Through the principles and teachings of the corporation's mission, drug addicts were changed to sober profitable citizens, criminals to good neighbors, and the hopes of the down-and-outs were raised. This mission was our *raison d'etre*.

We took our mission very seriously. To us, it was certainly not "a game."

During the trial's formality, Brooks sometimes had no clue what the counsels from the law firm or the court requested. He was given no time to familiarize himself with the case, therefore he was not privy to the necessary facts. Our request was simply that the court allow us the right to present our evidence to try to debunk the web of deceit and lies which had been woven by the plaintiffs and their counsels.

We needed our closing argument to reflect the truth concerning our case. Therefore, the time had come for us to reach out to our formal counsel, Jim.

Jim Returns

Over the Labor Day weekend, the Board of Directors made a decision that we believed would alter the course of the defense as well as the offense for our case. Although Jim did not represent us during the trial, he understood this case backwards and forwards. If given the opportunity, Jim would have laid a thorough foundation for the trial.

As we prepared for closing arguments, I wrote Larry a note. "I will telephone Jim and ask him if he will represent us. We need him to make the closing arguments and assist us if we have to appeal." Counsel William did not have enough knowledge of the case. Therefore, he could not intelligently ask questions, nor did he interject during the Court's and the law firm's counsel's statements concerning membership.

The words from the song, "I Ain't Too Proud to Beg," by the group TLC summarized what happened the weekend prior to Jim's return. I left several voicemail messages and wrote him letters, but he did not respond. I took it upon myself to telephone each of the partners within his firm, leaving them voicemail messages and writing letters to them.

Had Jim chosen to ignore us? I refused to give up. I was tenacious. Not one of the partners returned my telephone calls, answered my emails, or answered my letters. I continued to telephone the firm.

By Friday night I had not received an answer to the many messages, voicemails, and letters I had sent to the law firm.

Labor Day Weekend – Saturday Morning

Our youth group had scheduled a trip to an amusement park. It was my routine to monitor each event prior to their departure to ensure we had enough chaperones. As we stood outside, the telephone rang. One of the youths ran inside and answered it. Returning, she casually stated to me, "Pastor, the telephone call is for you. It is someone by the name of Jim." I stopped in the middle of my instructions and ran inside the building, missing a step as I rushed into the office. I knew Jim would not ignore us forever.

I was so excited that I answered by saying, "Jim, I love you. Thank you for returning my telephone calls."

I could hear a smile in Jim's voice as he said, "Mr. S. (one of the senior partners at his law firm) agreed to allow us to return to the case."

I was excited. We could now prove our defense with Jim's return.

Jim informed me that it would take $30,000 in order for him to represent us. I assured Jim that we would do whatever it took to raise the money prior to Tuesday's court appearance. For the entire weekend, my staff and I placed telephone calls to anyone we thought might contribute to the legal fund.

By Monday evening, we had secured $20,000, with promises to raise the additional funds during the upcoming week. We were short of $10,000. I decided to take Jim what I had and wait for his response.

It was Tuesday morning and time to meet with Jim. As I waited for Jim, the receptionist escorted me to an empty office full of boxes of documents. Sue, Jim's secretary, walked into the office and greeted me saying, "This is our war room. We keep the documents for the Rogers vs. Richards' case here."

Jim's entrance into the War Room was like sunshine after a rainy day. Following our greetings, Jim asked me for the $30,000 check. "Jim, we only have $20,000, with promises to collect the balance during the upcoming week."

"I gave you specific instructions concerning my appearance. I informed the partners that you would bring in $30,000," he responded. I sat there in silence. I did not know what to say. We did not have the balance and were scheduled to appear in court for the closing arguments in less than one hour.

Jim wasted no more time. He sat down and immediately went to work. He questioned me about specific details concerning the trial. Jim thoroughly understood the legal intricacies of our case and the political dynamics of the Giant law firm, and he was acquainted with the plaintiffs.

As he opened the folder, Jim explained how he planned to represent us at the end of the trial.

It was quite simple. "The Court could not legally order an election for our church, as it was forbidden by the law to determine who the members of our church were. Further, the First Amendment and Religious Laws secured this law."

Jim briefly outlined his closing argument on a white board, outlined in red, which would be easily visible to each person in the courtroom. As he explained to me the purpose of the board, we walked out of Jim's office. Jim was prepared to present our closing statement.

It was then I remembered my dream of Jim's disappearance. Another dream had come true.

36
JIM ARRIVES

J im's arrival in the courtroom had stunned the counsels from the law firm and their clients. Jim spoke kindly to the counsels, turned his board around, and took his seat.

Although the trial was all but finished, we needed the court records to reflect our position and the truth regarding our charter, our by-laws, our non-elections, our membership criteria, and the ecclesiastical authority of the Pastor. Jim's return for the closing arguments made us much more comfortable than we had been throughout the entire trial.

No one objected to Jim's return.

Jim's first question was, "So, there has been no waiver of their ability to state who they believe the members of the church are at this point?"

The Court responded, "Right."

Jim, "Very good."

Jim then took a seat and waited his turn to present our closing argument.

Jim's Closing Argument

Jim's presence was captivating. As he stood to present his closing argument, he picked up the board and turned it in the direction of the court. He began by quoting the profound words from Rogers's testimony,

"In the words of Rogers, 'If a man does not pay tithes, he is a thief and a robber.

Your Honor, you might say that a lawyer who does a closing argument after not having attended the trial has somewhat of a disadvantage, and that's probably true. But in one sense, I am not, and that is in the sense in which I believe the defendants are entitled to judgment in this case, mostly as a matter of law. And I will certainly do my best to address points that refer to the evidence. But not having seen the evidence go in and not having seen transcripts written, I am obviously not going to be able to cite directly to the evidence.

From the beginning, the defendants have argued that these plaintiffs have no standing to bring this case. The principal reason they have no standing to bring this case is that none of them are directors in this corporation. And in this corporation, only a director would have any standing to sue concerning corporate governance and corporate affairs on behalf of the corporation to recover alleged misdirected assets or corporate procedures. There must be a basis. This is a not-for-profit corporation. It owns its own assets. There aren't any stockholders. There must be a corporate law basis to have standing to sue; a real injury to oneself that the law would recognize.

Somebody claiming to be a director does not have standing. And at least on the face of the complaint, Rogers, who claimed to be a holdover director, has standing. It begs the question of whether he really is a director. But if he is, he would certainly have some standing to bring this case.

The other plaintiffs who purported to be directors were only directors by virtue of having been appointed by Rogers. And the business they all conducted, that Mr. Bark referred to, are all the business of this group of people whose sole claim to governance of this corporation is that Rogers appointed them, and then I suppose you would say the fruit of that tree, the actions they took, in holding their own elections.

But really, it is all a house of cards because if Rogers never was a director or was not a director when he took these actions, none of the other individuals were authorized to do anything, and none of them have any standing in this case.

Now, I do understand that the plaintiffs' claim to be members of the church, as well, and on that basis, they attempt to bring this case. And this has been litigated in Brownlow and was not a basis of the Appellate Court's reversal, and this has been brought up at least in this lawsuit, as well.

This corporation does not have what the Not-For-Profit Corporation Act refers to as corporate members. There is a dispute about whether the members of this church congregation are entitled to elect the directors of the corporation.

Granted, that is in dispute. But the articles of incorporation nowhere establish that the not-for-profit corporation had called them 'corporate members.' It simply accords the right to vote on directors. According to the plaintiffs, it simply accords the right to vote on directors to the church congregation. And the articles of incorporation are consistent in referring to the people in question as members of the church, members of the congregation.

Never, nowhere, anywhere are they referred to as members of the corporation. That is a very important distinction.

So even if you indulge this notion that apart from Rogers these other plaintiffs are somehow members in the congregation as well, mere membership in the church congregation is not a basis and does not give standing to sue under the Not-For-Profit Corporation Act.

Now, it is the plaintiffs, who from the very beginning of this lawsuit, have told you that you are not going to run into a brick wall at the First Amendment and the ... Constitution because this is purely a corporate law lawsuit. You are only being asked to read, interpret, and apply the articles of incorporation and the ... Not-For-Profit Corporation Act.

It is they who have made a very strong distinction between the directors and the articles of incorporation on the one hand, the congregation, the church, religious law, and the role of Pastor on the other hand. And they have been clear from the beginning that this is not a lawsuit directed at the office of the Pastor.

That being so, you, even under their theory, are bound by those articles, and bound to hold that mere membership in the church congregation would not confer standing to bring this lawsuit.

Now, the point of all this -- the basis for standing and why Brownlow was dismissed, and this case was filed with Rogers as the lead plaintiff -- is a claim on the office of director. And Rogers has a very simple, clear claim. It is that he was a director named in the articles in 1980. His term ended. There was never an election after that, and so he remains a holdover director.

Rogers is not a holdover director. Rogers is not even a member of this church, and we know that for several reasons. First, we know it out of Rogers's own mouth in this trial. And I am relying on the report of what was testified to. There is more to it than that.

The point is, as the Court knows and as Mr. Bark addressed, in 1987 Rogers left this church. He left this state. He went to Mississippi and founded another church where he became the Pastor.

He may have visited Bethlehem on occasion and had a good relationship with Bishop Richards. That is all well and good, but he admits that he was not a regular attendee of church services at Bethlehem. He admits that he was not a regular player of tithes to Bethlehem. He admits physically departing to another state, joining a different church, and then founding and becoming Pastor of it.

Now, Bishop Richards himself was the Pastor of more than one church at a time, Mr. Bark told us. That was true. He was perfectly capable of administering both churches at the same time and of having full membership of both. That is not what Rogers did. He abandoned this congregation for a different one. It has been cited probably twenty times in this lawsuit, Rogers left and started a church in Mississippi.

Now, there is another reason he was not a member. At Bethlehem Healing Temple Church, ecclesiastical and doctrinal matters are under the religious authority of the Pastor, as founded since the 1930s. Both sides in this case acknowledge that true membership is an essentially religious test. There are other factors, like paying tithes or physically showing up. Nevertheless, on a more spiritual level, on a metaphysical level, on a religious level, you can only be a member if you meet these religious tests. Moreover, I am going to go into them in some detail a little later. For now, let us accept the fact that there are religious factors."

Only one person has the authority to say on behalf of this church who its members are and that is the Pastor of this church, whether it was Bishop Richards, Bishop Poole before him, or Dr. Marcenia Richards now. I think that one would call the neutral factors established that Rogers ceased being a member here in 1987.

I agree that we defer to the highest ecclesiastical authority. But what Mr. Bark has misunderstood is that this Court cannot place Bethlehem Healing Temple Church under the control of The National Organization on his say-so or on The National Organization's say-so. Look at the articles on which the plaintiffs rely. There is not one word referring to The National Organization. Nowhere is this church, by its own actions, subjected to the authority of any outside person or entity.

For one corporation and one entity to have that kind of hierarchical control over another, for a court to make the kind of inquiry that that the Appellate and Supreme Court has routinely approved of, requires the sort of neutral documents that a court can look at to simply see what the hierarchical system is, to recognize it for being there.

There are denominations in which there is something called a trust clause. All the Methodist churches have a trust clause in their local incorporations. The Episcopal churches also have trust clauses. This is the legal means for establishing the hierarchy that grants the mother church the ultimate authority to come in and take over if there is a dispute at the congregation or if a congregation wants to leave the denomination.

There is no trust clause in the Bethlehem articles of incorporation. These are the articles on which the plaintiffs rely. They tell you that is all you need to look at to decide this case, that there is no religious issue you must decide. So, the court has no authority to usurp the Pastor's power over this church, and historical right and authority are undeniable in this case.

I mean, no one disputed, for instance, that Bishop Poole created this corporation, put it together, decided what to do with it, organized it, got Rogers to sign up with it. That was his doing. Nobody disputed that the governance of the church was managed by the Pastor since organizing. The so-called relationship of trust that Mr. Bark is talking about still reflects this ultimate authority of the Pastor.

A court cannot usurp from the Pastor their right to say who is a member of the Pastor's congregation. And nothing in Bethlehem's neutral documents gives this court any different power. So, Rogers is not a holdover director. Why? Because the articles of incorporation specifically require that to be a director in this corporation, you must be a member in good standing in this church. That is undisputed.

Rogers waited around twenty-three years to file this lawsuit. He admits, in an affidavit he presented to the court, that Bishop Poole presented the articles of incorporation that he proposed, and he signed them. That was in 1980. If Rogers and the plaintiffs are correct, that every year on the second Tuesday of July, there was supposed to be an election of directors by the members of the church, then in July 1981, when there was no election, they were on notice that there was something very wrong in the running of this corporation. They didn't act in 1981,'82, '85. '89, or '90, or any time until this lawsuit was filed, not because they suddenly discovered this corporate right that they thought they had, but because they hate the current Pastor of the church and they want to remove her, which is, of course, what this lawsuit is about.

Now, Mr. Bark has told us that Mr. Rogers said, 'Oh, I signed those documents, but I didn't read them, and I don't know what they said.' He admits knowing he was helping to create a corporation and yet neglected to read the document he is putting his name to. I don't care what kind of position of trust the Pastor stood in relationship to Rogers. If neutral principles mean anything, they mean that this court is not going to relieve an individual of the obligation to read the piece of paper he signs just because the person presenting it to him is his Pastor. Bishop Poole didn't say, and Mr. Rogers did not claim, that Bishop Poole said, 'Don't read these. Don't read them, just sign them,' or 'Here is a signature page. I'm not showing you the rest of the document. Just sign it and give it to me.' He admits he was given the articles of incorporation in full. He admits signing them. He cannot today in equity in this chancery court profit from his negligence in not reading the piece of paper he signed. He is deemed to know what he signed.

And Mr. Rogers does admit knowing that there was a corporation that he helped create. So, if he had the slightest curiosity about what the corporation involved, he had only to ask the Secretary of State or even Bishop Poole or Bishop Richards for the articles.

He could have reviewed them. He could have known easily about the provisions in the articles that the plaintiffs refer to concerning elections. His delay is inexcusable as a matter of law. An inexcusable delay for 23 years is, in a case like this, sufficient to establish laches. The more severe, the more inexcusable the delay, the less the defendants are obliged to present evidence of prejudice. At some point, the plaintiffs' lack of diligence is what governs.

Now, I need to emphasize that word. Mr. Bark kept talking about knowledge, but the standard isn't knowledge. The standard is reasonable diligence, due diligence, and you are not relieved by lack of knowledge from laches by your own failure of due diligence.

Most obviously, this is a dispute about the true meaning of a portion of the articles relating to the election of the directors. The defendants say those are provisions telling you what would happen if there were an election, but they don't require one, and there are no corporate members. The plaintiffs say those provisions say that the members of the congregation are supposed to elect the directors.

In 1981, one year after these articles were filed, we had the draft of the articles available. We had the three original directors and the incorporators available. We had the participants in the church who knew how it actually functioned at that time and for the 50 years, almost forty-five years, the church had been in existence before incorporation.

In all of that time, board after board after board was in place and corporate actions have taken place. Now, twenty-three years later, it is all invalid. The entire history of this corporation is invalid, according to the plaintiffs.

That is highly prejudicial. That is a change of position by the defense. It is to conduct their corporate affairs without addressing this alleged ambiguity because nobody is saying to them, 'You should be holding elections.' At this late date, it is simply too late to come back and take over Bethlehem Healing Temple Church. Rogers's claims are barred by laches. The plaintiffs' claims are barred by laches. And in addition, if he can't claim to be a director because of laches, he again lacks standing to bring this case.

There has never ever been an election. Now, that tells you that nobody seriously believed that that is how this church ought to be governed by election. That tells you that there wasn't some secret fraudulent cabal somehow hiding this.

You can't hide the fact that you are not holding an election. People knew that the Pastor appointed those in governance of the church – deacons, elders, members of the Board of Directors. Now, some of the plaintiffs claim they didn't even know there was a corporation. But Mr. Rogers admits he did know there was a corporation. And other plaintiffs can't deny they knew there was a corporation because they admit being privy to corporate business. So, how can you watch for twenty years and participate in the running of the church under the rule of the Pastor and then somehow claim that, all along, there were supposed to be elections?

We have cited law in this case already, earlier in the proceedings, showing that law does recognize that through corporate practice, through custom, and through corporate history, there can effectively be amendments that a chancellor can recognize in the articles and by-laws of a corporation.

If there was ever a case where, through disuse or contrary practice, the articles of incorporation have been effectively amended, it is this one. There is another basis for the same conclusion, and that is that the corporate model I am talking about mirrors exactly the model of polity, the polity of this church. It was a church under the control, almost dictatorial control, of the Pastor from the time Mattie Poole founded it in the 1930s.

But it is very interesting that the plaintiffs want you to forgive Mr. Rogers's negligence, because he didn't even read the paper that he signed and is now saying that this church somehow changed its form of ecclesiastical polity because Bishop Poole incorporated under the Not-For-Profit Corporation Act and not the Religious Corporation Act.

The church polity was consistent and unbroken from the 1930s through today. And while there has been a lot of conflicting testimony on other subjects, the authority of the Pastor within the congregation has not been contested. That polity was reflected in the operation of this corporation, and that is another reason that you should agree that these by-laws do not require an election or, if they did, that that was effectively amended.

There are a number of important reasons that religious liberty principles require this Court to dismiss this case. Technically, I suppose that is a lack of subject-matter jurisdiction and so dismissal rather than verdict would probably be the proper form to ask – relief to ask -- from the Court.

The Board of Directors has nowhere given the authority to make ministerial decisions, ministry decisions, about what goes on at Bethlehem. That is the Pastor's authority. If the Court orders the church to hold elections to essentially accede control of the local church to the congregation in that democratic way, the Court would be changing the polity of this church. Those sorts of decisions, that kind of decision-making has never historically been vested in the congregation. I know what the articles said, and I have addressed that. But at this point, it is also important to remember the 50 years during which no member of the congregation voted on anything, 50 years before incorporation, and then another 23 years since. That tells you a lot about what the real polity of this church is.

So, you would be doing violence to the current members of the church, to the church itself as a religious institution, and to the religious rights of the Pastor if you, by fiat, say, 'From now on, you are a congregational polity and the members of your congregation vote on things.' Mr. Bark wants you to rely on The National Organization. Except for these problems: first, as I said before, The National Organization has no authority over this church. Nothing in the church's own documents, including those that predate this dispute, and especially the articles of incorporation, grant The National Organization any authority whatsoever. Number two, getting back to the *Milivojevich* case, the Supreme Court admonished the ... Supreme Court not to delve into church constitutions and to start making fine distinctions about how things worked under them. I think that was the point Mr. Bark himself made. This Court can't redesign a polity for Bethlehem simply because it will conveniently provide an out in this case. The 'neutral principles of law' approach does not exist to create convenience for courts so that they can make decisions no matter what. Rather, it says that when you can decide based on neutral principles, you do. When you cannot, you don't.

But let's start with the heart of the matter, and I alluded to this earlier in my argument. It is the Pastor who has the right to say who the voters in an election are because it is the Pastor who has the right to say who the members of the church are. Why is it the Pastor only and not this Court? That is because membership is not solely based on who has paid tithes or where someone lives, if you consider Mississippi to be close enough to the City to make Mr. Rogers a member.

It is based on these factors, as well, which the plaintiffs have admitted to, whether the person is baptized in water, whether the person is filled with the Holy Ghost, whether the person pays tithes, and then, of course, whether the person attends regularly. The Court cannot apply at least the first four of these factors to anybody, ever, and I think the plaintiffs recognize that. So, to get around that, they tell you to authorize Lloyd and The National Organization to do so.

But that is where you run into a brick wall, because Lloyd and The National Organization have no power and no authority to say who the members of the Bethlehem congregation are. They don't because the articles grant no authority to any other corporation or any other person. They don't, because The National Organization has never exercised internal management control over Bethlehem Healing Temple Church. As everybody in this room knows, it was Bethlehem that was founded in the 1930s, not The National Organization.

It is The National Organization that eventually grew out of Bethlehem and not vice versa. So, not only do they not have the power as a matter of law, think of the serious egregious interference by the Court on this church in this purely ecclesiastical question. If the Court were to rewrite this polity and say, 'Well, now we are going to write in The National Organization over Pastor of Bethlehem. Okay. The National Organization, you are the Pope, and the Pastor is now just' – I don't know – 'Cardinal George.' The Court can't do that. Only Bethlehem can submit itself to The National Organization, and nothing in this case is evidence that Bethlehem has done that, certainly not on a matter such as who is and is not a member of the Bethlehem congregation. The Court can't impose that on Bethlehem. So, where that leaves us is, a plaintiff claimed for an election in which no secular power can say who the electors will be and, I can tell you, in the view of this Pastor, the electors will not be the plaintiffs and their people.

So, what position does that put the Court in?

It puts the Court in the position that Mr. Bark called for, that you defer to the highest ecclesiastical authority and power to make the decision – the Pastor -- who knows who the members of this congregation are. If you are going to do that, what is the point of ordering an election? You know what will happen and so does Mr. Bark.

There is a whole history of members of the congregation. More to the point, the three hundred or so members of the congregation today are members in good faith in this faithful exercise. They have a stake in this church. They are the congregation. They are the people who come to church, who pay tithes, and who meet these other tests."

Jim continued, "Mr. Bark and the plaintiffs want to disenfranchise the people who have been going to church at Bethlehem for years now simply because they are not on his side of the case. The Court must respect the rights of the current members of the congregation to participate. We can't exclude them. That violates their rights to religious liberty. It is their church. Now, Mr. Bark told you that the people on the plaintiffs' membership lists didn't abandon this church. They didn't leave the church. They were kicked out.

A few individuals who committed acts of violence in the sanctuary of the church were ordered not to return and were told that if they came back, they would be arrested. And my letter refers to those people. Even if you take the general word 'plaintiffs,' there were only five or six plaintiffs in the Brownlow case. No member of the congregation at large was forced to leave, asked to leave, or even made to feel like they ought to leave. Anybody could attend the church freely. No former member who has joined the plaintiffs' group was precluded from being a member of Bethlehem. They did, in fact, leave voluntarily. They have abandoned their membership in this church. Again, under *Hines*, they lose.

And so, the plaintiffs went out and found themselves a better-named plaintiff than Clay. They voluntarily dismissed that case, and they went with this one. Live by the sword, die by the sword. This is the man who sat on his rights for 23 years. The Court should not reward that lack of diligence, should not interfere in the governance of this church, should defer to the Pastor on matters of church governance, and should dismiss this case. At a minimum, the Court should render a verdict for the defendants on the grounds that because of the corporate practices, there is no requirement for an election."

After listening to Jim's closing arguments, the entire courtroom was completely silent. The judge was the first to move. He arose from his seat, appearing to have stumbled, and stated that he needed to find his glasses. Located on his desk, just in front of him, were his glasses. The judge seemed to have been so stunned by Jim's facts and history of religious law that upon his return to the courtroom, he asked if Jim had argued this case to a higher court. Jim replied "No." There was no doubt that the facts surrounding this case were supported by the laws of justice.

Surely this should have been the end of this litigation.

But it was not.

The court proceeded to determine who the members of our church were for its upcoming election.

37

NEVER MIND WHAT THE LAW SAYS

The Court Defined the Membership Qualifications for Our Church

The judge returned and attempted to make sense out of the Court's predisposition to order an election for our church. It was not difficult to see that the court had no concept as to how to determine a member of a church. The Court inquired, "The articles of incorporation don't define what a member is…Now, I think … at least three of those criteria can be analyzed …, but a voter would come up and check them on the list of people *that I have ruled are members* eligible to vote." We listened attentively as the judge stated his predisposition to determine who the members were of our church.

The trial court unapologetically determined that there would be an election regardless of the law. The Court defined who the members were for our corporation, as well as our church. Immediately following its decision to allow anyone walking off the street to participate in its election, the trial court then named the election administrator as the authority to confirm who the members were that the court defined. We aggressively objected to the court's decision to determine the membership of our church. However, it was to no avail.

Jim asked, "Your Honor, what evidence of that is there besides their lawyers' say-so that there was an election held for a Pastor?"

The Plaintiffs' Counsel, Bark, replied, "At this moment, we don't have any evidence."

The court delivered its rulings for the membership selection. Seeming to shrug with a sort of "Oh, let's not keep anyone out of this if they want to vote" decision, the Court decreed that basically whoever wanted to vote could do so. Never mind that there was no evidence to support what the court desired, besides the counsels from the law firm's "say so." Never mind any of the evidence we held which was denied by the court.

We were "fighting on the lie," just because the counsels from the Giant law firm "said so."

Jim's Objection

Jim refused to allow the court to slide or get away with its determination of membership for a church. Changing the course of history and delving into religious matters, the Court continued to insist on determining who the members of our church were.

Jim allowed the court to complete its statement about who could vote in the ordered election and said, "We object, Your Honor."

The court refused to listen or rule according to the laws governing our case. It continued its predisposition to determine who the members of our church were. Jim reiterated to the Court that the membership criteria was solely based on religious practices, that an individual must repent of his sins, be baptized in the name of the Lord Jesus Christ, baptism of the Holy Spirit, speak in other tongues, be a tithe-payer, and a member in good standing, as confirmed by the existing Pastor, to be classified as a member.

To begin exploring the Baptism of the Holy Spirit alone was in and of itself a spiritual challenge for the court. Therefore, how was it possible for the courts to determine if a person speaks in tongues, rather than another language? Additionally, if we had explored a member in good standing, one would not have been declared a member in good standing who had ceased to be a part of the church and brought a lawsuit against the church.

Distract and Attack – The Property Dispute

The court dismissed Rogers as being the holdover director of our corporation, but still proceeded to conduct its election. The facts relating to the case were entirely overlooked.

While the law firm's amended complaint was to be filed to determine if Rogers was a holdover director, it appeared that the court deliberately chose to ignore the true reason for the complaint.

The court further ruled that Rogers was not qualified to be a director. Yet the court proceeded further with the case. Plaintiff Rogers was brought into this case supposedly to add credibility to the plaintiffs' outrageous claims. As one of the original Board of Director members, Rogers's role for the plaintiffs and their counsel was to bring clarity to their preposterous lawsuit, given that all the other original directors were now deceased. In a legal system, true justice would have ended with the statement that Rogers was not a director of Bethlehem's corporation. However, this in fact would not be the end. The court continued its predisposition for its election.

Throughout the trial, and in affidavits, Rogers denied his knowledge that the corporation was, in fact, incorporated. He also denied having knowledge of participating in meetings of Bishop Richards's appointment as successor of Bishop Charles Poole.

As disclosed in the statement of their counsel, there seemed to be only one objective.

Plaintiff's Counsel Bark said, "And it is only the property here that is at stake, not the ecclesiastical entity. If, in fact, Marcenia Richards has the authority to damn us all to Hell as an ecclesiastical matter, she will still have that authority after Your Honor gives the property to us. The issue is not who has ecclesiastical authority. The issue is who has the property."

The Amended Complaint for the clients from the law firm was merely a means to an end. It was the goal of the counsels of the law firm to devise a method by way to seize the assets of the corporation. There was no other way to justify the plaintiffs' claims.

Following the court's ruling that Rogers was not a holdover director, it was understood that he also was not a member of the church. The court then failed to share its reason for the insistence of a court election and why it addressed further proceedings in this case. We could not help but conjecture that the statement the judge made in the beginning of the trial was true: "I don't even think it's really that important to the decision."

The only way to obtain the corporation's assets, however, would be through control granted by the court's ordered election.

The Court clarified, "You, Mr. Bark, simply want possession."

Plaintiffs' Counsel Bark affirmed, "This is a corporation, Your Honor. We not only want possession, but we also want her bank accounts, her vehicles, her properties; we want possession of everything she has. She, Your Honor, should have nothing."

Following the admission of the counsel to strip me of not only the corporation's assets, but of my personal assets, we waited for litigation to run its course, including the court's election.

38

THE COURT'S ELECTION

The issue concerning the evidence was never satisfied. Several days were filled with arguments by our counsel regarding the church's membership and the court's predisposition to impose an election on the corporation. Jim stated, "It's really for a church to decide who the accountable members of the church are, not for the civil law or corporate law. We must default to the church's decision of who the members are. It's still the church's decision."

Even the court admitted that there was no evidence to support the plaintiffs' claims.

The judge ordered that each side pay $3,500 to cover the anticipated costs of the election. Jim opposed this, since our side had already put out so much money over everything and now, here we were, being ordered to split the cost of the election that their side wanted. and, of course, we knew where their side's half was ultimately coming from.

You Stopped Payment?

Once we remitted funds for the Court's election, our Finance Director, Marge, stopped payment on the check. Marge telephoned me and stated she did not believe we were responsible to remit any payment for a court ordered election. "Doctor Richards, I stopped payment on the check to the court because, not only do we not have the funds, how are we going to pay for the court's election?"

Horrified, I exclaimed, "You stopped payment? On the check to the court – for its election? Please tell me if you are kidding. We have enough problems." I telephoned Jim and left a voicemail message informing him that we had stopped payment on our check for the court's election.

Subsequently, when we arrived in court the following day, Jon, one of the leading counsel from the law firm, ran around in circles in the courtroom stating they had to take care of a financial matter. Jon went to the clerk and stated he believed the check for their clients was not clear.

Shaking his head very slowly, Jim looked at me, and mumbled, "I hope that was not our check. Marci, I hope that our check is cleared." I did not respond, because I knew it was not that our check was not clear, but rather that Marge had stopped payment on it. Marie stared at me, as Jim said, "Marci, tell me that is not our check." From Jim's response, I gathered that he had not gotten my voicemail message. Therefore, I thought it best to wait and have a conversation with Jim about the check after we left court. I did not respond.

The check was not our check. We observed as the plaintiff's counsel went through the mechanics of presenting a check to the clerk. Jim continued to shake his head. I turned to Marie and said, "Jim must not have gotten his email." Jim continued to shake his head. I was not about to stand up before the court and announce that we had stopped payment on the check. We had experienced enough humiliation in that courtroom.

You Will Be Arrested

A day or two later, I received a call from Jim. He was very annoyed with us, "Marci, you sat in the courtroom knowing all along the court was referring to our check."

"That was not our check. I left you a voicemail message stating we stopped payment on our check. Jim, the reason we stopped payment is because we could not afford to pay for the Court's decision to determine who the members of our church are."

Jim could not believe what he was hearing. "The Trial Court's clerk has informed me that if we do not immediately remit payment, the court would order the arrest of those responsible for stopping payment on the check. That goes for you and whoever else signed that check. You will be arrested and possibly taken to jail."

The litigation had already sent me through hell. Nothing could have compared to the anguish we experienced because of the faulty lawsuit against us and the corporation.

I telephoned Marie and informed her of what Jim communicated to me. Marie started gasping for breath. "Did you say arrested? Did you say jail?"

"Are you okay?" I asked.

"I will call you back later." I had no idea what happened to Marie and why she abruptly hung up the telephone.

About twenty minutes later, Marie telephoned me, "I paid the court."

"What happened?" I asked.

"I was so terrified that I hung up the phone, ran to the courthouse, and paid the Court's election fee. I could hardly believe it. The only word I heard was "jail" – after that, my brain completely shut down." For Marie, as a faithful churchgoer, the serious use of the word "jail" was perhaps more than she could swallow. We teased Marie at the office.

39
COSTLY CONVICTIONS

Boycott

It was the Sunday morning before the court-ordered election. An emergency board meeting was called with the Board of Directors regarding the election imposed by the court. It was a unanimous interpretation of the Board members of the court's decision that anyone walking off the street could participate in its imposed election. Therefore, we chose to exercise our rights and participate in an invalid election.

There were certain rights and laws established by our nation that the justice system is bound to be governed by. Even if those laws are tampered with and perverted by those representing that system, it does not nullify the existence of these laws.

Following our Sunday morning worship services, we shared the details of the courts' orders concerning its election with our congregation. The news concerning a court-ordered election was known throughout the church and the members had been telephoning us for the details. That Sunday, the church was full. Members and non-members arrived to hear the details and procedures for Tuesday's election process at the courthouse. We presented the facts and the truths relating to our cases, including the history of appointing directors and the laws referencing our First Amendment Rights as well as the Religious Liberty Act. We shared our decision to honor those rights and to respect the customs and practices of our organization. After receiving an overwhelming share of support and respect from well-informed individuals, we upheld our stand and moved forward. Whatever the results and the decision of the court, we were compelled to accept responsibility for our convictions and to seek further justice.

Two days prior to the court's election, following several board and management meetings, we addressed the congregation. We shared our position on the court's decision to allow an election which was to involve individuals who were no longer members of our church. We also shared the restraints of participating in an election ordered by the court.

That Sunday, hundreds of individuals agreed corporately to not participate in the election being held outside of the corporation's by-laws and church polity. Following this decision, we signed petitions and hundreds of affidavits. The petitions and affidavits were presented to the court, along with all of the documents confirming those who were members in good standing of our congregation. We also presented to the court a copy of a privacy disclosure letter presented to all members, which stated our responsibility not to disclose their information with outside sources without prior consent.

While we respected the Court's opinion, the church and corporation were bound by their governing principles, laws, and beliefs.

The Cost of Our Convictions

Sunday evening, we worked untiringly organizing our affidavits, membership criteria, and other legal documents for our case. There were volunteers throughout the building categorizing our records to present to the court. We did not complete the process of systematizing our records until nearly 3:00a.m. We desperately wanted to be confident that our legal documents were properly placed in order.

Frequently, a person's convictions will affect not only the individual, but ultimately others as well, including others who are not inside his or her immediate environment. It was a very natural thing for me to teach tenets of faith and convictions. However, when those convictions were expressed throughout an entire group, the group could come under punishment for its convictions. One of our leaders reminded us that it had been demonstrated throughout the years that a person is often only as good as their last popular decision. To make an unpopular decision can bring unnecessary duress on any organization. After reading through the laws and studying the supporting facts of our case, we resolved that the law supported our position. And we held that we were the legitimate Board of Directors. We were having difficulty comprehending the Court's ruling concerning the membership of the church, without the ecclesiastical authority of the Pastor. Nor could we conceive how the Court had forced an election and allowed individuals who admitted that they started their own church and corporation to participate in the court-ordered election that would have consequences for our church.

On the day of the court-ordered election, we hauled our documents into court as evidence concerning our membership, as well as about defining our membership criteria. We sat there in total disbelief as the Court informed us to place the documents in a back room. The Court did not appear interested in the evidence we presented. The fact that the Court did not review our evidence was not a deterring factor for us to continue presenting the facts. Just as the counsels from the Giant law firm held to their conviction – that this case was a "game" that they sought to win – we held to our convictions of the church polity, the corporation practices, the rights of the First Amendment, and the laws of the Religious Rights Acts.

We had originally been quite amused that the Court ordered its election and anticipated us partaking in it. But things were not so funny once we expressed our opinion and rejected the court-ordered election.

40

A NEW WAR

The Day of the Court's Election

The morning of the court-ordered election, we remained resolute in our decision. We were not going to participate. Such an election went against all of the practices and history of our corporation. Also, the election was governed by the Court's appointed Election Administrator, who had no concept of the religious history of our church. No one had any idea where the appointed Election Judge appeared from or what his background or qualifications were.

In our exhausted plans for managing our records to submit to the court, Pastor Larry took responsibility for driving downtown to present our petitions. Jim telephoned me and asked if we needed him to oversee the process of the election and I hesitated for a moment. But I just could not bring myself to tell Jim that we had decided against participating in the court's election. It would have involved too many details. Jim explained to me the cost associated with his appearance in court during the election, and that made it quite simple for me to respond by saying we did not need him to appear for us in court that day. There was no need to incur any additional legal fees, much less unnecessary legal fees. I declined to get out of bed. My mobile phone was ringing, but I refused to answer it.

Near 4:00 p.m., I decided to phone Larry. Larry observed the process of the plaintiffs and their friends participating in the court's election. The plaintiffs, their family members, friends, and others working with them were lined up outside of the courtroom to cast their ballots.

Larry called me from the courtroom as he observed the plaintiff's counsel, named Jon, positioning himself to demonstrate to his clients how to complete and file their ballots for the court's election. "They are lined up. Jon has set-up a table outside of the courtroom demonstrating to them how to vote." I did not wish to hear of the details of the election. Instead, I asked, "Larry, were you successful in dropping off our petitions?"

"Yes." He replied.

"I will see you later." I was convinced the court-ordered election was strategically designed.

How could the court determine that individuals who were not members of our church were entitled to vote in an election that it ordered for our church? The judge himself had been confused about our practices. Thus, we could not understand why the Court demanded we participate in an election that was outrageously prejudiced against our corporation and its long-standing practices.

We were content with our decision not to participate in the court-ordered election.

Was the Election Fixed?

A few days later, we received the results from the court-ordered election. We realized that it had clearly been in our best interest not to participate in this election after reviewing the results. This was perhaps one of the most crucial decisions of our corporation, and it proved to be one of the best decisions we could have made.

We discovered the election had become a hoax. The court ordered that there was to be an election of five directors. The goal of the plaintiffs was apparently to elect three board members in order that their clients might control our corporation.

Ironically, Rogers's name was omitted from the list of candidates because he was not a member of the church.

The Cost of Convictions

A week later we arrived in court to hear the ruling. The judge entered the room, scowling. He barked at Jim, "Counsel, not one of your clients voted in the election." Jim was flabbergasted. I stared directly at the judge. Jim refused to believe the judge. The judge then offered Jim the chance to review the cast ballots.

Jim rushed into the room where the courts' ballots were stationed. It seemed as if Jim was in there forever. Larry looked at me and asked, "Did you not inform him?"

I shook my head no, and said, "I couldn't reach him."

Jim returned with an astonished look. There was not one vote cast from any of us or the members of our congregation. He saw that we had submitted petitions choosing to exercise our First Amendment and Religious Rights.

Unable to believe his eyes, he returned to where we were sitting and said to me, "You did not vote. Not even you voted." He was stunned. He sat there as if we had totally humiliated him. I decided it was best to wait before explaining our convictions. The truth was that each of us had tried to reach Jim.

William looked over at Marie and me, "Well, all of you have certainly offended the court."

"No kidding. We managed to offend the court every day of the trial because of your daily tardiness. Further, the court was offended on the very first day of the trial," I replied. We knew our convictions would cost us dearly. However, we were not prepared for the total price.

Convictions are Costly

We accepted our convictions for exercising our rightful ecclesiastical authority. As the Pastor of the church was the only ecclesiastical authority or individual possessing such authority, exercising that authority would be the only way to determine who was or who was not a member in good standing of the congregation.

Following Bark's outburst regarding my ecclesiastical authority, the judge proceeded to read its order about the election. I held my head down reading the Bible. As the judge continued to read, he stated that we were shepherds without a flock. I did look up to witness the faces of those who were sitting with us.

Excited, I said to Marie, "I am ecstatic." Handing her the Bible, I added, "I have just read the story of Pharaoh and his army being drowned in the Red Sea." I told her to read the passage for herself. Marie did not respond. Those who sat along with me were witnessing the reality of the cost of our convictions.

Gene, one of the plaintiffs, reached out to shake my hand as he said, "Marci, you would have won if you had had a good lawyer to catch us up on the witness stand like the one who gave the last statement."

I responded, "It doesn't end here. We will continue our search for justice against the lies and evil each of you have fabricated in this courtroom."

A New War Begins

Indeed, we had offended the court. The greatest offense, however, was against us. That offense was that the court determined those who were not members to be members and even leaders of our church following its election process.

The two days after the court's orders proved to be brutally painful for us. The plaintiffs and their supporters telephoned the Pastors throughout our city and around the globe, crowing about their clever victory. Our office telephones were ringing off their hooks with an average of more than one hundred additional calls during the next three days. Our corporate voicemail box was full. The doors of the church were constantly swinging open. Individuals were coming in and out to inquire about the court orders.

This was the beginning of a new war.

"You Will Have to Fight from the Wilderness"

Following Jim's initial and overwhelming astonishment of our not participating in the court's ordered membership election, Jim said to me, "Marci, we can win on appeal. However, you will have to fight from the wilderness."

I interrupted him, "Wilderness? Wilderness? Jim, I have been in the wilderness since the death of my father." Jim was extremely patient. He listened to me, allowing me to express my confusion concerning the decision of the court.

"The court has declared that Rogers was not a holdover director of our corporation. That was the genesis of the law firm's amended complaint, to include Rogers as a holdover director to grant substance to their case. The court made its decision regarding Rogers."

Jim allowed me to continue ranting and raving until I was exhausted and placed his hands over his ears. Finally, he said, "Marci, as your counsel, I cannot listen to those statements."

I removed his hands from his ears and continued talking.

Jim did not judge me for my words or my tone. He simply stated, "We must come up with an immediate strategy."

I placed my confidence in him. "I know you will, Jim. You are exceptionally brilliant and your understanding of the laws governing this case will bring us a strategy."

With those words, Jim and I said our goodbyes. I was determined to keep fighting.

41
THE RED SEA

Traveling to the office, I asked Larry, "Should we allow the injustice to be the end of our story?"

I repeated to myself, "How dare the Court call us 'shepherds without a flock'? The Court never once took the opportunity to allow us to present evidence. This case was decided prior to our appearance in court. The trial was a mere formality. We will fight this injustice with all our might. We will find the laws governing our case. We must not give up. We are farther ahead than we were yesterday. I am not at all concerned by the Court's decisions. That order will not be the final verdict."

I said to Larry, "I am exhausted. How far are we willing to go to fight for justice?" Everyone around me was also exhausted. Each of us had poured our resources and energy into the litigation.

The vindication for justice did not happen the way we had hoped.

The day following the trial court's decision, Jim informed me that we had better start packing. The office staff were at a loss. The employees of our corporation were scurrying around. There were so many personal decisions for me to make that I decided to go home and relax.

I refused to believe that the trial court's decision was the end of our journey with this case – just because the counsels from the law firm "said so." Is that how we should live our lives?

Thursday evening, I learned that vehicles were patrolling our property throughout the evening. At 11:30 p.m. I asked the staff to close for the night.

"Now You See it, Now You Don't"

"This is not about me. If only others would get off the sidelines, something incredible would happen," I repeated over and over.

Not only did I not assist in packing any of the boxes, but I could also not move any of my personal belongings from my private residence or the corporate office. I decided that the convictions of our organization were greater than the court's error in determining who the members of our church were. Our beliefs were in line with our mission and convictions.

It was seven o'clock Friday morning when the telephone rang. Mildred, one of the assistants working in the office, informed me that police officers were patrolling the perimeters of our property. I quickly prepared to leave. I grabbed a shirt and headed straight for the office. A female officer met me as I was exiting my car.

"Good morning, officer, is there a problem?" I asked.

"We have received numerous telephone calls stating furniture was being removed from the church, and I am here to investigate." As she spoke, she patrolled the outside of the property. I stood there frozen. Before I could take a step, the officer returned, "I am not sure of the reason for the telephone calls; however, everything looks fine."

She radioed the station. "Everything looks fine."

When I opened the door to the church, four-foot-tall Kelle was pulling a thousand-pound machine on a dolly to the back door of the church.

"That is my personal copier. I loaned it to the church. "I tried to catch up with her. "What are you doing? Why are you guys moving the furniture?"

Kelle explained, "Whatever location we move our offices to, we will need a copier."

I ran to the back of the church. There were vans everywhere. The office staff was moving the entire office. I decided to take a tour through the church.

Mildred sent a message: "There's a lieutenant from the police district waiting to see you outside in front of the church."

As I opened the door, the lieutenant stuck his foot in the doorway. "We have received numerous telephone calls that the furniture is being removed from the premises." As the lieutenant and I walked up the stairs, I noticed the custodians coming from the sanctuary pulling the organ towards the back of the church.

I attempted to stall the lieutenant, but he was too quick.

There was only one door left preventing the lieutenant from stepping inside the main hallway of the church. He noticed that I was stalling and said, "Madam, can you please open the door to the inside of the building?"

I opened the door. The lights were out inside the hallway, and the guys were still pushing the organ out the back door. Other volunteers moving heavy boxes. There were large garbage bags filled with items from the office, thrown into the hallway.

The people moving the furniture spoke to the lieutenant and kept working.

As sweat poured from my eyebrows and ran down my face, the lieutenant asked if I was okay. I simply nodded my head, yes. Words escaped me.

The lieutenant asked, "Are you removing all of the furniture and equipment out of the church?" Before I could answer, someone walked past the two of us dragging huge boxes.

Unbelievably, the lieutenant said, "I don't see anything unusual."

When the lieutenant walked out, I was terribly exhausted.

I walked into the sanctuary to have a seat, only to notice the microphones, the audio system, the organs, the chairs, the podium, the cords, and anything that was not nailed down had been removed from inside of the sanctuary. I stood speechless.

I left the sanctuary and walked upstairs to the War Room. The War Room was now completely empty. Each room I walked into was empty. I walked into the ladies' room and wondered what, if anything, could possibly be missing there. The only items left in the ladies' room were the bathroom accessories.

How was it possible to empty an entire church of more than seventy thousand square feet in one day?

There was one unmarked car positioned outside the church for the entire day. We considered ourselves so blessed.

Had the officers taken a trip to the back of the church, they may not have been able to contain themselves, as the entire parking lot was full of items we personally purchased when I became Pastor.

Whoever telephoned the police officers was correct in reporting that we were moving all the furniture that we had personally purchased. These were our personal items, and our office staff had no intention of leaving any of our items alone.

"You Are at the Red Sea"

Friday afternoon, the office was in total chaos.

When my mother stopped by the office to console me, I sat in silence. I believed if there was one person who would understand the fearlessness in my heart, it would be my mother. My mother expressed her concerns and said a prayer for me.

Motionless, I stared ahead as my mother prayed, "God, you must send someone to speak to my daughter in order that she can make the right decisions from her heart. She needs to be strengthened and encouraged. Guide her in your grace and mercy." My mother hugged me and assured me that whatever happened in my life, God was actively involved.

"Mom, do you think we did the right thing by not participating in the court's election?" I inquired.

"What do you believe in your heart?"

"I am not sure what to believe," I confessed.

I walked outside and noticed someone ringing the doorbell of the church. It was Pat, one of my spiritual advisors. It was unusual for Pat to be at the church. As I opened the door, we started walking toward the sanctuary. Pat was a very spiritual individual and was extremely sensitive to me throughout the stages of the litigation. Pat informed me that her daughter, Katessa, shared the Court's decision with her and had encouraged her to visit me.

Pat continued, "Pharaoh and his army were drowned in the Red Sea." I did not tell Pat that that was the story I had read as the Court delivered its decision. I waited to hear the entire story behind Pat's statement.

Pat continued to recite the story of Moses and the Children of Israel against Pharaoh's army. She recalled how the Children of Israel were at the Red Sea and were completely outnumbered. She reminded me that the Red Sea was in front of the Children of Israel and Pharaoh's army was behind them.

Then Moses cried out to God in fear of the huge army pursuing the Children of Israel. She reminded me that, as Moses cried out to God, God spoke to Moses and asked why Moses was crying.

Pat said to me, "God told Moses to use what he had in his hand." Pat continued, "God is with you. You must use what you have in your hands. Moses had a simple rod in his hand. However, when he used the rod, the Red Sea parted, and the Children of Israel walked through on dry land."

As Pat continued telling the story, a friend named Mat entered the area. Mat looked at me and said, "It's not worth it. This church and litigation have been the source of your pain and heartache. You have lots of bad memories because of the litigation."

Pat told me to ignore the negative advice and stay focused. "You are at the Red Sea. You must use what you have in your hands."

I sat in silence as I considered my mother's prayer, "She needs to be strengthened and encouraged."

Pat's words were so encouraging.

My heart was resting on the story of Moses and the Children of Israel at the Red Sea. The end of that story was phenomenal – Pharaoh and his huge army were no match for the Almighty God of Moses. Pharaoh and his huge army drowned in the Red Sea.

Friday evening, as we met with the leaders of our church to discuss the strategy for our organization, I realized that every battle ever won was won mentally prior to the victory. I braced myself to continue fighting the injustice against us.

Saturday Morning

Our teenage dance group had an early rehearsal at the church. We heard many rumors that the plaintiffs were set to march into the church Saturday morning.

Arising early, I began my day with prayer and revisited the story of the Red Sea. Larry decided to manage the daily affairs of the organization while managing the Court's decision.

The maintenance supervisor called to warn me that the plaintiffs and their supporters were on our property trying to seize control.

As I headed for the church. Larry, who had also received the news, greeted me. He was prepared to drive me to the church and asked if I had our emergency motion filed in court requesting a new trial. I nodded yes.

The lieutenant, along with other officers from the Twelfth District, were on the scene. One of the teenagers, Janell, refused to allow the officers or the plaintiffs access to the church. There was a previously scheduled rehearsal for the teen dancers, but the Pastors had neglected to cancel the dance rehearsal.

The plaintiffs' arrival with the police had frightened those youths. The police threatened to arrest the youths and to take them to jail, but the teenagers stood their ground, unafraid to stand up against the injustice of the plaintiffs and their supporters.

The plaintiffs had hired locksmiths, who were attempting to change the locks. Refusing access to all the locksmiths, Janell stood in front of the door.

Driving up to the church, I jumped out the car and saw crowds of people circling the front of it with the police officers. Directly in front of the church were the plaintiffs and their supporters, who had parked vehicles throughout the community.

The locksmiths were looking at me as they waited to change our locks. One of the teenagers approached the locksmiths, "You have no authority to change these locks." The locksmiths then waved their hands and said, "We're out of here."

I turned to the officers, "Let the teenagers leave the property. They have nothing to do with this." The officer did not answer as I scrambled for the papers Jim had filed in court for us.

Larry managed to speak with the officer. Once I located the documents, I handed them to the lieutenant and said, "They have no right to possession as we are scheduled to appear in front of the judge on Monday."

The officer asked me if we were aware that these people were allegedly now the Directors of our corporation. As I proceeded to explain to the lieutenant about our emergency court date, one of the supporters of the plaintiffs, Roy, started to yell at me.

I told Roy that this was not his war, and he had no right to speak to me, much less shout and be part of my conversation with the lieutenant.

The lieutenant asked if Roy's name was on the papers, and Roy said it was not. The lieutenant then warned him that if he made another outburst he would be taken away.

Larry stepped inside the office to telephone Jim. As I talked with the lieutenant, Roy jeered at me, "When the police leave, we will get you. We got the biggest law firm in the city."

Larry returned just in time to prevent me from losing my temper. Glaring at Roy, Larry turned to him and said, "Do not speak to her." Then he asked me to step inside the church. I was grateful that one statement from Larry silenced the entire group.

Inside the church, the teenage dancers were horrified. I assured them that everything would turn out fine.

I headed toward the sanctuary where there were pictures of Mattie Poole. As I stood there, I wondered how she had survived the vicious attacks against her character.

Watching the activity outside, I heard the police officers say, "If you guys do not calm down, we will begin making arrests."

The officers agreed to allow the teens to leave the premises.

Larry entered the church to tell me, "The lieutenant would like to speak with you. Don't speak until he has completed his statements."

The lieutenant pointed to the court documents in his hand. "Have you read these documents?"

"Yes."

"Do you clearly understand these documents?"

Again, I simply said, "Yes."

Standing in front of the lieutenant were the plaintiffs and their supporters.

He addressed them. "She has stated she clearly understands the court order. We are only peace-keeping officers. We have no right to evict her. She does not have to leave these premises. Take this matter up in court on Monday."

That statement made me gasp for breath.

As I left, Gene and one of the supporters of the plaintiffs attempted to deliver more documents to me. I placed my hand up in Gene's face. "Get out of my sight."

Later the Lieutenant pulled me to the side, "Do you reside on the property?"

"It has been nearly twelve years since I became a resident on the corporate property. Furthermore, since I am Pastor, they are aware that I am a resident."

Several of the plaintiffs' supporters screamed, "You will go to jail on Monday!"

Gene asked the officer if it was possible to arrest me onsite, and the officer replied no. We went back into the church to phone Jim, who had prepared a motion for Monday morning.

Monday Morning – In Court

The first words from the judge were, "Are you back so soon?"

Terri from the Giant law firm immediately pointed at me. "Have her arrested! Hold her in contempt."

Bark, the leading counsel from the law firm shouted, "Have her removed from the property. Get her out now!"

After listening to the complaints, the judge refused to hold me in contempt of court. He believed that the police officers acted according to the law.

Bark shouted, "She removed all of the furniture from the church!"

Jim interrupted. "Your Honor, I informed my clients to remove their personal property from the church."

We had never known Jim to back away from a legal fight, and he did not back away this time. He understood the law. Jim was present in a rare form. The judge agreed that we had a right to remove our personal property.

Once the plaintiff's counsel finished complaining, Jim presented our request for a new trial or modification of the previous trial.

As Jim and I stepped outside of the courtroom, I requested that he ask the judge to allow us three days before making his decision.

I desired to complete a three-day spiritual journey to determine our next strategy. Jim told me that we did not have three days. "I doubt if the Judge will give us one day."

I told Jim not to worry. "Please ask the court for three." Jim shook his head and returned to the courtroom.

The Court immediately denied our request. The judge ordered that we should be removed from the property by means of the sheriff's eviction, but the court held up the sheriff's notice for eviction for six days.

I was thrilled, confident that we would continue to fight for justice.

A Different Universe

Following the court appearance, Jim said we would appeal. Equally, Jim was aware that the trial court would not entertain, much less grant our motion for a new trial.

Our motion to the Appellate Court was prepared. It was necessary that we petitioned the court for a stay until the appeal was decided. Jim advised us that the court rarely grants a stay and that we should be prepared to fight, even if it meant we had to fight from the outside. Jim further informed us of the cost to prepare the motion for a stay in the Appellate Court, as well as the cost for filing our appeal -- every step of the process. Jim said, "This is not a common case. I do not want you to be surprised if you must fight from the wilderness."

"We will pray and hope for the best," I replied.

Jim turned to me, "You are from a different universe. My concept and understanding are strictly legal. However, I must remember that your concept is completely different from mine. While you go to your planet," he said with a smile, "I will perform my responsibilities as your legal counsel."

"I will go to my universe and talk to the God of my planet. He will help us. Just do what you must do and allow the God of the universe to show his power."

Jim constantly reminded me, "Marci, I know we are right. However, we need to *prove* that we are right."

As Jim turned to walk away, I wondered how we would be able to continue and prove that we were right, as our legal fund resources were rapidly depleting again. I only prayed that we would have sufficient funds to continue the fight for justice.

Another Miraculous Court Ruling

Tuesday morning, I started my spiritual three-day journey. Whatever our fate, I decided to leave it in the hands of God.

On Friday morning, my spiritual journey was complete. Late Friday evening, as I drove to my mother's house, my mobile telephone rang. Jim's voice was filled with excitement. "Marci, we have just received word from the Appellate Court. Our motion was granted. We have a stay."

I pulled over to the side of the road, leapt out of my car, and started jumping up and down for joy. "I told you, Jim, I knew something great would happen for us!"

Jim assured me that it was a miracle.

He shared with me in his years of experience of being a legal counsel that he had never witnessed an event such as this.

"Jim, miracles happen every day; we are excited that you are a part of our miracle."

Each day, we came to realize that our battle is not against an army made up by the hands of men. Our army is a spiritual army.

The Holy War Aftermath

Like so many of the international wars we have been witnessing and enduring – al Qaeda, Taliban, Sudan, Hamas -- our holy war for justice consumed more than a decade. We spent every day of that decade in battle, whether in courtrooms or newspapers, street corners, or our own pews and sanctuary. The losses on all sides were astronomical.

The seeds of that war had taken root long before my father heeded to remove Mike from his prominent role. Mattie Poole's struggles to reduce dissension and defeat conspiracies were at the heart of her dire prophecy that "God shall sweep this church clean. Those of you sitting in this congregation will one day come against this church to destroy it."

It seemed Mike may not have been a satisfactory leader, in some individuals' viewpoint, but he did possess certain skills, for he managed to fan the flames of revolt among disgruntled members and to mobilize supporters who were willing to believe that he had been treated unjustly. Although Mike did not become Pastor, the impulse to establish a new and different church did not die with him.

Deb persisted in building loyal advocates for her cause throughout the holy war, and as the plaintiffs' secretary, she initiated every confrontation that occurred. including the lawsuit after Mike's appointment. Mike and the deacons were used, enlisting especially the seniors who had watched her grow up, to achieve her goals.

The plaintiffs' secretary dedicated herself to a personal mission of acquiring the same degree of autocratic power that her adoptive mother, Mattie Poole, had wielded. The fundamental difference, however, was that

Deb never made the mistake of trying to become Pastor. She was fully aware that an attempt to put yet another woman in that role would fail against opposition from men throughout the congregation and leadership and would compound the disasters that had already occurred after my father appointed me to succeed him. Instead, Deb managed to establish her loud, aggressive husband, Jimmy, as Pastor – a brilliant stroke. Jimmy not only obeyed Deb's directives, but also never saw a microphone he did not like.

As the Pastor's wife, Deb runs the church founded by Mattie Poole.

The Holy War Ends: Case Dismissed

The decision of the Giant law firm to provide legal services *pro bono* presented an existential threat which the judicial system not only failed to counter, but also behaved irresponsibly and even unlawfully.

Many legal battles persisted for more than a decade. The Giant law firm waged a vicious, highly personal battle against me, resulting in the loss of all my belongings in a lawsuit.

As a personal policy to ensure my health and sanity, I decided to ignore the incessant court dates in favor of getting a good night's sleep.

One day, unexpectedly, I received a message that the case had been dismissed.

There was no fanfare, no brown envelopes, no courtroom filled with the plaintiffs and their supporters, no more fabrications, and no outlandish outbursts from the plaintiffs' counsel, Bark. Unlike all of the long orders previously received throughout the trial, it was a very simple order of dismissal without prejudice signed by the court stating "…it is hereby ordered and decreed that all claims asserted by the plaintiffs against the defendants are dismissed without prejudice, with each party to bear its own cost and attorney's fees."

I have always believed that my life was always in the hands of God. Therefore, there was no need for me to worry about the case, the plaintiffs, or the counsels from the law firm.

At the end of the litigation, I was left with nothing material that I had acquired and worked for all my life, including my special pieces of art from Israel and across the world where I had traveled. The plaintiffs succeeded in taking all my personal assets, excluding the few pieces of clothing that I wore to the hospital the day of the first warrant for my arrest and my Mercedes Benz, which was sold to pay legal fees.

There existed one asset that neither the courts, the plaintiffs, nor their counsels could have ever taken away from me; and that was my faith. In the beginning of the litigation, I started with my faith and in the end; it was my faith that sustained me.

Were it not for my faith in God, I would never have withstood the scandal, psychologically, physically, emotionally, spiritually, or financially.

I was exhausted, yet full of hope. My faith in the judicial system was quite challenged, but I believed in the prospect of justice in a different format.

From this experience, I learned a valuable lesson. As long as there is greed and evil within any system, injustice reigns, but only temporarily, for it should never override true justice.

A fundamental outcome of the war between faith and justice has been that the church of Evangelist Mattie B. Poole and of Bishop Arcenia Richards no longer exists as a vibrant religious community – a spiritual congregation.

I have not given up the fight for justice.

As Jim observed, I thrive in a different universe.

"Failure is not an option."